The Spiritual Crisis of the Intelligentsia

Articles on Societal and Religious Psychology
(1907-1909)

Nicholas Berdyaev

Translated by Fr. S. Janos

Revised Edition

frsj Publications
Mohrsville, Pennsylvania

The Spiritual Crisis of the Intelligentsia

Articles on Societal and Religious Psychology (1907-1909)

ISBN: 978-0-9963992-1-0

Library of Congress Control Number: 2015942837

Revised Edition

Printed in the United States of America

Printed on acid-free paper.

For information address:

frsj Publications
Fr. Stephen J. Janos
P.O. Box 210
Mohrsville, PA 19541

Contents

II.
Religion. Church.

Dedicated to the Memory
of
Peter Pastore († 18 January, 1982)

* * *

Note on Revised Edition

The purpose of this revision to the year 2014 original publication (by Vilnius Press, now since "fallen by the wayside") corrects in our present text a serious previous flaw -- that involving "clipped sub-titles" on the Contents pages, regarding, i.e.. *Struve, Weininger, Rozanov, Nesmelov...*

This present revision also does away with the needless and unseemly hyphenisation of words initially in the "Translator Preface", and thereafter...

Otherwise, this revised edition maintains the textual intergrity of content with the original edition. On aesthetic grounds, however, the text has been reset and reedited. Unavoidably, the pagination consequently now differs. Those quoting citations from the text will, of course, properly provide annotation differentiating which of the two editions they have in hand...

Other circumstances also have prompted this revision, -- among which, is the oversight of my above "Dedication" lacking from the initial version.

Fr. S. Janos (8 May 2015)

Translator Preface

The name of the Russian religious philosopher, Nicholas Berdyaev (alt. Berdiaev, 1874-1948), is likely unknown to the typical English speaking modern reader of any erudition; likewise, he might be surprised indeed to learn that there has been such a thing as "Russian Religious Philosophy". Hence, some rambling words and thoughts for purposes of clarity and perspective seem in order. As an example, -- how can the present text, published in 1910, speak in a past tense concerning the "Russian Revolution", when those with a penchant for historical dates know, that the "Russian Revolution" occurred in the year 1917?...

There are, of course those over the course of years who will, seemingly by "pure chance" or "felicitous fate" [Jn. 3,8], have stumbled upon and perused this or that tome by Berdyaev. And yet, irony though it be, many if not most of us will have first encountered Berdyaev's name in our adolescent years unaware, in the opening page epigram of Aldous Huxley's "Brave New World", an epigram in French attributed to Nicolas Berdiaeff. History is indeed replete with irony.

In 1922 Berdyaev, together with a number of other prominent Russian intellectual figures[1], was banished into exile from Russia by the Communist government, in the process of consolidating the new Soviet order with the collapse of the Russian Civil War. A famous anecdote involves Berdyaev's father-confessor, Fr. Alexei Mechev (since canonised as "Saint"), telling the distraught Berdyaev that, "You must go, the world must hear what you have to say!".

---

[1] Vide the invaluable recent book by Lesley Chamberlain, "Lenin's Private War: the Voyage of the Philosophy Steamer and the Exile of the Intelligentsia", St. Martin's Press, New York, 2007. This book, to its great merit, lists also the names of those who were deported from Russia on these 2 "Philosophy Steamships".

Perhaps evidencing the truth of the saying, -- "Blessed are those cast out for the sake of righteousness, for theirs is the Kingdom of Heaven" [Mt. 5, 10], -- another historical irony is that Berdyaev seems a man "fated for exile". Had the "old regime" not collapsed amidst WWI giving rise ultimately to the Communists, who banished Berdyaev to the West, he would have instead have been banished to the East, to Siberia for "blasphemy"; his lawyer indeed is alleged to have described his case as "hopeless". What occasioned this? In 1913 Berdyaev penned a fiery article, "Quenchers of the Spirit" ("Gasiteli Dukha"), expressing the public outrage against church authorities resorting to tsarist troops with bayonets to discipline and rough up infirm aged monks on Mt. Athos, such as were recalcitrant in their hesychiast "Name-Praiser" ("Imyaslavtsi") convictions.[2] But what symbolically is the source inspiration for Berdyaev's title, "Quenchers of the Spirit"? He does not need to indicate it, since it is transparent.[3] But why is this lengthy digressive anecdote relevant? In the rich extent of Berdyaev's religio-philosophic thought, not always is the origin of his insights apparent or attributed, and Berdyaev's own inner reworking of whatever a theme renders this all the more challenging.

---

[2] Berdyaev's complaint is moreso on the manner that the church authorities handled the issue. rather than the theological nuances involved. One need but remember the churchly scandal a decade earlier, over the "Excommunication" (or "Self-Excommunication") of the world reknown Russian author L. Tolstoy by the Holy Synod of the Church.

[3] St. Paul, 1 Thessalonians 5, 19, "Quench not the Spirit". St Paul speaks this in nearly the same breath as the far better known exhortation to "Pray Unceasingly" [5, 17] -- which forms the basis of the mystical hesychiast practice in Eastern Christianity with the constant inner repetition of the "Jesus Prayer", the "Prayer of the Heart": "Lord Jesus Christ, Son of the Living God, have mercy on me a sinner". In certain foppish circles of recent times in the West, this has assumed almost the guise of a sort of "New Age mantra" syncretised with elements of yoga. And significant as well in Berdyaev's philosophy, St. Paul in the very next breath exhorts: "Contemn not Prophesyings" [5, 20].

Banished from Russia in 1922, Berdyaev ultimately settled in Clamart near Paris, where he continued to write extensively until his death in 1948. His many books written during this period of his life were virtually all translated and published in English, as well as many other languages. Many in the West came to form their concept of Russia and Orthodox Christianity through his writings, and through his involvements in religious and intellectual European circles beyond the Russian emigre community. He was chosen to become "editeur" of the Parisian Russian language publishing house, IMKA Press[4], which published both books by many significant Russian religio-philosophic authors of the time, as well as the 1925-40 Journal "Put'" ("The Way").

Berdyaev, together with others of his generation, was part a dynamic creative cultural and intellectual phenomenon, variously termed the "Silver Age" and the "Russian Religious Renaissance". For this portion of the Intelligentsia, the movement involved initially a critical questioning of rigid ideological assumptions, and then making transition from naive positivism and Marxist dialectical materialism to instead philosophic idealism, and then back to a Christian faith. "My faith hath passed through the crucible of doubt", -- quoted by (St.) Mother Maria Skobtsova in her 1929 booklet on Dostoevsky. "Suffering passes, but what has been suffered/ experienced remains always with us", -- a similar quote from Leon Bloy with which Berdyaev begins his 1927 book, "Freedom and the Spirit". The rediscovery of one's religion, having perchance lost it at

---

[4] IMKA Press was initiated under the financial auspices of the international YMCA, and became a major source for works written by authors "forbidden" in the Soviet Union -- in later years including such famous authors as B. Pasternak and A. Solzhenitsyn. The greater portion of IMKA Press materials were subsequently "repatriated" to Russia following the 1990's collapse of the Soviet Union.

Two excellent sources on Berdyaev's life are, of course, his own autobiography, in English entitled "Dream and Reality", and "Rebellious Prophet" by D. Lowrie (written in collaboration with Berdyaev's sister-in-law, E. Rapp).

some phase in adolescence, and then passing through the "Crucible of Doubt", the "Gornilo Somnenii", and finally being able to believe, results in far different an experience and perception, than for someone never subject to doubt. Many there are, that lose their faith forevermore, and are not troubled by it, since often it mattered little to them when they had it; others are transfixed with grief into "passionate atheists" like Nietzsche; and yet others in their myopic conversion angrily denounce and repudiate the strange pathways by which Divine Providence has led them to faith. How central to Russian Religious Philosophy are the insights of Dostoevsky! The experience of "God-forsakenness" upon spiritual pathways is twofold a process: man's questioning the love by God in times of extremist trials and tribulations when put to the test, and conversely, God's questioning of a man's alleged love for God when put to the test, whether it be a love authentic and genuine, or mere lukewarm lip-service. On another plane, this is similar to the intimate relationship between husband and wife, where each through innumerable a variety of non-verbal probing tests attempts to ascertain a response, that the alleged love is true and genuine. Failure can lead to tragic results! This is part of the dynamics of the "I and Thou" relationship, grounded in freedom, variously touched upon by both Berdyaev and the Jewish philosopher, Martin Buber. Three of Christ's Apostles might serve as symbolic an example: John the "Beloved Disciple" stood firm at the foot of the Cross, Peter in crushing fear ran away but tearfully returned for the rest of his life, and finally Judas Iskariot "the Betrayer", who in ultimate frenzy of despair did away with himself. It is far easier to deeply fear, than it is to deeply love God. An unrequited authentic love is possible only when the element of fear is transcended. The "fear of God" may be, according to the Proverb [1,7], "the beginning of wisdom", but it is only *the beginning* and not the full fruition of wisdom.

In 1907 this intellectual transition resulted in a sbornik, or collection of articles, entitled "Vekhi" ("Signposts"), which included articles by Berdyaev, P. Struve, S. Bulgakov and S. L. Frank among others. "Vekhi" evoked a virulent firestorm of protest from the revolutionary Intelligentsia. Our present 1910 text, "Spiritual Crisis of the Intelligentsia", represents a follow up response to these protestations. Especially in his pre-exile period, Berdyaev tended to "recycle" his published articles into books, and the present text is an example of this; it includes also his "Vekhi" article, "Philosophic Truth/Istina and Intelligentsia Just-Truth/Pravda".

What was the situation in Russia -- socially, culturally, religiously -- in 1907 when "Vekhi was published, in 1910 when our present text was published? It was a time of societal unrest, worsened by the humiliating defeat of Russia in the 1904 Russo-Japanese War, and exploding on "Bloody Sunday" 22 January 1905, when tsarist troops fired on a peaceful procession led by Orthodox priest Georgii Gapon, which shocked public opinion and helped set in motion a "Russian revolution", nearly toppling the autocracy, and which unleashed "Red Hundredists" from the revolutionary left to commit maximalist acts of violence and outrage, thus crippling the revolutionary momentum, and in turn evoking the virulent "Black Hundredists" acts of reactionary violence and rhetoric. It is this 1905 failed "Russian revolution" that Berdyaev speaks of in the present text.

Intellectually and culturally, this "Silver Age" was a dynamic era of creativity in literature, poetry and the arts. It was also a time of the start of the Religio-Philosophic Societies in St. Peterburg, Moscow and Kiev. It was also a time of rapprochement of certain "God-seeker' elements of the Intelligentsia and the Church -- hitherto two "mutually exclusive worlds" in Russia -- which began initially in 1901, a mere year after the death of Vl. Solov'ev, when a small group centred round D. S. Merezhkovsky managed the quite unexpected, in getting approval for the Meetings from K. P. Pobedonostsev, the Prokurator of the Holy Synod of the Church. It was a vibrant time of intellectual efforts, of profound books and journals and trends, from a plethora of gifted talents.

Strange a co-incidence, one might note, that in August 1900 died two significant philosophic figures, both solitaries of a sort -- the German Friedrich Nietzsche and the Russian Vl. Solov'ev. In various subtle ways their thoughts intertwine within the legacy of Russian religio-philosophic thought. Nietzsche, suffice it to say, has been understood rather differently in Russian thought than elsewhere, when viewed through the profound prism of Dostoevsky. And Vl. Solov'ev, a few years but recently in the grave, our text acclaims as the first truly genuine Russian national philosopher.

Both "Vekhi" and Berdyaev's choice of title in 1910, "Spiritual Crisis of the Intelligentsia", are an attempt to provide a bridge back over the "Crucible of Doubt" to a solid footing, with principles grounded upon solid rock rather than sand. Berdyaev is already exploring what will become major themes in his mature philosophy: person, freedom, spirit, creativity. His religious themes are refreshingly vibrant and bold in their significance, -- so very in contrast to the droll insipid religious hucksterings of our day, of a "salt that hath lost its saltiness"... And bridging the opposite side of the divide, with striking audacity Berdyaev boldly and publicly challenges the churchly authorities to allow the Church to be truly the Church of Christ.

What was the condition of the Russian Orthodox Church at this time? Structured upon the Byzantine model, church and state always exist in an uneasy harmony, where the state is wont to regard with suspicion undue influence and interference by the church. In Russia previously around 1700, Tsar Peter the Great "reformed" church administration upon the Protestant Synodal models, with a bureaucracy similar to the civil reform, which resulted in the Russian Church under the direction of a layperson rather than hierarch, serving as Prokurator of the Holy Synod. But even earlier, Tsar Ivan the Terrible had St. Philip (Kolychev), Metropolitan of Moscow, executed in 1569. Astonishing or no, the Church had been "tamed" with a civil Prokurator heading its governance -- even the initial Religio-Philosophic Meetings were convened only by official permission of the arch-conservative Prokurator, Pobedonostsev. Long anticipated hopes for the convening of a reform "Church Great Sobor/Council" to address matters in the Church were obstructed for many years by the authorities, and the Great Sobor only occurred later and in hurried fashion in the beginning days of the 1917 Bolshevik "October Revolution".

Regarding the Church, the terms "white clergy" and "black clergy" bears explaining. The "white clergy" are married clergy, priests and deacons and minor orders, serving in the parishes, and long a semi-hereditary class between that of peasants and nobility; indeed, only around 1900 were seminaries opened for study to non-clergy. Economically stressed, large white clergy families often suffered alcohol abuse and similar dysfunctional familial problems, contributing significant apostate youth to the atheist revolutionary movements. In contrast, the "black clergy" are monastics, celibates at ordination or else widowed priests choosing monasticism, from whom the churchly hierarchs, bishops, are chosen. And for those especially ambitious at fast-track careerist opportunities of advancement, since often "like begets like", this at times has worked to the detriment of the Church, with differing priorities between the white and the black clergy, as somewhat evident from our text. Noteworthy is Berdyaev's final article, his "Open Letter to ArchBishop Anthony", acclaiming this opened door to the Church for the Intelligentsia. Here too is bittersweet an historical irony: this Vladyka Anthony Khrapovitsky will head the "Russian Church in Exile" after the 1917 Bolshevik Revolution, whereas Berdyaev in exile will remain faithful to the Moscow Church to his death.

This rambling overview of course neglects to explain much that is addressed in Berdyaev's book, in part to satisfy an approach for the general reader, and to allow the moreso specialist reader to let the primary text speak for itself.

Berdyaev's religio-philosophic thought and literary work might be seen as comprising two overlapping periods, -- the "formative period" while still in Russia, and the "mature period" following his 1922 exile to the West. As previously mentioned, virtually all of Berdyaev's books written during this "mature period" were translated into English and published during his lifetime. In contrast, a number of his books from this earlier "formative period" continue to remain untranslated into English, and it is only in recent years that the Russian texts of such have become generally available. They are important on their own merit, sharing the wide scope of Berdyaev's intellectual investigations, but also in contributing to the forming of his mature thoughts and themes. Our present tome, "The Spiritual Crisis of the Intelligentsia", is but a first step among several such intended, towards completing the corpus of Berdyaev's works in English.

As regards the present English translation -- portions of it, all which comprise Berdyaev's "recycled" periodical articles, were translated by the translator well over a decade ago, and other portions only but recently for purpose of publication. Hence, certain inconsistencies of form or style may obtain, or certain eccentricities of the translator prove evident. Yet whatever the faults of the present translation, the alternative, -- after so many fallow years of waiting for other far more gifted individuals to take the initiative, -- the alternative remains what it has been: nothing! So please accept this humble attempt to honour the memory of the Russian religious philosopher N. A. Berdyaev, to prove true the words of St Alexei Mechev.

Fr. Stephen Janos, translator

Introduction

I.

The present collection of my articles, according to its themes and direction, parallels closely the critical task of the selection of articles in "Vekhi"[1] and, it seems to me, can add its own small bit to that total, which seeks to discern paths of egress out from the spiritual crisis, now being experienced by the Russian intelligentsia. I stand firmly on the viewpoint, that every serious crisis with its social and political side is a manifestation only superficial, only on the surface, only an effect, the roots of which lay within the spiritual and mysterious depths of being, and therefore also an escape from the crisis is connected with a regeneration in these depths. Political reaction -- is in its appearance an effect, on the surface, quite ephemeral, and the near-sighted might tend to get fixated upon it, as now the tradition-following radical intelligentsia are wont to do. The spiritually perspicacious perceive, that in the depths of our life there transpires subterraneous a working, the consequences of which still are not manifest and the significance of which lies still ahead. Both in the Russian "intelligentsia" and in the Russian "people" is occurring an upheaval of will and of consciousness, which leads to different a feeling for life and a different understanding of the world. A new spirit is being born, undiscerned by the intelligentsia. But every profound crisis -- is first of all a crisis of faith, every setting right to the crisis leads from a worshipping of idols to a renewal of faith in the living God. Now it is that the radical and revolutionary (in the deep, the spiritual sense of this word) can be termed one, who to the utmost of his powers contributes to a radical regeneration in the

---

[1] Long before the appearance of "Vekhi" [Engl. "Landmarks" or "Signposts"], in articles of mine I already had dealt with questions, raised by this ["Vekhi"] anthology.

intelligentsia, who consciously affirms a new sense of order to the soul and not to an idolatrous faith in God; and in the same way, one who would seek to hold back this process of regeneration, who defends the intelligentsia's old-faith, the intelligentsia prejudices and defending the old sins, -- that one namely ought to be called the conservative (in the bad sense of this word) as well as reactionary. The tragedy of the Russian revolution has aggravated the already long growing crisis, and one, who has gone through this crisis, can no longer put up with the old intelligentsia ideology, the old, the demoralising tactics. I have had profound an experience with this crisis, which I conditionally term as the spiritual crisis of the intelligentsia, and if, on the one hand, what has been experienced and put to the test comes off with a subjective passion in tone, and which might suggest the suspicion of a lack of objective impartiality, then on the other hand, in this setting of a seal to life I see as a chief justification for the appearance of my article collection. I shall leave untouched, what directly issues forth as a reaction in life.

The anthology of articles in "Vekhi" united people of various positive ideas and confessions, but the important thing all the same, is that it was united. And as it seems, I can formulate the positive aspect, to which all the participants of "Vekhi" appealed, in place of the traditional ideals of the intelligentsia. We all sought to set at the basis of a societal world-view the idea of *the person* and the idea of the *nation* in place of the idea of *intelligentsia* and *classes* (and of "the people" in the class sense), by which the traditionally minded intelligentsia had always been inspired. The person self-identity and nation self-identity ought to take precedence over an intelligentsia or class self-identity. For the regeneration of Russia it is substantially important, that each should be conscious of oneself as an human person in its absolute significance and a member of the nation in its absolute fore-ordained destiny, and not the intelligentsia aspect or the representative of this or some other class. This shifting in self-identity and in the awareness of ideas presupposes an altogether different philosophy, than that which up to the present has held sway within the intelligentsia medium. The ideas that have prevailed among us of "intelligentsia" and "class" (likewise also "the people") rest upon phenomenalism and empiricism; the ideas of person and nation presuppose an acknowledgement of their substantiality. Person -- is substantial, and nation -- is substantial. Their substantial aspect is a given not in a philosophy only mental, but also in living experience. We have to pass beyond the vapidity of phenomenalistic illusionism and comprehend the substantial aspect of our own person and our nation. Realism has to win out over nominalism, just as in life, so also in thought. Classes, including the "intelligentsia" class, possess a significance phenomenalistic, empirically derivative and subordinate, whereas person and nation possess a significance as substance and real and therefore to them belongs central a place in our world-concept. Both person and nation -- are living organisms, the roots of which are lodged ineffably deep, they are ineradicable; whereas classes -- are transitory forms. Therefore the spiritual reform, for which the "Vekhi" collection and also my own anthology here contend, transfers the centre of gravity of life, on the one hand, to the depths of the experiential person, in the heightening of its creative energy, in its religious experience, its moral, aesthetic and philosophic culture, and on the other hand, with the broad sweep of the national, the life of all the people with its historical perspectives and a connection of these perspectives with the historical past.

A new intelligentsia from this point of view cannot be a social group, nor can the belonging to it be defined by any particular societal current and particular moral frame of mind. A new intelligentsia can consist only from an assortment of *persons* of the highest qualities: to belong to suchlike an intelligentsia ought only to be those, in whom obtain high qualities mental, moral or aesthetic, or especial areas of knowledge, energies or a gift of creativity, talent, genius or the prophetic. There might be *select persons*, but there cannot be select classes, nor select social groups. Indeed can it possibly be said, that among us a belonging to the intelligentsia is to be defined by genius, talent, capabilities, knowledge, energy, an in-general selection process of the qualities of the person? An intelligent by far does not always mean for us one who is intelligent. The psychological type of the intelligentsia rests upon social-group peculiarities, and not upon spiritual powers. Then only will the renegade character of the "intelligentsia" change, and its time-bestown opposition to "the people" be erased, when the intelligentsia becomes the spiritual blossoming of the people, through its select persons, and not by small-circle pretensions to save the fatherland, independent of its *qualities*. The broad segments of our historical "intelligentsia" has to become merged with "the people", with the "inhabitants", to enter into the thick of national life and to grow from the womb of the people's life its best qualities, and by them to lift the inhabitant life upwards. The old intelligentsia have to get out of the way of the person and its creative initiative. The "intelligentsia" figure in the old, the social-group sense of this word, with the traditional emotional mannerisms and the traditional views is on average, nowise higher than the merchant, the land-owner, the official or other inhabitant. Better to be a good merchant than a feckless intelligentsia figure. And it is time already to stop arrogantly separating oneself off from the national life of all the people, it is time to stop with the worshipful bowing to the "people" as to an idol, and setting oneself as a select group apart from "the people". And indeed the "people" itself, as constructed by the intelligentsia renegade mentality, ought to give way to the *nation*, -- to the people in the religiously-real sense of this word.

I would further want to stress, that the reform work of "Vekhi" strives towards the creation of suchlike a spiritual atmosphere, as to make forever impossible another "Azefovschina" [i.e. the early 1909 scandal surrounding the "double-agent" Yevno Azef, revolutionary assassin and police informer].

II.

At the core of a new world-view for the Russian intelligentsia ought to be placed not only the idea of the substantiality of person and nation, i.e. the extra-temporal and indestructible organic roots of person and nation, but also the idea of *freedom*. There are two manners of feeling in the world: at the basis of one is that of feeling wronged, and at the basis of the other -- is a feeling of culpability. To these correspond also different philosophies. Our intelligentsia up into the present has confessed a philosophy of feeling wronged, of victimisation, i.e. a slave-like philosophy; whereas it ought to confess a philosophy of culpable guilt, i.e. a philosophy of freedom. Only one who is free can sense himself culpable with blame, only an awareness to guilt gets to the deepest depths of one's freedom. The philosophy of culpable guilt is also a philosophy of the sons of God, of free beings. The philosophy of feeling wronged, victimised, is a philosophy of slaves, sons of natural necessity. Christianity -- is a religion of culpable guilt and of freedom, a religion of the nobility and honour of man, of his free filiation in sonship to God; this liberates man from a feeling of slave-like dependence, from the shackles of natural necessity and leads man to an awareness of his own free culpability, an awareness, so contrary to the slave-like sense of injury amidst natural necessity. The socialistic faith and hope -- is a religion of wronged injury and slave-like dependence upon the natural necessity, and therefore so often stokes feelings for malice and revenge. Those conscious of their own filiation of sonship to God, of their own higher nature, of their own primordial freedom, cannot be driven by feelings of malice and revenge, cannot be gripped by a slave-like feeling of wronged injury, they first of all have a sense of their own culpability and they are conscious of their own freedom, from that upon which the structure of the world depends. If from a feeling of slave-like necessity there is wont to be begotten a revolution of wronged injury and revenge, then from a Christian feeling of free sonship to God there is wont to be begotten a revolution with the aspect of culpability and free renewal. Redemption -- is the answer to the torment of guilt. Regeneration and transformation -- is the path of the free. Spiteful revolt -- is the reply to the torment of feeling wronged. Destruction and negation -- is the path of slave-like shackling. To take upon oneself a sense of guilt and responsibility can only be done by a being aware of the unfathomable depth of one's freedom; this freedom however is revealed through

Christ, through the filiation of sonship to God rendered perfect by Him. From an immeasurable sense of wronged injury is begotten malice, from an immeasurable sense of culpability is begotten love. The path of wronged injury and necessity -- is a path destructive, the path of culpability and freedom -- is a path constructive. The awareness of one's own sonship to God and one's own immeasurable freedom is likewise an awareness of one's own chosenness, but this awareness of chosenness is revealed as open to all, and is not something elected upon by those, who by a free act of their will depart the realm of injury, malice and necessity. The basic religious dividing line in the world is a division into the culpable and the wronged, into the free and slaves, into the noble and the ignoble. In each human soul, the consciousness of the free culpability of the sons of God ought to win out over the slave's outrage amidst the sons of necessity.

III.

And in regard to the Church, the psychology of wronged injury and pretension ought ultimately to be conquered by the psychology of culpability and answerable responsibility. With the Church it is impossible to make entry dependent upon contractual agreement, it is impossible to pose to it conditions for one's own entry into it. It is impossible to impute to the Church the responsibility for human sins. The Church is a Divine-human organism and a Divine-human process. In the Divine-human organic dynamics there is a Divine side, of ineradicable sanctity, of the graced gifts of the Holy Spirit, nowise dependent upon the human; and there is the human side, the human willful activity, striving towards Divine life, and it involves a creativity, which God awaits from mankind. Aspects of weakness in the Church, its sickness is only in the aspects of weakness and sickness of the human willful activity. The life of the Church courses its way within a mysteried unity of humankind and the Divinity, and this life is wont to fall and decay, when the will of mankind gets oriented away from the

Divinity. Therefore only upon oneself ought we to lay blame for that "abomination of desolation" [Mt. 24: 15], which we see in place of the sacred. The churchly hierarchy could become corrupted from top to bottom on its human side. Yet still the Divine Sanctity of the Church would remain ineradicable. And this Sanctity ought to be assumed as a child would, since it is only like the little children that we can enter into the Kingdom of God [Mt. 18: 3]. A rationalistic critique of the Church is non-belief. The Church -- is a mysteried communion of all the living and the dead, a "memory eternal" for the dead and also for the living. The churchly bonding with the departed, with the fathers, is the sacred basis of a true conservatism. Vile indeed would be a societal aspect, based upon forgetful oblivion. The Church is the pathway to those, for whom history is a pathway. But the churchly Christian idea has a side that is not only conservative, but also creative, oriented towards new life, eternally begotten from the striving of the human will to God. The creative side of the religious life ought particularly to be promoted, since churchly life has become moribund, i.e. the human activeness within the Church has become moribund.

IV.

Under the influence of the Russian revolution and the experience of recent years, I have come to feel rather more deeply an awareness of the lack of viability of the abstract, fleshless, rationalistic solutions to questions on the societal aspect. Both life itself and the work of thought pointed me towards a *conscious historicism*. I had a sense of the mysterious aspect of the source-flows of history, the mysterious thousands of years span operative within historical forces. The mystical and the mysterious involve not only the Church, but also the state,[2] and nationality, and the whole of

---

[2] I resolutely reject any mystical sort of connection between Orthodoxy and autocracy, but I assert a mystical aspect to the state, a mystical aspect in the attitude of people in regard to it, independent of the

culture, and all the greater body of history. Everything enormous, protracted, significant within history evokes a mysterious palpitation and cannot be rationally denied and rejected. A rational rejection of the flesh of history is all the same as the psychology of iconoclasm. An iconoclastic sort of rationalism rejects the mysteried symbolic aspect within history, upon which rests not only religious life, but also the whole of "culture", deriving from the "cultus".

It is easy to proclaim, that absolute freedom is a supreme aim, that within it is the meaning of the world process. But they are wont to preach an exiting from history coursing along its mysterious paths, and they proclaim absolute freedom at a given moment, and still there ensues chaos, slavery and non-being. Absolute freedom comes to be realised through history and historical bodies, through a mysterious historical succession, churchly and cultural. The state is not a limiting end of societal developement, this purposive end is in a free power of God and powerlessness, but only through the state and power[3] is there realised this end. It is necessary to relatively affirm the state, in order absolutely to surmount it. The churchly hierarchy is not a delimiting purposive end of religious developement, this end -- is in an all in common priesthood and free love, but it is only through the hierarchical churchly succession that that this end should be realised. Likewise also the finalative unification of mankind into one body is realised through nationality, and a new creative culture is created through successive cultural traditions. Only a deep religious awareness can heal us from sterile utopianism, from abstract resolutions on societal questions detached from historical times and spans, as well also from the utopian denial of the evil rooted in human nature and the almost inhuman difficulty in the struggle

---

forms of state. Towards the state we have the same supra-rational relation, as also towards culture. This nowise excludes the struggle against despotism, the rising up against moribund and evil forms of the state.

[3] Again still by power I am not thinking of whatever a given form of governance, but rather the idea of power in its opposition to anarchy.

against it. Only faith in the living God can provide healing against the abstract social fantasies, and against the idolatry of transforming limited social objectives into a god. One who has had experience of the living God and the real path of communion with Him, that same one has no need further for crafting himself the false gods, in social utopianism, in abstract constructs of perfection upon earth, and that same one comprehends the conditional and relative aspect of everything outwardly societal, whilst also grasping the unconditional aspect and absoluteness of religious life. And I do not believe, I definitely do not believe in some religious regeneration, which would have external an impetus, societal and non-religious. A religious regeneration cannot be created either by societal revolution, nor by societal reforms. Both churchly revolutionaries and churchly reformist-restorers start not from this end, yet they subconsciously subordinate the mysterious depths of religious life to societal reforms and turnabouts.[4] But a genuine societal regeneration can only proceed from the depths of religious life, from a religious discipline of the will. A religious shifting of our will is however the primary thing, and without it we shall get nowhere.

V.

The path to a new life -- is a path creative and constructive, not destructive and negative, not a rendering of the past with our departed ancestors into a *tabula rasa*, a blank slate. The radicalism of creative path cannot be properly measured by the old criteria of "rightist" and "leftist". We want finally to get beyond rightist and leftist, to unite and divide along new criteria. The extreme rightists and the extreme leftists breathe malice and hate, they thirst for disruption, an intensification of collapse, a laceration of the life of the people. This very principle of division and repulsion, with malice and

---

[4] There is repeated the selfsame fatal mistake, that obtains also with churchly conservatives and reactionaries, who in like manner subordinate the religious life to the state and to an external power.

hatred, the forgetting about the human face, has already become intolerable. This principle of party, narrow circle, of class, class-hatred and animosity are alike characteristic to both the right and the left, they all lodge their pride into hatred towards enemies and in the power of shoving back. I have no love for the black and the red colours, since these are colours of a false division and false hostility. Russia is suffering bloodshed from this discord and animosity. All have forgotten about Russia. I seek for a principle of attraction, calling for love, which is alike missing in the recent-most pathos of both right and left camps. Our sword would divide not the right and the left, not the reactionaries and the revolutionaries, not the bourgeoise and the proletariat, not societal classes and groups, but rather those of a will, directed to good, to love and to Divine life, from those of a will, directed towards evil, towards hatred and non-being. Russia -- is a suffering living being and it is necessary but to love it, rather than to seek to steer it via partisan classes, "rightist" and "leftist".

VI.

From former times up to the present day, a basic division within Russian self-consciousness remains the division into Slavophilism and Westernism. The Slavophil and Westerniser elements quaintly interweave at times: thus in Vl. Solov'ev, a Slavophil in his source ideas, there was very strongly a true Westernism; in the Russian revolutionaries however and even the Marxists, in their source ideas Westernisers, there was very strongly a false Slavophilism. Russian national self-consciousness cannot be exclusively Slavophil, nor exclusively Westerniser. In it ought to be revealed the great mission of Russia -- to be the intermediary between East and West, to realise the Slavophil dream in union with Western culture and in transforming it into its own flesh and blood. Eastern and Russian principles have to become inculcated with principles Western and cultural. Otherwise, disintegration and ruin await Russia. The Russian spirit bears within it the seed of a new and great life, but, left to itself and taken abstractly, torn off from the universal culture, it will fatally become transformed into a spirit of self-immolation and self-destruction. The sect of the self-immolators -- is very characteristic an effect of the Russian spirit. But this selfsame Russian spirit in the person of Peter the Great, of Pushkin and other of its geniuses revealed its all-human character, its extraordinary gift of a creative transformation of universal Western principles. Whosoever loves the Russian idea and desires a real mightiness for its realisation, that same person ought to be not only a Slavophil, but also a Westerniser, i.e. ought to reveal in our national self-consciousness the *universal* principles of the truth and freedom of Christ.

VII.

In conclusion there has still to be said: I believe, I believe invariably, that the world is heading towards the "religiously new".[5] With all my being I await within Christian life the victory of freedom over compulsion and the revealing of the prophetic and creative sides of our faith. But that which is new within our religious consciousness, is yet still for me inseparably connected with the old and eternal religious consciousness, with the sanctities and the priesthood. Only through the sanctity of the Universal Church, based upon Christ Himself, only through the sacred succession and sacred tradition of the Church can and ought there to be an approach to new religious shores, to delve into mysterious and only remotely discerned prophecies. Upon the path of modern searchings for God stand the dangers of rationalism and sectarianism, which can be

[5] This is the expression of a certain inspiring man -- V. A. Ternavtsev, the religious ideas of whom, regretably, remain largely unknown to any wide circles.

guarded against only by an involvement with the people's sanctity and the people's cultus. Therein is the authentic universality and the authentic mysticism. In the abstract-literary constructs concerning Church and theocracy I cannot still believe nor do I desire to in areas of human self-conceits and human pretensions involving the holy. The holy mysteries and sacraments cannot be the doings of our hands, they are given us from above, and people for nigh on two thousand years live by their graced power. The Temple of the Body of Christ long since is already constructed, and we do not set in place the foundation stones. But this does not mean, that the Temple is finished, that the roof is already raised, that "Orthodoxy is complete as given" and that the Divine-human process has ceased. Do not those perchance commit blasphemy against the Holy Spirit, who consider the eternal and mystical existence of the Church as completely identical with an old and temporal existence, such as was quite still pagan? And can there be justified in place of the Universal Church a church nationally-local, having lost its spiritual freedom from an attachment to pagan a way of life? In churchly conservatism, in guarding the sanctity of the cultus there is an healthy grain of truth, but it has nothing in common with an inertly-mannered and superstitiously-pagan religiosity. One, who has made a transition from religious thought to religious life, ought to light the lampada before the icon and fall prayerfully down on his knees before it, and one who in the Spirit of Christ lights the lampada and prays before the icon,[6] -- such a person emerges from the inertness of existence, and he is terribly free, terribly free, and oppressed and crushed by pretension to everyday an existence.

The religion of Christ is a religion liberative, and not enslaving, a religion rejoicing, and not oppressing. From the Spirit of Christ are born gusts of uplift, and not in this Spirit is there cringing and denigration. The Spirit of the freedom of Christ is alike contrary both to the human evil-willed, rationalistic self-conceit, and to human

---

[6] I am speaking all this while about the lampada and icon in the literal, and not figurative sense of the word.

cravenness and suppression, to superstitious cringing. A Christian regeneration ought equally to refrain from a fleshless wont for abstraction and inertia of existence, to refrain from rationalism and superstition, from iconoclasm and externalistic ritualism, from the exclusiveness of a new consciousness and from the exclusiveness of the old consciousness; it ought likewise to flee any denying of the historical Church and measures to halt churchly developement, to avoid both hostility towards the past and ancestors and hostility towards the future and descendants, to avoid the self-smugness of sectarian apostasy and the self-smugness of historical way of life, as well as the exclusive affirmation of the human aspect and the just as exclusive affirmation of the Divine aspect. The task is nowise easy, but it points to a directing of the will. "Thy Kingdom come, Thy will be done, as it is in heaven, so also upon earth" [Mt. 6: 10]. "Thy Kingdom" is a perfective co-uniting of the Divine and the human, and this co-uniting is wrought through the arduous paths of history, the mystical actings within it of powers and will, by inward regeneration, and not by abstractly-maximalistic declarations, nor by excitedly-exaltive expectations. When they assert the Divine against the human, then by this they have expressed the selfsame apostasy from the Divine, that is also in the assertion of the human against the Divine. Christ revealed the path of deification for man and mankind. The great teachers of the Church and the great Christian mystics have taught this. The religion of Christ cannot be responsible in this, that its very essence has become forgotten in the pagan existence of Christians. Christianity is the revelation of God-manhood, the revealing of the religious truth concerning man and mankind. But in the active realisation of this truth, God awaits a response from human freedom.

Khutor Bobaki,
Khar'kov guberniya,
25 September, 1909

I.

Intelligentsia. Revolution. Nationalness. Literature

DECADENTISM AND MYSTICAL REALISM [1]

Decadents readily pass themselves off as mystics, and frequently they express mystical pretensions. Russian decadentism especially gravitates towards mysticism, it speaks about the mystical. The approach is to jumble together decadentism and mysticism in certain of the literary circles, but the academism and mystifications get entangled along the way and hinder the decadentism from passing over into an authentic, a real mysticism. In the select, the cultured, the refined literary circles they speak much on mystical themes, they employ mystical terminology, but they speak in too literary a fashion, they display too historico-philological an attitude. The experts can speak about Medieval mysticism or the mysticism of antiquity, they employ in line with the character of their specialty a mystical terminology, which was learned via an historico-philological faculty, but does this indeed mean, that these people have a real attitude towards mysticism, does it mean that they are full of mystical hopes and expectations, a mystical faith and love?

Certainly, no. They are positivists perhaps, they do not believe in the real-mystical, yet they can academically examine the interesting theme of the past, the mystical outlook of the old days. But lift away the literary historico-philological veil, speak the language of your soul, of your experience, your real hopes and beliefs, speak about the modern, about our mysticism, then we shall see, of what sort is your authentic and vital attitude towards mysticism. For indeed, the mystical in history can only be taken up in a non-dead and real manner only in connection with the contemporary mystical, with the mystical stirrings and hope of our own day. It is necessary to grasp not at the outward historical thread,

---

[1] Published in "Russkaya mysl'", June 1907.

but rather at the inner, the truly real mystical thread, connecting us both with the Middle Ages and with antiquity, in their mystical activity, in their eternity, and not in their temporality. The academic, the archeological attitude is as though towards a corpse, with it there is so little to be learned, everything remains superficial and a matter of mere words. The danger of an academic, a literary attitude towards mysticism -- is in its full the absence of realism. I would the more give credence to the realism of the mystical words of whatever the physicist or economist, rather then the literateur coming from the historico-philological school, since in accord with their specialty the physicist or economist would find it quite perplexing dealing with the academic and exclusively literary approach towards mysticism; there would be no correspondence of terminology at their disposal, often they would not know the words, denoting things mystical in the past, and for them the mystical proper would not be a matter of words only. And it becomes strange, when one ceases really to differentiate mystical words from mystical activity, when one fails to distinguish literature from being, the refined positivists from the genuine mystics, when everything is veiled over by a cloud, when the foggy mist of clever positivism is passed off as mysticism. It is important instead to establish the genuine distinctions, since then only can there be established any affinity and correlation. The distinctions however can be sharpened only upon the basis of a realism on mysticism, a real relationship to mysticism. Every mysticism, and ours modernly also, strives towards a new way of being, and not towards a new literature only, and the distinctions connected with it -- are of a way of life itself, and not of mere literary words.

I shall speak not about decadentist art, but rather about the decadentist condition of the human soul, about the decadentist world-perception and world-concept. My theme is not literary aesthetic, but religio-philosophic. I have to caution beforehand, that the "decadentist" literature and art I deal with here is only as a symptom of an illness of spirit and it is only under this one point of perspective that I shall investigate this illness. I say "illness of spirit", although I set a very high store on the so-called decadentist art, and I regard it the sole genuine art in our era.

The decadentism has been criticised from various points of view, and accused of many a transgression: some have seen in it foolishness and an outrage against healthy thought, others have decried its immorality, a third group -- its non-societal aspect, and a fourth group have found in it an infraction of aesthetic norms. It is impossible to say, whether all this customary criticism of decadentism has demonstrated any especial effect or proven any danger for decadentism. In the majority of instances the criticism has tended to miss the mark. But the decadentist world-view and the decadentist state of spirit can be criticised from an altogether unique point of view, quite rarely put forth. The terrible aspect presented by decadentism, its authentic tragedy -- is in its loss of the sense and awareness of realities, in its extreme anti-realism. Decadentism is the reflection of the illusory aspect of being. Therefore it is not without basis that they should term decadentism as a neo-romanticism: in it there is anguish over being, but not the reality of being.

Analysing the relationship of decadentism to the real, to the mystical-real, we first of all have to take note of its extreme anti-individualism, its hostility to person. It would be very superficial and erroneous to see an individualism in decadentism, to suggest its pathos as serving to the affirmation of person. In the decadentist experiences, the person is disintegrated into momentary instants, impressions, fragmented conditions, with the loss of the centre for the person and its own organic connections to life. Decadentism has no right to speak about individuality, since it denies to deny the objective reality of such. For an affirmation of individuality there mustneeds be a pulling oneself together, a concentration around the centre, and not a disintegration into momentary fragments. The idea of person -- is normative, person is not some aggregate of whatever the favorable condition, without any sort of bearings to some objective centre. In order to sense the limits of person, in order to set it apart from all the world, in order for the person not to be disintegrated and blasted to bits across the dimensions of the universe nor narrowed down within the dimensions of the lower forms of being, there has to be an objectivity and realism, there mustneeds be an objectivity of distinction, the sensing and awareness of the realities of the world in their inter-relationships. The decadentist attitude towards the person is illusory; decadentism senses individuality as a disintegration of being and it snatches at the morsels, the fragments, in the experience of the moment it seeks after all fullness, and in having despaired of any real fullness of person, it does not believe in the attainability of being.

Having lost its own sense and self-awareness of person, decadentism herein by this loses the sense and awareness of all the realities of the world, of all the objective distinctions of being. The decadentist world-perception jumbles together the "I" with the "not-I", it mixes together that, which is, with that, which is not. The decadentists are as it were afraid of real encounters, they want to reserve for themselves the possibility to say, what is not reality, what is nothing, they have an aversion towards a connectedness with anything real. The decadentist experiencings too much reckon upon the possibility of enlarging the extent of the person, by an acknowledging of illusory being, having abolished all the boundaries of the fictitious but not of the real, surmounting these limits in a transient mindset and word, but not in an eternal actuality. The decadentists have hopelessly confused mysticism with a psychological subtlety of refinement, with the discovering of new empirical states, and upon this jumbled confusion they have based their mystical pretensions. The decadentists have ceased to be able to differentiate the light of the moon from the light of the streetlamps. The London and the Peterburg fogs have provided many a new experience, they have enriched experimental psychology, but in them was hidden and dissolved a mystical sort of being, a mystical realism was misted over. Upon decadentism, like a curse, lies the seal of its derivation from naturalism: the naturalism has become refined, has decomposed imperceptibly and passed over into its opposite. Both in the coarse lineage of naturalism and in the most refined lines of decadentism there is alike a triumph of illusionism and not the reflection of absolute mystical being. The positivist naturalism is also at the root of all an illusionism and anti-realism. From this taproot it is difficult for the decadentists to tear themselves away, and they all confuse as mysticism the refinements and pretty flowers, sprouted from this selfsame root.

It is impossible to confuse the mystically real with a mere experience, with a testing of factual conditions, with a subjective given. The most vivid, the most powerful, the most irrational experience is still not reality and is still not mysticism. The experiences in a certain sense are all in general undifferentiated; the experience is set in opposition to nothing, is not distinct from it. And in the experiences, in the subjective states there can reign a total illusiveness of sight, it can be that there is not a single drop of reality to it. Realism enters in only then, when the experience, the subjective testing is applied towards objective centres, towards existing monads, when there are established distinctions in objective being. The most intensive experience -- is illusory, if it is directed at an object, not endowed with reality. An objectless experiencing, a sundering of experience from objects makes them illusory, non-real: the experience of love cannot be without object, the experiencing of freedom cannot not have an object of striving. Each experience, in order to become a genuine actuality, ought to have a bearer, ought to be connected with an existing centre. Mysticism, real mysticism, enters in only then, when the experience is applied towards absolute being.

Decadentism in the darkness grasps at being and strikes up against the illusory, upon the torn off fragments of reality, upon mere splinters of being, -- in the darkness it is difficult to distinguish that, which is, from that, which is not. They seize hold the first thing they stumble upon in the darkness, they clutch at it convulsively, they want to get a feel of its depth, but too often they embrace only emptiness. The decadentists are not hospitable to empirical reality, they sense its insipidness and they thirst for a mystical reality. But the decadentist attitude towards mysticism is so frightened by this, that it thus readily substitutes for it a mysticism of *mystifications*.

Decadentist mysticism is replete full of mystifications. It is tempting indeed in the absence of a real mysticism to console oneself with a mysticism not real, illusory, contrived. The mystification only is thus also reprehensible, in that within it there is not attained the reality of being. The non-real, the as it were "idealistic" mysticism is also mystification, since that it is too real a mystification to become mysticism. With the decadentist world-outlook the boundary line, separating mysticism from mystification, almost without notice too much tends to fade away: the decadentist mysticism to a remarkable degree is a mystification, it is non-real, in it there is not quite yet the sense, that it is but a bad joke, but then the decadentist mystification sometimes comes close to mysticism, it would seem a mystical reality, unaware of the danger of playing with fire. Within the bounds of decadentist experience there can never be an awareness of all the infinitude of difference between mysticism and mystification, between reality and illusion. Decadentism remains in a fatal manner within the closed-in circle of subjectivity, it is tempted by solipcism, it refines and gets entangled in the human, but it does not unite with the Divine. Mysticism is always a rupturing of the boundaries of subjectivism, a surmounting of the human, an uniting with a supra-human reality. Decadentism has taken upon itself the torment of longing for mystical reality, for supra-human being, it has reflected within itself the loss of taste for the everyday world, but it suffers the illness of impotence to attain to the reality of being. The frightful aspect of decadentism is in this, that nothing is attained, that there are no joyful encounters. This new romanticism is situated at far greater a remoteness from being, than was the old romanticism.

Decadentism denies truth as an objective reality or else it accepts a multitude of truths, all which are equivalent with their negation. Truth however is something binding, it empowers and compels, it does not permit for itself an attitude of mystification. Only an objective acceptance of truth -- is real. To know the truth -- means to have a real object, to be merged with a real object. The decadentist world-attitude has wanted as though to preserve an illusory freedom from truth. i.e. from reality. Decadentism has wanted as though to reserve for itself the possibility to spurn every reality, to step back upon some happy remoteness from real being, to call an halt before the truth, i.e. before the having of reality, before a merging with reality. The decadentist sense of feeling is directed upon itself, and not upon the world, and therefore it fails to unite with it; the mystical sense of feeling unites with other existents, it penetrates into the intimate being of the world, it is as it were -- conjugal.

Mystical realism is connected with an acknowledging of the distinctions within objective being. Real mystical experiences presuppose a certain light, a gnosis, they cannot transpire within total darkness and blindness. In order to mystically experience the real, it is necessary to know truth, i.e. to have mystically-real objects of being, to be merged as it were conjugally with that, which is authentic. The sensing and awareness of mystical realities is a sensing and awareness of real *existents*, of a real being with its own proper name. Mystical realism enters in only then, when we call all and everything by its own name, when we recognise the existents, from which the world is comprised, when we can say: this here is such and so, and there -- is that such and so. The dogmatism, this unacceptable, repulsive wicked dogmatism is also, perhaps, the recognition, the sharpening of mystical insight, a calling by their own names the real objects of the world. In this sense mystical realism always is dogmatic, it wants to know the realties, to name them, to be involved not with the experiences only, but also with existents. The indeed real is not the experiencings, the only real are the existents, -- the conveyors of experience. Mystical realism presupposes an intuitive comprehension of being, the grace of an absolute reality, entering into the human being and as it were ravaging him. In decadentism there is not yet this dawning light, since the decadentists are caught up only with themself, and are not yet given to involvement with universal being.

In the decadentist world-approach there is no intuition, no entering of an universal reality, this world-approach is closed in within its own human subjectivity. Mysticism always involves a graced element, always includes within itself intuitive knowledge, in it the Divinity is immanent to the human soul. A refined positivism can with great ease pass itself off as mysticism, since it is all -- the same colour, all jumbled together, if there is no objective criterion, if there is no objective norm for the establishing of realities, for the distinguishing of being from non-being. Positivism at present has gotten quite refined and has become so liberalised, that it is ready to recognise even the sphere of mystical experiences. It never alone avows any sort of positivism, or any sort of subjective psychologism -- the mystical reality it never avows, whereas the mystical illusions it already avows. Within the sphere of mystical literature there can circulate the cultural and refined positivist, and here there can be the academic and archeological interest, but ultimately still the positivist is unable to enter into the sphere of mystical being. Decadentism furthers the jumbling together of a refined positivism with mysticism, it obscures the differences, and does not sharpen them in focus. And if mysticism for us is the striving towards new being, then we ought to avow an absolute norm, distinguishing being from non-being, a norm not logical and not moral, but rather an ontological norm, *a norm of being*. Only in accord with this norm will the decadentist world-approach become mystically real. Mysticism is first of all a discipline of will.

Decadentism lives now through a crisis, it wants to transcend itself, to pass over to mystical realism, but it cannot, it is lacking in powers to sense reality, it is afraid to get bound up with being. This powerlessness, this inability to pass over to real mysticism finds expression in the "mystical anarchism", -- begotten of the crisis of decadentism. Mystical anarchism -- is not mystical realism, it is too fearful of truth, it does not want to accept the binding realism of truth. Mystical anarchism keeps itself at a remarkable distance from the realities, at a distance, amidst it is impossible to call any one reality by its own name, and it is impossible to sense the existents, which comprise being. The mystical anarchist reserves for himself the possibility to deny every reality, he desires that being should only depend upon his arbitrary will, and he thus guards the darkness, in which so little can be discerned. In this -- is the anti-realism and anti-mysticism of mystical anarchism. In the mindset of the mystical anarchist freedom is set in opposition to all the entirety of being and therefore it is an empty freedom, bereft of real content, and in its wont for illusion it is hostile to the perception of mystical realities. Mystical anarchism does not overcome, but only intensifies the decadentist feeling of freedom, as a desire for that which is without object and without content, as non-being set in opposition to being, frightened at its connectedness.

Decadentism opens up the sphere of the subconscious, it expands the circle of possibilities and provides an experimental tool in the struggle against rationalism, it lifts from life the fetters of rationality. But the subconscious is only an element, in which there ought to begin movement towards realities, towards new, different, non-disgusting realties. The subconscious element can be dawned upon by light, issuing forth from real being, wherein it proceeds as a revelation of absolute activity, and thereupon the subconscious becomes supra-conscious, supra-rational. Rationalism is conquered not by blindness and darkness, but by the ultimate and absolute light, the phantasmic and loathesome aspects of empirical being are conquered by absolute real being.

Decadentism is faced by the threat of degeneration and vulgarisation, should it not find the strength to conquer subjectivism, illusionism and irrationalism. Decadentism remains totally in a negative opposition to the acceptance of the values of this world, to the staleness of empirical being, but it is time already to turn round to the values of the other world, to the depths of mystical being. At the summits of its consciousness, our epoch stands beneathe the standard of a passing over to objectivism, realism, universal meaning.

Decadentism confuses mysticism with aestheticism, it mistakes aesthetic experiences for the mystical, in the aesthetic perception it seeks a mystical activity. A religion of aestheticism, -- here is what decadentism comes to approximate, here is by what it comforts itself. In this transformation of aesthetics into a religion, in this confusion of aesthetic illusion with mystical reality it expresses most of all the anti-realism and illusionism of the decadentist world-approach. Between the aesthetic experience and the mystical experience there is an enormous difference, there lies between an impassable chasm, and it is not so difficult to determine, in what consists this difference. Mystical experience is distinct in this from the aesthetic, in that it real, i.e. it is accompanied by the sense and awareness of the reality of the object, of the object of its striving; the aesthetic experience, abstractly taken, -- is illusory, since that it does not yet relate to any particular reality. The object of aspiration of every aesthetic experience is beauty, but it remains uncertain, whether there actually is beauty, whether it is being, whether it is reality. Mystical experience likewise can strive towards beauty, can perceive beauty, but here the beauty -- is reality, beauty -- is being, beauty --- is absolute an activity. The decadentist religion of aestheticism was disillusioned in the seemingly stale "realities" of positivism, it was stung by the monstrously empirical, but it can only oppose to this world a phantasmic non-real world of beauty, since it cannot accept mystical beauty as an existent. The religion of aestheticism arrives only to a new literature, and not to new being; this is a bad, pitiful, unreal religion and it predisposes its followers to live, to be in ugliness. We want to accept the absolute active beauty of the world, we want being as beauty, and beauty as being, and not merely an illusional experience of beauty. Beauty is not only in art, not only in our experiences, phantasmic and foggy, -- there is beauty, but in being itself, in the very existence of the world. The revelation of the Cosmos, of God's creation, is a revelation of beauty. Beauty is a supreme and authentic reality, an actuality, but the approach to it can only be mystical, and not abstract aesthetic.[2] Aestheticism remains in the sphere of the seemingly apparent, mysticism leads across to the sphere of the real. The inward punishment of every

---

[2] Schelling in his "Philosophie der Kunst" ["Philosophy of Art"] says: "Schoenheit ist das real angeschaute Absolute" ["Beauty is the real contemplatible Absolute"]. Vide Schellings Werke. Dritter Band [Vol. III], 1907, p. 46. This is a very profound definition, from which is evident, that the contemplative extent of absolute being is beauty.

experience of an aesthetique transformed into a religion lies in this, that being is not attained, that the thing most desired, most loved -- beauty, -- is not sensed as a reality, that having been saved from the ugliness of being, they remain in a beauty of non-being, wherein life is transformed into literature. It is not necessary to abolish the aesthetic, but rather to overcome its self-satisfied and smugly abstract character, to subordinate the aesthetic to the mystical organism, to pass over to a mystical aesthetics, in which beauty is not only accepted and experienced, but also is endowed with reality, beauty -- is of a vital existence, and not only of literature. Beauty will save the world.

"Decadentism" -- is the sole thing now in our literature and our art. Only in the camp, signified by this indefinable word, can there be found both talent, and a genuine love for art, and creative impulses. There is apparently already the time, when disputes over literary trends will be decided by this fact, that there will be no sort of art for us besides the decadentist, and therefore there will no longer be even a "decadentist" art. There will be a new art, long wished for, but meanwhile yet situated in a condition of potential being. Inside the decadentist camp there will result a crisis, a decomposition, a self-determination. Decadentist art of an inner dialectical necessity will dissociate into an academic, Parnassian, classical form, and into a mystical, religious, theurgic form.[3] Classical art is a very venerable and fine art, possessing its own mission in the world, it rests upon the abstract ideal of artistic beauty and lacks for any mystical pretensions. Not to have mystical pretensions, when one cannot fulfill them, -- is a fine quality and from this perspective the trend of decadentist art towards academism and classicism (Valery Briusov can be hailed.

Mystical art has theurgy as the goal of its striving. Theurgic art posits as its aim the creation of new being, of a new mankind. This -- is the practising of a mystical realism. In the final end there

---

[3] Its most imposing representative for us is Vyacheslav Ivanov.

are only two directions in art -- the classical and the theurgic, everything else is but a transitory state. The so-called realism in art has merely been pseudo-theurgic. Classicism is the ideal of a self-sufficing art, of art as an abstract principle, an ideal of literature, but not vitally of life. I repeat, that by this I do not want to condemn it, I highly value classical art. Theurgy however is the ideal of religious art, transfigurative of being, creating the new man, an ideal vitally of life, and not only literary. Theurgic art is already a religious activity, and it existed always in the organic periods of the life of the people. Art is born of an insufficiency, a failed reach of being, in it there is filled up the emptiness of this world with the riches of the other world. And within the scope of mystery the creation of beauty by art coincides with God's creation of the cosmos.

Decadentist art, insofar as it is a genuine art, stands higher than a decadentist religion, in it there have been authentic insights and there is the potential of a theurgic art. Still, in Russian great literature there have been genuine mystical realists, filled with expectation, -- Tiutchev and Dostoevsky. In modern Russian poetry (of the "decadentist" camp) there is many a talent, but no one still can compare with Tiutchev in his power of mystical realism. There is the strangest desire, that a new Russian literature might find expression: let it be sought, just like in its great past, not only in life, but also its meaning, i.e. that it be religious, theurgic. Then only will the crisis of decadentism result in an happy end. But God preserve us from a false understanding of the tasks of religious art: not upon assigned religious themes and not from a religious tendency ought the artist to create. Most of all it mustneeds be understood, that it is not a matter of religious themes, since all themes, all themes without exception -- are religious. With the artist there ought not to be religious tendencies only, but rather *a religious world-feeling*, and then in his art will be manifest the religiousness of everything in the world, the religious depths of everything being disclosed in this. The decadentist world-sense hinders the artist from immersion into the depths of the religious mystery of the world and only great artistic talent can catch sight of the religious realities, despite the decadentist rendering asunder from being. Authentic genuine art is as it were a photo-imaging of absolute activity, a reflection of eternal ideas. It is necessary most of all to be rid of that prejudice, that religion is of something else, some sort of special sphere. Religion -- is everything, religion -- is in everything, or it -- is nothing. The religious world-feeling reveals the depths of being in everything, it as it were is an opening to the mystery of creation.

Mystical realism inevitably bears a religious character, it becomes religion, does not remain mysticism. Once it becomes clearly apparent, the connections namely of the mystical realities, then only but a religious attitude can be established towards them. The mysticism is an as yet imperfect and transitional form of religion, this is a religion blind and as yet insufficiently real. Religious mysticism is not something connected only with fictitious experiences, but with the facts of world life. The religious stirring is bound up only with universal realities, with that, which -- is being within history. With the traditions of being, of being and not of lifestyle, mystical realism cannot and ought not to split, for it continues the universal line of authentic being.

Anti-realist decadentism dwells with the fluctuating tastes over decades, over years and months, and not eternity, it yields to the enticements of fads and the interests of the season. In this is an inward punishment of decadentism and the danger of its vulgarisation. Decadentism is a transition of flesh into word, of being into literature; mystical realism is a transformation of word into flesh, the creation of new being. One might say: every literature is a transformation of flesh into word, and therefore one would want to abolish literature in revolting against this. What I want to say is not this: let flesh be transformed into word in literature, since a fine literature is born of this and great is the significance of this literature, but let it not be transformed into life, into being itself, flesh into the word. Decadentism has an inclination towards the transformation of flesh into word within life itself, and not only in literature, and in this is its anti-realism.[4] And the eternal criterion of distinction, the light determinative of this distinction, is neither literary nor academic, but rather of existence and of life, it remains an attitude towards the historical accomplishing of the Incarnation of the Word. Those, for whom the Incarnation of the Word occurred not symbolically only, but mystically-real, and who believe in the real Resurrection of the Word, such only can be mystical realists, striving towards new being, and for the anguish regarding Heaven is transformed into a thirst for the new real flesh of life. Mystical illusionism either passes over into mystical realism or it degenerates and becomes vulgar, extinguishing being.

---

[4] The transformation of flesh into word was characteristic of the Alexandrian epoch.

RUSSIAN GOD-SEEKERS [1]

The history of Russian self-consciousness in the XIX and beginning XX Centuries is of tremendous interest. This history is still not written, and many a page, very dear for us, is absent, many faces remain in the shadows, in the back alley-ways, not leading out onto the main thorough-fares. The typical liberal and radical histories of Russian self-consciousness have worked out their stereotypes, they have established banal criteria for defining what is the "main road", what generally obtains, and much that is original, the most of all valuable for us, has ceased to be visible, has been omitted, has been skipped over in the book about the Russian soul. The vital worrying of official conservatism has prevented this book from being written, and has created in the area of thought an official progressiveness. There was created a moribund state cabinet of the progressive camp, a special sort of bureaucratism of consciousness, reflecting in itself the hated bureaucratism of the state lifestyle. Against everything, that that seemed imputable to the conservative camp, sometimes with foundation, sometimes without basis, there were adopted bureaucratic measures, similar to the way the government had taken bureaucratic measures against the progressive camp. In such manner, off and to the outside of the official-progressive horizon of view proved to be almost the whole of Chaadaev, the Slavophils in what was progressive in them, half of Gogol, Tiutchev, Dostoevsky, Lev Tolstoy in part, Konstantin Leont'ev, Vl. Solov'ev, V. V. Rozanov, Merezhkovsky, all the Russian decadents, the whole of Russian philosophy. They penned instead an history of the progressive self-consciousness, which they accepted as the triumph of the positivist world-view, and all the religious cravings, essentially, fell off by the

---

[1] Originally published in "Moskovskii Ezhenedel'nik", 28 July 1907.

wayside from this history, and they were treated as either individual quirks, or as reactionary. But in history there was the so-called "conservatism", the non-official, the non-Katkovite, moreso romantic than it was realistic, and in it was hidden much wealth, many creative and not altogether "conservative" ideas. It is necessary to get to understand these ideas and discover these riches.

A great pining, an incessant *God-seeking* is lodged within the Russian soul, and it was expressed over the expanse of an entire century. The God-seekers reflected our spirit, rebellious and hostile to every philistinism. Almost the whole of Russian literature, the Russian great literature, is a living document, witnessing to this God-seeking, to an unquenchable spiritual thirst. There is something heart-rending and together with this tragic in the fate of the Russian God-seekers. They go unrecognised, misunderstood, spurned, they perish from the torments of their languishing.

The first such God-seeker in the XIX Century was Chaadaev, and no fate was more sad than his. In answer to his religious thirst, his search for the Kingdom of God, they declared him a lunatic, and then they forgot him. He remained a stranger for both the Westernisers and the Slavophils, for both those on the left and on the right, and successive God-seekers failed to comprehend their kinship with him. In the school-manuals it has become commonplace to speak a couple trite words about the scepticism of Chaadaev in regard to Russia, and about his going over to Catholicism, but they failed to see into the depths of his searching, and that which was prophetic in this man -- they failed to appreciate.[2] Chaadaev had a presentiment already of the passage over of historical forms of Christianity towards the supra-historical Universal Church. With It he connected his hope for the Kingdom of God upon earth. In this regard, Chaadaev was to

---

[2] Not so long ago, M. Gershenson opened up almost all that there was in Chaadaev within his articles in "Voprosi Zhizn" for the year 1905, and in "Vestnik Evropy" for the year 1906. And thereafter the work of Gershenson came out as a separate book.

a greater degree a precursor for Vl. Solov'ev, than for the Slavophils, although this connection was unclear even to Solov'ev himself. Chaadaev's thirst senses the Universal Church and subjects to it all the history of the world, something which torments us even now. He was not a Catholic, nor could he be only an Orthodox, for in him there was the potentiality of a great religious idea. *Universality* upon a religious ground, the search for a theocracy -- here is what Chaadaev bequeathed to the subsequent generations of God-seekers.

The Slavophils fared incomparably better, they constituted an entire camp, they founded a school of thought, and the influence of their current is felt even in our own time. But the actual influence of the Slavophils upon subsequent generations is a distressing drama, filled with historical irony. The religious thirst of the Slavophils and the mission of faith in the supreme vocation of Russia decayed into the moribund official churchliness and the official state patriotism. With his enormous intellect, his religious visionary dreaminess, his aristocratic spirit, what does Khomyakov have in common with those subsequent nationalists, all those "truly Russian people", the Russian groups, the "Union of Russian People", etc? The only thing that had historical success was the conservative teaching of the Slavophils about sovereignty and their false veneration of nationality as a fact, as an idealisation of the past, and not as an ideal norm, not as something which ought to be realised. This -- is what has obtained in the camp of official conservatism, which has guarded the temporal in place of the eternal. And in the progressive camp they only scoffed at or just plain ignored the Slavophils, since before their eyes they had only the degenerated legacy of Slavophilism. And at present, when someone wants to get into Kireevsky, Khomyakov, K. Aksakov, their feet tangle upon the likes of Gr. Sharapov, and they hesitate to go further.

And Gogol, the great God-seeker Gogol? His fate was something terrible. True, he is esteemed by everyone as a first-class artist, he was put in the Pantheon, but his religious torments met with general censure, his anguish was misunderstood. He sought God and His Kingdom and he perished amidst the inescapableness of his longing. Further along came our great geniuses, Dostoevsky and

Tolstoy, having merited world acclaim, revered by everyone, but moreso as artists, than as God-seekers. Dostoevsky is quite still regarded with suspicion, and the progressives do not forgive him his "reactionary" streak. Everything, that in Dostoevsky was religious and prophetic, everything such failed to make it out upon the main thorough-fare of Russian history, it remained the dostoyanie-merit but of few. And the fate of a remarkable Russian man, extraordinarily original and talented, tormented and anguished, -- was that of Konstantin Leont'ev, almost a genius of a reactionary, with a fate even more pitiful than that of Chaadaev. Political fanaticism was the undoing of Leont'ev, and no one wants to know him. Who would guess, that in this reactionary there was something in truth revolutionary, in whom stormed religious passions?[3] Vl. Solov'ev has begun to be appreciated now, but this extraordinary man spent all his life isolated and ended in gloomy despair, he lost his faith that mankind would turn itself to God, as a sign of Christ within itself. Then there is Rozanov, together with the religio-philosophic gatherings, and too the most recent searchings and experiences -- all this by-passes the main thorough-fare, it all roosts off in the corners. Why does the God-seeking get valued so lowly, why does it evoke such derision and malice? Or is this a thirst for something vile? Sometimes one arrives at despair, one loses faith in mankind, the hope in the coming of the Kingdom of God. It may be that we, being weak, have not the gift to move hearts, nor inspire by example, but indeed behind us stand those great and strong ones, and their fate is sadder than ours. Some day they will write down the rightly just

---

[3] Here however there ought to be mentioned the remarkable thinker N. F. Fedorov, a bit strange and with flashes of genius, having had influence upon Vl. Solov'ev and deeply revered by him. In Fedorov is seen already a passage over towards a new religious consciousness. Concerning Fedorov, vide the interesting book by V. A. Kozhevnikov, which regrettably was published not gratis for free, as was the work of Fedorov himself.

history of the Russian God-seekers, whose universal thirst will be quenched in those, for whom the hour of historical reality draws nigh.

The God-seekers were of little use, they were unable to give practical directives, they did not transform stones into bread, and so there has not been forgiven them their dreamy uselessness, their apparent inactivity. The official conservatism had nothing in common with this religious thirst, it declared every thirst illegal, every manifestation of spirit it regarded with suspicion, and in essence it is merely positivist. But the idealistic conservatism, romantic in its hostility to everything civil and official, has lodged within it greater spiritual values, than the official, the governmental progressiveness and revolutionism. The civil conservatives in the spirit of Katkov and others worshipped imperialism, they worshipped the idol of abstract statecraft, the kingdom of this world, but the God-seekers, even though they outwardly and to casual glance might be imputed to the conservative camp, actually instead craved for the city of God, they sought in this world the kingdom not of this world. It may be that Dostoevsky and Vl. Solov'ev were tempted by the idea of autocracy, and they displayed their political naivete and made crude mistakes in their political arithmetic, as is apparent now to any gymnasium school-kid, yet all the same they never worshipped the idol of imperialism, the Katkovism, they never avowed autocracy, as something not limited by the law of God. Government life, the practice of official statecraft did not however recognise this limitation of every rule of power by the law of God, and therefore every God-seeking as such was inwardly directed against the reactionary rule of power, against the demonic imperialism. A free theocracy, the replacing of the state by the Church, -- was an utmost dream of all the God-seekers, and insofar as there has never yet been a theocracy within historical Orthodoxy, our God-seekers strove towards an higher, a supra-historical form of Christianity.

In modern Europe there is no such religious craving, and a different spirit has prevailed there. There each day the spirit of the earth conquers out the sphere of its kingdom, it deadens the age-old eternal dream about heaven and the thirst for the meaning of life. The mechanistic in Europe conquers everything organic, both in the theoretical consciousness, and so also in activity. Man herein -- is an outright machine, society -- is an outright machine, the whole of culture -- is an improved mechanism, the whole of thought is non-organic, is rational judgement, wherein the whole world-sense has lost its organic centre of being. Only *God's* world is an organism, whereas the godless world, naturally improved, is a mechanism, a pseudo-organism, a substitute for authentic life. The prevailing European philosophy is likewise mechanistic, torn off from the absolute centre, irreligious, just as in the prevailing European politics. Observations upon European culture tend to stoke the faith in Russian missionism. This missionism readily assumes false forms, and it degenerates into the nationalism, against which Vl. Solov'ev so brilliantly contended. Nationalism, national self-praise and self-affirmation, the rendering of nationality into an idol for oneself, a doltish chauvinism -- all this quite flourishes also in the West, and in this we cannot even compare with the French, the English and the Germans in national exclusiveness, in national greed and self-worship. Our "truly Russian" people -- these are people demonic and sick, evidencing for us moreso the absence of an healthy and strong national sense, rather than its abundance. Russian missionism, which was always present in the Russian God-seekers, is least of all an earthly nationalism and state self-affirmation. This missionism, intelligible only for the religious consciousness, is totally foreign to our official imperialism, it is opposed to it and a danger for it; those seeking out the city of God have nothing in common with our nationalists, statesmen and political reactionaries, tempted by the prince of this world. In Slavophilism itself there was a twofold understanding of the missionism: that of a religious vocation and calling, which ought to be realised by Russia on the world stage, though it be by way of great self-renunciation, or otherwise that of an idealisation and regarding divine the fact of national lifestyle, i.e. a purely pagan self-affirmation. The first sort of consciousness of a Russian missionism was further developed by Dostoevsky, by Vl. Solov'ev, and passed on to Merezhkovsky and the most recent God-seekers; the second sort of consciousness was developed by Katkov, by the state nationalists, and it passed on into reactionary obscurantism and the "Union of the Russian People". The missionary consciousness is a duty, and not a privilege, an arduous historical task, and not an outward primacy. The pagan, the non-Christian and anti-Christian attitude towards nationality and statecraft all still prevails, and our official conservatives, Katkovites, nationalists, "truly Russian" people stand firmly on the soil of this paganism and anti-Christianism.

In the revolutionary epoch at present, the position of the God-seekers, in seeking out the City, is very difficult, tortuous, complex. Truth has too much become mixed up together with falsehood. It is necessary to contend both against the official statecraft, with its reactionism, and also against the official revolutionism, with its nihilistic hooliganism in revolution, since both with the one and the other there is temptation with the kingdoms of this world. Lovers of the kingdom not of this world seem like foreigners in the bustle and the crowd, finding themselves there no joy. All these, whether Chaadaev, Gogol, the best of the Slavophils, Dostoevsky, Solov'ev and the others, did not find actual and practical applications for their extraordinary ideas, they did not find points of application, wherein their ideas would overturn all the world; they seemed in comparison with others to be inactive, and for matters of this world poorly adapted. All of them rendered unseen a great deed, but they did not bequeathe us clear methods of visible historical activity. And we too stand helplessly before a great historical task. In the official-progressive and Westerniser camp only infrequently is there to be encountered any hidden God-seeking, always instead there is the veiled-over struggle against God, and the ideas of this camp in the majority of instances are banal, but they had with them clear methods of action, techniques for liberation, and with them there is much that might be learned whether for Dostoevsky, or Vl. Solov'ev, and all the other people of this type. When the Slavophils made a great practical deed (participation in the emancipation of the serfs, they then worked in concert with the Westernisers; whereas, their own original methods almost always were mistaken or utopian.

Someone once mentioned about the day and night aspect in the history of Russian self-consciousness, in our searchings, in our literature. With us only the day part obtained an official right to existence, and was acknowledged as progressive. In this day aspect of the history there is little that is original, it all follows along on its trite models, though too it served a needed and useful service. But our God-searching has transpired as though in the night, amidst the light of the stars, and not by that of the sun. Nocturnal -- is all the poetry of Tiutchev, all the creativity of Dostoevsky. Nocturnal -- is all the Russian metaphysics and mysticism. For people of the day and daytime work, the nocturnal represents all the consciousness of the religious meaning of life. Only the nocturnal, the transcendent, the supra-empirical consciousness leads to the sensing of God, though in it too can be manifest the devil (about this, much can be learned in Dostoevsky). Amidst the night, the trans-rational, we do not reason upon the darkness and gloom, but on something higher, passing beyond the bounds of the consciousness of this world. To transform the nocturnal insight and vision into the mighty powers of the daytime sun -- in this is our great task, perhaps, our historical mission. The rift between the "nocturnal" and the "daytime" consciousness, a dualism of the transcendent and the immanent -- is likewise a sickness of spirit, and in it is all our tragedy. It is exactly as when in oversleeping we waken from the night-time dreams and our eyes are in a blind daze, and our mind is tormented by the fright of actuality, by the terror of the reality of day. We are powerless to transfer to the daytime God's truth, as borne from out of the nocturnal searchings. The Russian missionism, lodged within the night, the transcendent consciousness of the finest Russian people, is shaken to its roots by *the immediacy of day.*

There has been lost faith in the people, which proved such a slave on the day of its emancipation. How could the God-bearing people in a notable extent prove so nihilistic hooligan-like or be so black-souled rowdy? How could the sacred standard of liberation become polluted with criminal acts, wild licentiousness and brazen impudence? Hath the people, as a mystical organism, said its say, and where is it, this great people? The Social-Revolutionary fabrications of the people's soul just as little resemble -- the people, as do the fabrications of the state-cabinets. We believe, that the people is neither the Black Hundreds nor the Red Hundreds. Within the people there has always been suchlike a religious thirst, amongst those lower down in national life, in Russian sectarianism, and in the people's Orthodox piety there has been the same God-seeking and God-responsiveness, that there is at the summits of the people's organism, with the God-seeker thinkers, artists and prophets.

But, perchance, in our nocturnal visionary dreams and insights has there been a greater reality, an absolute reality, than that which exists in daily activity? Those, who believe in the sole finality of empirical activity, may laugh at our questions, but they will not have the last laughs. It is not about romantic dreams that are being discussed, for even without this we have had sufficient of such, but rather about actual, real, to the utmost a directing with real power the awareness of God to history, to the fate of Russia and the world. If we and our predecessors were all only mere up in the air, day-dreamy God-seekers, then it would be ludicrous to speak of real power and historical action. But we indeed speak about that God-seeking, which also together with this was a God-finding, a coming upon and following of God: the religious future in these searchings is bound up with the religious past, which is imbued already with an absolute and utmost reality, an uniquely absolute, unrepeatable, salvific and redemptive fact of world history. With Christ, with the faith in Christ the God-Man, our Saviour, is bound up the Russian religious movement, the seeking of the Kingdom of God, the thirst for the God-manly path of developement; in Him, and only in Him is all our hope, and the possibility for us to become a real force in history.

The movement follows from whence Christ leads, apart from Christ it would be bereft of all reality. But the martyrs of the new religious thirst have awaited and await the fulfilling of the promise and prophecies about the Kingdom of God even upon the earth. Often along unperceived and varied pathways, from varied and quite apparently contrary scenes of modern culture there occurs the working out in consciousness and the preparation in practice of a new idea of theocracy, neither Catholic nor Old Testament, alike opposed to both the Western Papocaesarism and the Eastern Caesaropapism. At the various ends of culture there is conceived an awareness of dissatisfaction and apprehension at the dissociated and abstract being, the impossibility and the madness of human self-affirmation and self-deification. A melancholy anxiety is taking hold, close like to that, with which the ancient world was sickened in its era of decline and decay. The most refined summits of culture are grasping at mysticism, a mysticism chaotic, anarchistic and irreligious, just as remote from worldly meaning, as are also positivism and materialism. Contemporary trans-cultural man is experiencing a profound spiritual decadence, the loss of an objective, absolutely real, religious meaning of life and he substitutes for it his subjectively contrived meaning.

The ultimate liberation is possible only by God-manhood, and the ultimate joy is possible only in God. From this perspective of consciousness there inevitable results a twofold attitude towards revolution, towards the worldwide liberation movement, now bursting forth upon Russia. The humanistic side of revolution, the liberation of man from slavery, the affirmation of the rights of man and the unconditional significance of the human person is part of the truth of God-manhood. But the abstract and exclusively self-affirming humanism, an humanism, which would idolise the human element as a god, passes over as something not only godless, but also inhuman. The revolutionaries, the humanists and atheists too often with an inhuman ferocity struggle against man, they do not respect the human person, and they lay waste the human soul. The very idea of the inalienable rights of man and the unconditional value of the human person cannot be affirmed on the grounds of an abstract humanism, it presupposes inevitably an higher and supra-human will. To spurn God and the God-Man -- this means together with this to spurn both mankind and man as the idea of God. The natural man of nature is still a beast, the offspring of a chaotic element, a child of death and decay, not a person still; the natural mankind of nature is still impersonal, subject to the law of hostility and decay, a phantasmic being. Only the God-Man was a true and absolutely real Divine Man, and a true, absolutely real Divine Mankind can only be in God-manhood. All our God-seekers, whether consciously or unconsciously, sought after God-manhood, they moved towards a sociability of God-manhood and therefore they seemed foreign to a sociability merely human, they gave the impression of being lovers of God and as it were seeming indifferent towards mankind.

The conditional, the superficial criteria of conservatism and progressivism, of the right and of the left, are inapplicable to these searches, ineffective for this spirit. One can but say, that a thousand times more radical are those, which go down deep to the very roots of being, who get to the transcendent fundaments of all phenomena, rather than those, that accept the phenomenality as the essence, and see not the roots.

To go along the path not only of an European but also a world liberation does not signify an as yet for certain becoming subject to vulgarisation, to philistinism and spiritual devastation, as tended to think Konstantin Leont'ev, an odd, extraordinarily gifted reactionary and genuine God-seeker. Russian God-seekers, perhaps, as no one nowhere, sensed the absolute void of emptiness in the end-point of the natural, the merely human progress, and they were terrified at the shrill vividness of their insight. But this was indeed only one side of the world developement -- a foreseeing of the kingdom of the prince of this world. There is also another side -- the prophecy about the Kingdom of God upon earth, into which will enter everything good that was created and conceived in the world. And there can be further developed the invested pledges of an *organic* thought and an *organic* world-sense. These rich investments we see in Russian literature, in Russian philosophy, in the unique religiosity of the Russian people and in the religious searchings of the finest segment of the Intelligentsia, creative investments, prophetic about the future. It has fallen to our lot to undergo onerous tribulations, but a great people has need of such trials, in order to prove the strength of its spirit. At present the very idea of the people has been shaken; the religious idea of the people as an integrally whole organism has been falsified by both the right and the left, it has had substituted for it various classes, social classes and every sort of social category. The will of the people has become splintered, fragmented, unseen by us, and everyone alike takes cover under the veil of the people's will: with it all justify themselves the Black Hundreds, and the Red Hundreds, and the government, and the people's freedom parties. Two Dumas have already expired, and neither one of them has discovered the authentic and mighty will of the people, there has been discovered only dissonance and discord. The people's will has sickened with a grievous illness, and this inward infirmity can hardly be doctored with but outward, politically-abstract measures. Then only will the people's will be integrally whole and organic, then only can it find itself expression and fulfillment, surmounting the malice and hatred, when it inwardly becomes conjoined together with the will of God, when it becomes a God-manly will, and not merely human a will.

We do not share the earthly utopias of other dreamers and we believe it to be a poor thing the general deification of mankind, though also we ought to aspire to this. But we believe and we hope that there will be discerned the God-manly centre of world history and around it will coalesce the full scope of God-manly life. Vl. Solov'ev, in whom there was much of the prophetic, finely said, that if prior to Christ the world moved towards the God-Man, then after Christ the world moves towards God-manhood. When upon the world historical path there acutely arises the problem of God-manhood, when the purely human paths will have been traversed, when the godless efforts yield all their results, when religious anguish takes hold on people not only separate and as it were torn off from the great historical path, and there be many, whole masses, whole peoples, then they will remember the Russian God-seekers. These names, sometimes forgotten and always misunderstood by people, will be inscribed onto the list of heroes of world liberation, not an illusionary, but quite real liberation. The anguish of the God-seekers will be appeased. “Blessed are they that hunger and thirst after righteousness, for they shalt be satisfied”.

AS TO THE PSYCHOLOGY OF THE REVOLUTION [1]

There has been exasperatingly much dispute, about whether Russia ought to go the peaceful and constitutional path, or a path militant and revolutionary; while there has yet to be decided the preliminary question, of whether in Russia there does exist the "revolution", which so readily has been transformed into a fetish? All the "leftists" believe blindly and limitlessly in this being, named revolution, almost an absolute being, almost endowed with divine attributes. It has been transformed within life into the idol of "revolution", just like long ago already it has been transformed in theory into the idol of "progress".

The criteria of revolutionness and progressiveness have replaced the old criteria of good and evil, of truth and falsehood, of beauty and ugliness, of godly and godless. To be a leftist, a progressive, a revolutionary, this means also to be a proper fellow, to be moral and just, to have the truth, almost it means to be intelligent and handsome. True, even in the realm of the "left" we too often encounter stupidity and ugliness, moral corruption and falsehood, but all this it is acceptable to either deny or to account accidental, a carry-over, connected with remnants of the "right"; within the left itself and revolutionness already as regards tactical considerations it permits of no inward defects. As regards trite concepts that are not "leftist" or insufficiently "leftist" there is immediately suspicion, the moral propriety is subject to doubt, greed is perceived in each word, each action, to speak with such wantonness is possible only with a person, corrupted by evil. But this sort of fetishism, this idolatry, this creating for oneself an idol and everything like to it, seems to me a dangerous

---

[1] Published in "Russkaya mysl'", July 1908. Written in July 1907. [trans. note: "Revolution" here refers to the 1905 Russian revolution].

sickness, a grievous illness for the Russian soul, which ought to be attended to and doctored in what still can be done.

I tend to think, that the Russian revolution has ultimately been fetishised, undergone an apotheosis, been transformed into an idol, after having ceased really to exist. The revolution in Russia has been ended, in extreme measure for the present it has ended. It has forever gained much, it has made impossible a return to the old, , but half has been rendered a gamble, since it has taken a false direction and made fatal mistakes. After this, as a revolution it has been rendered really impossible, ineffective, the dream about it sent ablaze by reactionary forces has been transformed into a fetish. The revolutionaries cannot really make a revolution similar to that, as was done in the historical and national October general-strike, there is no longer still that period of societal array, nor still such a psychology within the masses. But nonetheless they believe this still all the more passionately, that there is suchlike a god, under the name "revolution", in which absolute bliss is conjoined with absolute might, and this mysterious being, though still invisible, will do it all itself, it will punish the guilty and realise the hopes of the oppressed. It is to this being that the revolutionaries appeal with their shouted cries, with intense desperation, and they hope to beseech from it a miracle. The revolution has died, it has been canonised and made sacred, and now all hope is on the graced action of its relics.

The Russian revolution has ended, long since already it has passed over into the decaying process, into an anarchisation of society, into disintegration. Painfully this has to be acknowledged. The murderings, the expropriations, the hooligan incidents and loud words -- are not revolution, the doings of "maximalists" -- they are a proof of the end of the revolution, the beginning of its disintegration. There is no historical revolutionary activity visible in the near future, and it is impossible to substitute for this activity with any sort of mere noisy shoutings. There is no strong, crystal-clear social consciousness within the masses of the people, and in this consciousness -- is the essence of the revolution. The national historical task in common involving all the people has dimmed, The collective liberating consciousness has fallen into ruin, there has begun a petty process of mutual devouring, the skinning the hide off of a not-dead, and perhaps even, non-existent bear. The enthusiasm and inspiration have been replaced by demonic fury and beastliness. The process of disintegration and decay has proven itself uniform both in the reactionary sphere and in the revolutionary sphere. Both there and here -- is frantic obsession in place of a clear consciousness and strong senses. The maximalists of the right and the maximalists of the left in the final end both serve the same god of violence, and one and the same insane and greedy will lies at the basis of the existence of those and others, the same apostacy from the Absolute Will.

To superficial the political glance, Russia is entering into the phase of an out of sorts and uncertain constitutional monarchy with strong a reactionary bent, a typical thing after the revolutionary excesses. But a constitutional order is something won only slowly and organically. From this it suffices but to study the experience of Western Europe, especially England, where it took centuries to accumulate their government by law. In Germany and Austria at present there is nothing especially good, merely the startings from a very puny constitution. It would as though seem, given where we are at, that we might outstrip Europe; if only that we should stop clambering about on all fours. But with no few a Slavophil among the Russian revolutionary type, they suffer a self-conceit and they think, that Europe for them is no indicator, that Russia has its own mission to realise socialism earlier than Europe. This is a curious psychological fact, and once again merely emphasises our non-political aspect. Russia is positively ungifted a land politically, it has no talent to well arrange its own land. The ruling bureaucracy in Russia has been predominantly German, and it has held the land foreign to it in oppressive a grip. Even the revolutionary epoch has not created for us political talents, genuine leaders, worthwhile to follow. We have no sort of contrivances, no sort of creativity in politics, everything we do is in its trite pattern, and herein we put and decide world questions better than other lands. The deliberations of the two Dumas have revealed ultimately the powerlessness of our revolution. Neither the first, nor the second Duma was capable of consolidating itself within the consciousness of the people, so that their deliberations might become psychologically possible. The Russian people as it were does not desire for itself political power, nor does it have a taste for the rule by the people, it awaits an higher truth upon the earth. With the Slavophils there was a certain truth, which they did not know how to properly express, having distorted it with too obvious an historical lie; and it is this truth that our incipient religio-social movement at present anxiously wants to express.

I cannot call myself a believing constitutionalist, since I do not believe in an all-saving, ideal constitution; I do not await from it miracles, I do not see in a constitutional arrangement anything organic and real, I see rather a mechanical contract, reflecting the dissolution of the organism of the people, as having lost its religious centre. Regarding my religious beliefs I am likewise not a democrat,[2] since religiously I repudiate the principle of the people's sovereignty, I seek guarantees of the rights of the person not in the people's will, not in the human will, but in the will of God. I also do not believe, as do the Constitutional-Democrats, in the salvational aspect of abstractly taken politics, political parties and political struggle, all promulgating the tactical lie on principle. To the ideal of a constitutional democracy I could only oppose the organic ideal of a free theocracy. But as to the relative coursings of politics, and consequently of both constitutionalism and democratism, it is impossible to deny, that this would be equivalent to a denying of history, an ignoring of the torments in its developement. Granted all this may reflect a tearing apart of the people's will, granted all this is mechanical, and not organic, but the splintering apart and mechanicalness -- is a fact, and this fact mustneeds be lived through and surmounted by a difficult, prolonged, tragic process as regards dissatisfaction with the most immediate results. A turnabout in

[2] But least of all does this mean, that I stand for class and social privileges against democracy.

consciousness does not yet make it a turnabout in life. It is always necessary to remember *the irrationalness of being*, begetting the torment within history. This irrationality cannot at present be overcome whether by revolution, or by constitution, nor by theocratic anarchism and there are no powers to overcome it in the name of reason itself. This tormentive irrationality is rooted in the primordial fall of the world into sin, in the invincibility of God-apostacised chaos. Only towards the end will there win out the completing process of the salvation of mankind and the world, and the annihilation of this tragic hindrance to ultimate harmony.

In the sphere of world politics, the People's Freedom party represents the least of all suchlike evil for Russia. This party, in the person of its finest representatives, understands as it were, that the inner educating of society is the most important matter, that mechanically it is impossible to create any sort of turnabout, that the people -- is a slave in its soul and cannot become free via the experiments of political alchemy. There is not in this party the immoderate human self-deceit, turning politics into a religion, there is not the political exaltation, leading to fanaticism and demonic obsessions. This is an humanitarian societal cross-section, and in its neutral humanism is included an indubitable truth. The Cadet [Constitutional-Democrat party] plan for the developement of Russia is however too rationalised; in a peaceful and healthy rebirth of the land there is little that is credible. The Constitutional-Democrat party serves its own good human purpose, it is free from the demonic obsessiveness of the blacks and the reds, but it is subject to make for itself the same sort of idol from the "constitution", as do the revolutionaries themself from the "revolution". A "constitution", even the most ideal, is the same as little Divine, as is "revolution", as is the "state" -- the idol of the right, and just the same does it little alleviate the thirst or weaken the anguish. The fetish of constitutionalism tempts the Cadets, and their neutral humanism cannot save them from this temptation, since it is only for the religious consciousness that there is ultimately apparent the relativeness, the temporality and subjugation involved whether by the constitution, or by the revolution, or by the state. howsoever harmful and howsoever dangerous, howsoever bourgeois (in the spiritual, and not in the social sense of the word be this worship of a constitution, transforming it into a solely-saving and divine being, howsoever false be this abstract legality, still worse is the obsession, the devilish obsession of the extreme left. Constitutionalism ought to be an experience for Russia, and God grant, that it be an experience with the least possible idolatry.

Revolution always liberates from many of the old idols and deities. Within the past several years, for the consciousness of the Russian masses there has been stripped off the mask from rotting idols, foremost of all the gilded idol of imperialism, and much discrediting what earlier was valued not in regard with its worthiness. But there has appeared the new idol of revolution, of the constitution, etc. Our revolution has made many a cultural conquest, it has forever won many a spiritual blessing, but together with this it has opened up something terrible, it has begotten something wild. It is here upon these cultural-psychological consequences of the revolution and upon the spiritual sub-soil of its many manifestations that I would want to have an halt. It is not in the struggle of the revolution with the government and its destructive policies that comprises the essence of the historical Russian drama, but in the condition of society itself, in its inner falling apart, in its anarchy of spirit. All the premiers, the ministers, the star chambers, the political combinations, the frightening outlook for reaction, all this -- is but the surface incrustation.

* * *

What has happened with the soul of the Russian people, what has the Russian revolution opened up within it? The revolution undertook the protection of the Russian societal aspect, and there was discovered rot, the body of Russia was covered with a rash of sickness, accumulated over centuries of slavery and despotism. Of inner buttresses of stability there was almost none, the fastenings holding it together were outward and mechanically contrived, merely sustaining the inward sickness. All the great revolutions have been accompanied by moral anarchy, all revolutionary epochs have been mere spiritual interregnums, but it would seem, there has not been a single revolution unaccompanied by suchlike a moral decay, that has not revealed suchlike an hooliganist nihilism, as in the intelligentsia, and so also in the people. There is arising a generation of hooligans, who do not know any law higher than that of self-assertion. This generation is given over into the grip of selfishness and greed, and is familiar only with the religion of self-worship and self-deifying. The consciousness of the value of human life has ultimately been lost, and disrespect for person has reached monstrous proportions. God long since already has died in the soul, the nihilist poison has seeped in drop after drop, above and below. Outward hitches have hindered the discovery of the full terror of the disappearance of God. Everyone believed, that the chains would be lifted off, and then man would stand up in his full stature, would discover all the wealth of his powers. But what a mess it has shown to be!

In the Russian liberation movement, beginning with the Decembrists, there was so much of the fine, the truly noble, the heroic. A passionate and visionary dreaminess over a just-truth upon the earth was lodged within this movement. It would be tormentive and terrible to think, that so much blood was spilt, that so much life was spent, that so many an hero made his effort, so many a thought was suffered out and Divine ardour of soul consumed for this, in order that the people's soul should have sickened with a plague of hooliganism and nihilism, so that indeed a dock-tailed constitution should have been fought over and won. Was it for this that the Westernisers fought with the Slavophils, and that Hertsen forever quit Russia, that Belinsky passionately sought truth, that [M. Saltykov-]Schedrin exposed, and Lev Tolstoy hurled his challenge to world history? The real political position of Russia and its most immediate perspectives are very pitiful, and the soul of the people is experiencing a grave crisis. The people itself, a great people, and with its great destiny as it were for naught. There is transpiring a revaluation of all values, according to the hackneyed expression, thus always it occurs during an epoch of revolution, and all will turn out well; but the terrible thing is this, that the revaluation so readily is transformed into a disregard for everything, into a loss of all values, into an obliviousness of the eternal distinctions between good and evil. By making a god of the naked human will, a freeing from everything sacred, it is impossible to create any sort of new values.

The tragedy of modern Russian life is rooted in this, that the struggle between progress and reaction has been transformed into a struggle of two self-asserting human wills. Both sides act in their own name, they do not know the Name of the MostHigh, and they therefore become beastly and wild, therefore they become puffed up with a mad selfishness and greed. A genuinely liberating word, overcoming the discord and hatred, is still not to be found in the Russian revolution, and therefore so pitiful and dreadful is its course, so elusive is the boundary-line separating the violence of the revolution from the violence of the reaction, so inwardly dependent is our liberation upon own enslavement. In our revolution there is no genuine enthusiasm amidst great ideas, our tremendous revolution is incomparably less inspired, than was the great French Revolution, but the political exaltation and political fanaticism assume among us still greater dimensions. This political exaltation is always accompanied by conceit and it readily passes over into a demonic obsession, -- a psychological truth, confirmed with each step taken. The demonic obsession of the priestmonk Iliodor [Sergei Trufanov] and [Vladimir] Purishkevich and the demonic obsession of the "bolshevik" and of the "maximalist" is of the same order, it rests upon the same style. Being in the grip of demons tends to express itself in the same manner of physiological type of shouting and physiological distortion of the face. Man becomes beast-like, when he acts only in his own name, when he asserts and makes a god of his own mere human will; suchlike is the law of being. Land-owners and peasants, factory-owners and factory-workers, rulers and revolutionaries, black-hundredists and red-hundredists alike, in accord with this selfsame law, they become wild, they lose the human image, become bereft of reason and conscience within their classes, their conditions and other self-assertions. The people is dying amidst this demonic possession of human wills, in this oblivion to an higher law.

At the basis of the old Russian governance, with its violence, its reaction, was that chaotic element, which was begotten in the primordial apostacy from God. The Russian bureaucracy forcefully and cruelly upheld its order, an order first of all of outward strength, seemingly united, but at the basis of all its activity, of the notorious state activity there lay chaos, disunity, a servile caprice of all and everything. Chaos reigns everywhere, where there is not a free acceptance within oneself of God, where external law has been substituted in place of inner law. In the Russian imperialism, despite the outward lustre, the mightiness and colossal extent, always there was sensed the nihilistic desolation of spirit, something morally suspicious, inward, hidden from the national drama of a fracture with the law of God. Peter accomplished a great deed, but after Peter something began going wrong, then impotent, then criminal. The Russian Church did not say its say about the earthly destiny of Russia, for it remained in subjection. And it burnt incense in honour of an imperialism, to which was entrusted to build up the land, but the imperialism did not know, how to build it up in accord with God. The Japanese war and the revolution hastened by it ultimately uncovered the illusion of the mightiness of the whole edifice, and the lie set within its foundation.

But the drama of the Russian revolution is inescapable, because that it prolongs the matter of the human self-assertion, the human craving for power and arranging the land in its own name; it lays waste the old imperialism and seeks to set up in its place a new, revolutionary, democratic imperialism, although it does not comprehend the significance of the state. The revolution likewise has not accepted God and His supreme law within itself, just the same as with the old state, and therefore the chaotic element, the element of ruination and hostility, veiled over by outward obligation and coercion, continues also to reign within it. The revolution likewise considers it inevitable to have a "militant position", just like the government, likewise it justifies force by necessity to safeguard the societal freedom, just as the government justifies it by necessity to safeguard the state order. The maximalists of the right and the maximalists of the left mystically are drawn in one after the other, all united in the elements of chaos and their demonic obsession. The revolution is connected not only with a thirst for freedom and justice, not only with a thundering of God, a threatening against godless might, not only with a struggle for the rights of man, praeternally bestown him by God, but also with a nihilistic consciousness, with atheism, with worshipping himself. The nihilism of the decade of the [18]60's, in its own time playing an enlightening role, has in fatal manner made a comeback in the course of the Russian revolution. In the majority of instances, not consciously so, the revolutionaries commit crimes, drawing suspicion upon the Russian revolution, and those who anoint themself for revolution, are superficially touched upon by its spirit. There is now nothing such as a thief and swindler, who has not cloaked himself under the guise of a revolutionary, with the ideas of socialism etc, every pilfering now is termed an expropriation, every murdering -- a terror. In this is the complexity of the revolution, in this is the difficulty to separate in it the truth from the falsehood, and in this is the woe of the revolution. In the nihilism, long since already having begun and gradually wasting away at the people's soul -- is the root of the moral decay, accompanying the revolution, of all that hooliganism, of all that horrid emotional aggregate. The new and saving word can only be in radical opposition to the beastly, the greedy, the selfish human wills by the Will of the MostHigh, this can only be a religious word. It is impossible to seek out this word whether in the adaption of the old faith to revolution, or in the negotiations of the new spirit with the old governance; it will be found in the ultimate ascendancy both over revolution and over reaction, both over the sovereignty of the people and over the imperialism, over the stale, old, thoughtless criteria of left and right. It is needful to go neither to the right nor to the left, neither forwards nor backwards, but in a different sort of measurement, towards the absolute and supra-human truth. Against the decay, in which unnoticed the revolution is transpiring, it is necessary to fight, but not by decay however, not by reaction. The chaos of murders and expropriations will not be conquered by the chaos of executions and military-police courts, but will only intensify and justify them. The hooliganism both reactionary and revolutionary, the hooliganism of the intelligentsia youth and of the popular masses -- is a process of rot, of the nihilism, decaying "society" from above and from below, and it can be contended against only by creative, genuinely radical and inspiring ideas.

But a genuine and deep *radicalism* has to be conjoined with a genuine and deep *conservatism*. There cannot exist a people, for whom nothing is to be preserved, who will have received no legacy, worthy of love. The denial of a genuine conservatism, of a reverent safeguarding of its eternal and absolute values, is always nihilistic. In the process of developement there has to be the seed, there has to be that, which underlies the developement, there has to be the stabilising subject of developement, there ought to be the accumulation of riches. Only organic growth is developement, and revolutions can only be especially strained moments of developement, with crises, with sick growth. In a revolution itself there is much that is forever organically won and it cannot be annihilated whether by reactions, nor by future revolutions. The mania for destroying everything, such as comprises the past, and the worship of everything to come is a filthy sickness or a superficial vogue, sustained by bazaar shoutings. Reaction with its apparitions of the past constantly holds revolution within its clutches, imposes its own imprint and bestows on it its own negative definition: revolutionaries worship the future, but they live in the past.

In revolution with its demonic-obsession there is too much of the mechanical, the outward, not corresponding to the inner growth of the land, to the organic rebirth of the soul of the people. In regard to my own religious beliefs and social ideals I am least of all an adherent to the ideal of an abstract state and would term myself an adherent of a free theocracy.[3] But I think, that it is impossible to conquer the statecraft and violence mechanically, by like violence, it is necessary inwardly to be rendered worthy a non-power and God's power. Outside the religious, the theocratic path, mankind never will be set free from the demands of the state with its compulsory character. This demand is rooted within the anarchy and chaotic aspect of the world, left to itself and its natural powers. The state appears also as a corrective, an outward weakening of the chaos, warding off an ultimate dissolution, but inwardly the chaotic element remains untouched. Mankind tends to subject itself to the outward coercion and force of the state, since that inwardly it is atomised and spiritually enslaved, held captivate by evil, and can set itself free, only by hacking out the root of the enslaving discord. political revolutions never get deep down to these *roots*, and therefore they are in truth *not radical*, they are but a change of clothing, leaving man in his former filth and falsehood. It is possible to announce that the slaves are free, to teach them the words and gestures of freedom, but they will become really free only then, when they inwardly cease to be slaves. Man long since already wants *to seem* to be free, he wears the clothes of a free man, a citizen of the world, but all the same he has not desired quite strongly *to become* free, *to be* free, to possess a free soul cleansed of all filth of body. This is not a justification of those that would place the shackles upon man, they themself -- are the first slaves, captivated by evil, they bowed down before the idol of externality, of outward appearances, the mechanical. And indeed it is not important, who and what imagines to justify himself by this, what is important is the existence of the deed, the truthfulness. Let the people free themself from the slave's feelings, from their violent instincts, from the devils of malice and greed, then and only then will they become a free people, then no sort of the might of the state will

---

[3] The idea of a free theocracy from the alive and concrete can be transformed into the dead and the abstract, a sin of many of us. The abstract promulgation of an absolute freedom upon religious grounds has little significance, but is important as an historical path towards this freedom.

have the strength to enslave and oppress them. every hooliganism, every nihilism, every decay of noble and supra-human feelings is a strengthening of violence and despotism, it is as it were a justification for the demonisation of power. Conquer the anarchy in yourself -- and then ye will become worthy of anarchism, surmount the violent chaos -- and ye will receive free harmony. Yet the so-called revolutionary "agitation" does not develope the consciousness, but only dulls it, it does not liberate from the anarchy of spirit, but rather enslaves it, it will not be the better but rather the worse instincts, it is oriented towards avarice and selfishness. they preach to the dark and yet wild people an exclusive self-assertion, they clutter their heads with unclear ideas, often malicious and always irresponsible. The slaves remain slaves and mutiny like slaves. This is an elementary truth, self-evident, but in our era they do not see it and fretfully deny it.

The Russian revolution is a very complex phenomenon: in it the good has become so mixed up with evil, the truth with falsehood. But one thing is indisputable: our hooliganistic, nihilistic revolutionism is inwardly unworthy even of that, what is demanded in the programme of the People's Freedom party, in general opinion -- a dead party; there is no growth, the inner revolutionary spirit no longer still merits it. The abyss between the people and the swarm of the revolutionaries is too great. In the mind of the Social-Democrats, long since already and with an extraordinary acuteness, has been the decay of the bourgeoise, and all are ready for a socialistic turnabout, but in actual life nothing of the sort has yet occurred, for this is merely the mental process of the Marxist brain, whereas our real being is irrational and not in accord with the brains of the intelligentsia. The schemae of intelligentsia-misfits have nothing in common with the real process of life: if in accord with these schemes there be imposed on us at present socialism or even anarchism, then as regards the real position of society and the actual correlation of forces we will have scarcely at all have advanced to the level of the demands of the party of peaceful restoration. We -- this is not me only and my thoughts alone, -- are not a select portion of society and not the upper portion of the intelligentsia, but rather the whole land, society as a whole, the people. And indeed it mustneeds be said, that the revolutionist and leftist for us often becomes so as a result of under-developement, of a lower level, and not of re-developement. The cultural level and spiritual figure of some of the extreme leftists approaches closely the level and appearance of Purishkevich and [Pavel Aleksandrovich] Krushevan.[4] If now the revolutionary mindset is widely dispersed in Russia, if it has taken hold with the broad masses, then this is explicable in that revolutionism has become for us something of a fad. Earlier among us, young men and women and the conscientious upper parts of the people went to revolution, saving themself from fadishness, from the darkness and emptiness of fashionable life, and in this there was something aristocratic. At present the fad of revolutionism is spreading like an epidemic, "the left" has become a new form of faddish drollness. Those, that not long ago were still indifferent or even worse, than the indifferent, those, that were given to toadyism during the gloomy epoch of [Vyacheslav Konstantinovich von] Pleve, now have become radical, they outstrip each other in revolutionary phraseology. Even talented writers, not having gone through the schools of political ethics, are ablaze with the faddish revolutionism, they relish the tantalising dishes new to them. The revolution indeed, in the banal sense of this word, defines itself not by a deep consciousness and not by the desire for justice, but by a degree of obsession, almost by a physiological power of demonic-possession. We shall become free, when we free ourself from the criteria of left and right, of revolution and reaction, when we in essence peer into that which is truth and just. This also will be a radicalism.

If we have lived according to false criteria of good and evil, then from this it cannot be inferred, that it is necessary to live without

---

[4] The possibility of the events with [Evno Fishelevich or Evgenii Philippovich] Azef clearly shows the spiritual collapse of the revolutionary medium. Only in a medium, in which the human soul is scorned, can an Azef appear and play a role.

any criteria of good and evil. the criteria of good and evil is deeper and more important, more radical than the criteria of left and right. The fight ought to be against evil, against the primordial evil, and not against the effects, the superficial aspects. It might be possible to push back the illness inwards, but this will not be a radical doctoring of the illness. The state coercion, the reaction, the black hundreds -- all this is but a boil on the body of Russia, it is necessary to treat Russia for that *decay*, which poisons with a corpsely rot the national organism. The rotting process, in which transpires the revolution, is indeed a legacy of the slavery, of despotism and savagery, it is begotten quite the same in the excesses of reaction and revolution, in the black hundredist pogroms and in the red hundredist expropriations and killings, in the beastification of the government and in the beastification of the revolutionaries. Those, that wish to save Russia from ruin, ought not to make for themself an idol either of "revolution", or of the "state", they ought to support the truth, ascendant over both revolution and over reaction. The rotting corpsely stench comes from the self-assertion of the human will in the demonic obsession of state power and the demonic-obsession of revolution.

Revolutionary upheavals are inevitable in the history of mankind, and mankind without sickness cannot grow, since it is begotten in sin. Revolutions cleanse the air, they appear as it were God's chastisement for historical God-abandonment, for the sins of the past. This resulting of revolution is from the evil of the past, and its having been begotten from the ruination of the past ought never to be forgotten. A revolution does not create anything, it does not create any sort of culture, neither spiritual nor material, it but flings off the veil of the lie from the national mode of life, it uncovers the real value of things. In the uncovering of the genuine realities, in distinction from their pseudo-reality, from the social fictions -- is the whole meaning of historical developement. But amidst this positive mission of revolution it indicates the impossibility of transforming it into an idol, the worshipping of it. Revolution itself per se cannot be called a good power, although it can serve towards the good, *revolution is a venerably formalised lie, of the scrupulously uncovered rot, a dealing with the entirety of the decay*. The aggregate of creative ideas and creative energy itself per se never leads to revolution, it leads to *developement*; what leads to revolution is the aggregate of evil and falsehood. Here is why revolution always is so servilely dependent upon reaction and thus reactionary in its psychology; it is but the reaction over the discovered lie, and nothing in it is to be worshipped. Here it is necessary to cry out, that the falsehood was so much, that the sin of the past was so great, and it is nothing to exult over. The Russian revolution is a colossal, an almost unprecedented within history uncovering of falsehood, a revealing of the rot. The ruling powers have lied, sinned and done violence, rendered craven and enthralled the people. It is not the revolution that creates the decay, but the revolution gives to it its course. The revolution is a mighty weapon of self-consciousness, of the knowledge of Russia, since it lays bare its body and uncovers the reality. But there is also a reverse side. If those that are wise recognise it, that the drunken elements of the revolution, which provides it an hypnotic effect of passionate dissipation by which is lost all consciousness, are prone to worship its new idols.

If there had not been the sinful irrationality of history, the mindless discord, killing the people's soul, there would not also have been revolution. The criminality of the ruling powers, the blood, its spilling by the despotism, its betrayal of God and people, all this poison but feeds the pathos of revolution, the blood rushes to the head and muddles the thinking. The political murderings ought to be condemned socially, morally, religiously, but can indeed the government share in this condemnation, having ruled with killings, can it sit in judgement of the transgressors? Every murder is terrible in its mystical consequences, it draws upon itself an historical retribution. The blood, spilt by the French Revolution, poisons through the present the soul of the French people, it hinders its happiness, allows it no joy, similar to how with the blood, spilt by despotic governments, cries out in revolutions, it draws down the government to its shameful demise. But the people, having lost the religious centre of life, with fatal inevitability enter upon the path of bloody quarrel, the path of reaction and revolution, the violence of the right and the left, the mutual destruction of classes and social conditions, of frenzied malice, poisoning every joy in life. Through this process of disintegration is passing, evidently, the whole of mankind , but wherein is no delight here. It is necessary to bear the cross. The most important thing of all is to discern here the psychological truth, that there is no antidote from revolution in reaction; quite the contrary, for revolution and reaction are of the same nature, twins literally. When the two beasts lunge themself one upon the other, then those, who recognise the sinfulness of every beastliness, ought not to incite the one beast upon the other, for one to win out over the other. But here it is especially needful to stress: not in the social demands of revolution is the evil, these demands in a majority of instances are just, but rather in the *spirit* of revolution is the evil. That it is "the land of God" -- in this social slogan is a great truth, but rather in the manner, by which the truth is introduced into consciousness, into the spirit, with which it is apperceived, that is the falsehood, the distortion, the evil self-affirmation.

* * *

What the Russian revolution has won, and it would seem, has won forever, is thus this comparatively great freedom of thought and of word. If one were to compare, how things are written now and how they were written two-three years back, if one were but to run and check out the old newspapers, then one would immediately sense, how colossal a turnabout there has occurred for us. A most sacred right has been won, not fully yet won, but to a remarkable degree: it is possible to write the truth, it is possible to denounce falsehood. But this freedom presents for us a great temptation. Will we find genuine *words*, will the Divine Logos be alive in our words, will truth be proclaimed, will the falsehood be denounced? In the interim we have not withstood this temptation. The waves of hooliganism have flooded over into our liberation printings and inundated them. Deadly triteness and the conditional lie reign even in the finest organs of our new press, of truth it is afraid most of all, since it is not sure that it is of use and non-dangerous. There has been born a new layer of the newspaper literati, very modernist, very leftist, the "modern times" radicals, without any ideas, without anything sacred of soul, -- the end product of a philistine democracy. The initial purity of Russian literature, its unique aristocratic quality, the anguish over truth lodged within it -- all this quickly vanishes, is swept off into the corner by the general flooding current. Democratism was a fine thing, when it was a visionary dream of the finest people in regards to justice. But an ugly stench has come from it, when its spirit has been realised in fact. This though is old history. In the greater portion of the newspapers, and indeed the journals, it is impossible to read without a gloomy feeling: there is the sense of something unclean, making for an involuntary disgust. They pronounce the fine words, the holy words -- freedom, justice, rights etc etc, but behind them is hid the total nihilism and lack of ideas. There is no assuredness of honour, of nobility, of veracity of those writing and speaking the loud words. Everything is of the second and third-rate sort. All the riffraff have taken up with the revolution and especially with the revolutionary literature, and the spiritual misfits having lost any sanctity of soul, they act the hooligan, they infect the atmosphere, they taint the soul of the people. The initial revolutionary activity was the apportioned lot of the few, of the finest, of the self-denying; the word of freedom was spread by [Aleksandr] Hertsen, [Pyotr] Lavrov, [Mikhail Petrovich] Dragomanov and others. But now revolution has become democratised, all have become revolutionaries, the moral level has dropped down to the point, that the word "revolutionary" no longer inspires its former respect. Yesterday's indifferentist, typical fellow and even conniver, a man of doubtful past, today rails against the moderation and non-reactionary good sense of people, by blood connected with the liberation movement, into its history having inscribed their names.[5] Revolutionism has become something gotten into in a few days, revolutionary ideas have become so simple, they are assimilated so lightly, and demand no mental exertion, nor mental anguish.

The whole of my conscious life I have lived with the hope, that the hour of liberation would strike for Russia, and that this would be an hour most joyous. But this hour has struck, and for joy there has been substituted grief, grief hath supplanted joy. It was impossible to have foreseen, that an hooliganistic and nihilistic generation would snatch into their hands the deed of liberation. It was a terrible thing for mankind to have become, when one sees, that the free word, the sanctity of the free word is snatched hold of by some sort of new, religiously droll, the new philistine from the street. With freedom it is impossible to be disillusioned, it -- is an eternal blessing, but one can be disenchanted with the human element, which is allured by freedom, but attracted to a new slavery. This torment of disenchantment is itself conveyed by our revolutionary words, by our revolutionary press.

The current literature of an higher quality shows the search for a new sanctity, a crisis of the old idols, but on the other hand, within it is disclosed a repulsive emotional dimension, a sort of neo-nihilism, all the same hooliganism, the same vileness, the same scorn for holy things. the most talented and creative literary current -- decadentism -- enters into an anti-natural connection with elements of the revolution, although it had always been indifferent to and had mocked the thirst for social freedom and truth. In decadentism, a very complex and profound phenomenon, there is an hidden nihilism, in its representatives there is the psychology of the kept mistress as regards the attitude towards sociability. I fear, that on these sides decadent art is oriented welcomingly towards revolution as a fact.

---

[5] Very characteristic of our mannerisms is the unjust, ignoble, ugly attitude towards P. V. Struve, one of the most noteworthy of Russian people, having done so much for the deed of Russian freedom, a man of exceptional moral valour and intense spiritual life.

Especially in the green youth a superficial revolutionism is readily combined with a superficial decadence, and this quite ever the newest type is so vexatious with its moral decadence and impudence.

The excesses of the revolution, its demonically obsessed elements begotten of reaction, are a danger for the future of Russia. We can possibly foresee twofold a reaction. First of all is possible a reaction of the temperance sort against drunkenness, the reaction of a bourgeois positivism, of a vital realism.[6] It is keen on material enrichment, it worships Moloch, its trifling practicality screens out the great historical tasks. This psychological reaction finds its justification in demands for the material developement of Russia, but it presents a great spiritual danger and serious temptation for us. Yet there will also be for us a romantic reaction, a reaction by the societally violated element of individuality. The romantic expectations of person, constrained and warped by the acute political struggle, demand to be fed, to find themself within the whole course of culture. Only a revolutionary realism can defeat in us the danger of every reaction.

* * *

A most substantial thing in the Russian revolution, which ultimately is expiring within it is the *mode of life*, which had fractured already back in the decade of the 60's. This -- was the nobility-landowner mode of life, the mode of life of Pushkin, Turgenev and Tolstoy; in it there was its own poetry and its own romantic memories, from it emerged the Russian great literature. But this lifestyle was nourished on injustice, as is otherwise almost every mode of life in this world, and it perishes ingloriously. The Russian nobility, in playing its role in Russian culture, scornfully ends its own existence, and certain of its noble features disappear without a trace, its legacy of fanatic followers reverting to beastliness, no longer possessing any sort of supra-individual and trans-class ideas common

---

[6] This reaction has already begun and contains within it an healthy grain of truth.

to all the nation, nor at all capable for the defense of their pitiful privileges. The nobility then either pour off into the common liberal-democratic current, or they go wild and vomit every foulness. The nobility has so degenerated, that it is incapable of self-assertion in the English spirit, nor of historical self-denial in the name of the truth of all the people, it cringes before the ruling powers, having become alien to all the groups of Russian society, it awaits an hand-out, undersigns its own death sentence, with the exception from its ranks for the participants of the liberation movement. Only certain singular representatives of the nobility even up til now still draw attention upon themself with a nobility of nature, with a chivalrous sense of honour, they evoke trust in themself, moreso, than certain of the plebian-rank revolutionaries. With the nobility everything however among us was connected with a singularly beautiful lifestyle, a non-philistine mode of life; everything else is either already the beginning of an escape from every lifestyle, or consists in a lifestyle monstrous and stinking.

Revolution is the fracturing of lifestyle in general, in it is subjected to doubt the value of every lifestyle, and it leads to the positing of a final religious problem concerning the relationship of lifestyle to *being*, of phenomenality to the absolute norm. For the religious consciousness there is no sort of lifestyle that ought to be, every lifestyle is non-obligatory, only being -- is real, and not illusory. All this world, all the empirical world merits the fire, and not only this or some other social order. Worthy of safeguarding is only the eternal, the non-temporal, only being, not lifestyle. Our revolution in particular as it were lays bare the antinomy of human existence and the impossibility of resolving these antinomies in whatever the societal lifestyle. And therefore the revolution, destroying everything in its maximalism both left and right, indirectly serves for a religious renewal. The illusory lifestyle passes over into authentic being, although the extent of this being seem not very large, in comparison with the extent of lifestyle, encompassing all the expanse of the earth.

But revolution leads not only to the crisis of the very idea of lifestyle, it creates a new lifestyle, in its most immediate results by revolution is created a repugnant lifestyle, impudent in its conceit and self-smugness, philistine down to its very roots. Thus it was in Western Europe, destroying chivalry and creating the bourgeois philistinism. The philistine lifestyle results of the European revolutions ought always to be for us a matter of serious caution. We ought to pray God about the saving of our organic conception of world freedom, of freedom from the philistine lifestyle, its having enslaved the most cultured lands of Europe.

About certain of the psychological features of this newly born, revolutionary lifestyle I have already spoken above. It is first of all to be characterised negatively: by the absence of every supra-individual and supra-human sanctity, but with the presence of many idols and objects of worship. The people, who worship nothing, who go not to pray in common a temple, who affirm only themself, can find unity only in an ugly lifestyle, ignoble, bourgeois as regards its spirit. The wretched lifestyle of the Russian peasantry was nonetheless aristocratic, non-philistine, since there was in it a real sense of closeness to God, there was alive in it an organic sanctity, transforming the least muzhik-peasant into a citizen of the universe. Only the consciousness of their ancient and eternal origin makes people aristocratic, lays up upon the lifestyle the human imprint of nobility. Those, that begin their history with the day before yesterday and delimit their formula of living with self-affirmation, always -- are bourgeois, philistine, and no sort of socialism can save one from this spirit. factory workers, torn off from the organic lifestyle of the peasantry, in a transitional period readily become hooligans, and then also intelligentsia of the third-rate sort. There is no poetry in this lifestyle.

God has died in the soul -- here is the basis of the most current lifestyle. In the youth, as the educated, so also in the people, there is sensed the demonic outlook in the most poor, altogether unpretty, but authentic meaning of these words. This -- is a nihilistic desolation of spirit, the loss of the meaning of life and of the value of the human person. The process of spiritual disintegration always accompanies revolution, but sometimes it becomes symptomatic of the begetting of a new religious light. Without God the people cannot live, man disintegrates. Russian life does not exhaust itself merely in lifestyle old and lifestyle new, within it there are seekers, searching out the City, ascendant over every lifestyle, thirsting for genuine being. These seekers will find their native-land, when in the people's religious consciousness there occurs the long since desired turnabout, when the people's life blazes up from a new religious fire and national developement will not be considered identical still with the falling away from every faith.

When the old religious consciousness dies in the soul of the people, lacking the powers still to transform life, to re-inspire dead matter, to save from the pitfalls of the reactionary and revolutionary hooliganism, there then remains the hope for a new, a more total religious consciousness, connected with the people's thirst for the truth of God on earth, with the chiliastic hope, with the promise, that this truth will be realised. Then there will be the kingdom not of this world, but still in this world. The forcible extortion of this "kingdom" of God's, the human demand, that this kingdom should arrive promptly at once as justice, can prove dishonest. Mankind is not prepared yet, has not yet made its act of self-denial, has not yet washed and dressed itself. The denial of the world historical working at the human developement of the material and spiritual task, the preparing for the *kingdom*, presents a great danger, a temptation of religious exaltation, akin to revolutionary obsession. If the idea of progress easily be transformed into an idol, into a substitute for religion, then the idea of the laborious developement of mankind is not strange at all, it is elemental in importance. The people's religious rebirth ought not to be mere visionary-dreamings and exultant awaiting of the thousand year kingdom, not a matter of throwing away everything in view of its impending onset, but of the toil in preparation for it, an inward cleansing, and corresponding to this cleansing, an outward liberation.

Only an inward revolution, life-creating anew by the Spirit, the eternal Spirit, will lead not to disintegration, not be accompanied by rotting ruination, only such a revolution -- is truly radical. And indeed this great sort of revolution would conquer both reaction and disintegration. The old revolution in Russia has ended, the old reaction evokes apparitions, is it not time for this new revolution to be begun?

ON THE PSYCHOLOGY OF THE RUSSIAN INTELLIGENTSIA [1]

The so-called "Third Element" has as it were a symbolic significance within the most recent period of Russian history, particularly in the history of these final days for Russia. The appearance of the "third element" and its large role in our societal life is a symptom of infirmity, a symbol of the falling-apart of the national organism. All the sins of our historical past have found their inverted upside-down reflection in some strange group of people, foreign to the organic layers of Russian society and esteeming itself the salt of the earth. A certain vice-governor christened as "third element" the Zemstvo intelligentsia, those serving in the district assemblies, the statisticians, physicians, teachers, etc. But it is possible to expand the content of this received right of citizenship title. Numerous of the stratum of the Russian intelligentsia, differing as regards origin, misfits as regards composite of soul, radical in outlook, can also be termed a "third element". With us it has taken the form of a special social group of the intelligentsia, with its own unique psychology, with characteristic features of face, which are easy to recognise even at a great distance. The intelligentsia "third element" includes not only statisticians -- this is a classical type of the average intelligentsia, -- those serving in the district assemblies, but also the newspaper literary sorts, the professional revolutionaries, the students, fleeing their lessons for social gatherings, the young women from their dental and midwife courses, beginning solicitors, small-time railway administrators, etc. In the mass of these people they are half-educated, outraged at the state of the world, but always attributing to themself the prerogatives of saviours of the fatherland. They are not greedy in their personal life, they do not secure themself

[1] Published in "Moskovskii Ezhenedel'nik", 27 October 1907.

a social position, but their idealistic visionary dreams are connected with greed on behalf of others, they always yield before the instincts of the masses of the people. These people read but little, but always according to trite plan, always the same jargon and the same memorised by-rote words that speak about a plan for the salvation of Russia. The "third element" is a new intelligentsia philistinism, not having grown its roots into the earth and therefore producing an impression of fickleness and being up in the air, quickly moving along and unstable. This peculiar world of its own, living in accord with its own law, opposing its own understanding of the "good" to all and everything in the world, hostile to the traditions of the universal good; this is a world, not knowing kindred and not remembering its origin. From this isolated world there emerge individual idealists, truth-seekers, freed from every lifestyle, always prepared for acts of self-denial. But the masses of the intelligentsia coalesce into an unpleasant lifestyle, and into the dull grey masses of the "third element" there tend to fade out the individual idealists, still seeking, full of utmost unrest.

The "third element" became the leavening of the Russian revolution, the basis of the revolution, its soul, and it set its own imprint upon our liberation movement. The "third element" -- the intelligentsia philistinism, aggrieved and not always a noble rebelliousness -- bestowed upon the Russian revolution primarily a negative, anarchistic character, bereft of creative spirit. Whole generations of the Russian intelligentsia grew up and were nourished in the spirit of nihilism, almost fully split off from the universal traditions, from the worldwide developing of the religious consciousness of the meaning of life. This nihilism expressed itself in the process of disintegration and decay, accompanying the Russian revolution. the nihilistic consciousness, the non-belief in the meaning of existence, the non-belief in the power of the Good and the absoluteness of its distinction from evil comprises the spiritual substrate of our revolutionary intelligentsia philistinism, and therefore it can create nothing, it cannot bring to realisation the revolution based upon it. The terror and the tragedy of the Russian revolution consists in this, that all its ideas -- are philistine-intelligentsia, rebellious. The Social-Democrats rely upon the workers and pretend to express the spirit of the proletariat; the Social-Revolutionaries have these same pretensions regarding the peasantry. But the ring-leaders and heads of the cadres of both the one and the other party are comprised of the "third element", of the materially and spiritually proletarised intelligentsia. All the Social-Democratic and the Social-Revolutionary committees are comprised of intelligentsia, concerned with revolution as a profession, esteeming themself the salt of the earth, singularly the saviours of the fatherland, with scorn spurning all other paths of salvation. This intelligentsia has splintered off from the people in the organic sense of this word, but it bows down as to an idol before the people in the societal-class sense: *foreign interests*, whether proletarian or peasant, have become for it *the ideal*. All these variations of revolutionary factions, the Social-Democrats and the Social-Revolutionaries, the Bolsheviks and the Mensheviks, etc -- are purely intelligentsia variants, a "third element" thing, rebellious wranglings, philistine ideologies. The workers and the peasants as organic segments of Russian society have little in common with this process of thinking, which transpires for the "third element" in an airless, empty expanse. The people most of all have need of an ideal, ascendant over their interests, but ultimately always they sense the falseness of rendering even the most just of their interests into an idol. It is the "third element" namely that creates a tragic rift between "thought" and "being": the wastingly-frail intelligentsia is too taken to its stuffy chambers to accomplish the great revolutionary turnabouts in "thinking". There has grown up a generation, capable in the person of its finest representatives for an heroic course of action, but with a refusal of real existence. Realist Marxism was experienced by the Russian intelligentsia as a process in the head, and in the head of the "third element" the bourgeoise has already begun to be destroyed, whereas actually it had only begun to develope. The "third element" is very greedy for power in its political passions, very impatient, but to the rule of power it has not been called, to decide the fate of Russia it is not capable.

In Russia there are two manners of intelligentsia understanding. One mindset, one understanding -- is of all the people and mankind in general, transcending class and station in life, external to party or circle: this intelligentsia -- are the finest, the select people of the land, the creators of the spiritual culture of the nation, the creators of Russian literature, of Russian art, philosophy, science, religious seekers, guardians of societal just-truth, prophets of a better future. To suchlike an intelligentsia in the best sense of this word belonged Pushkin and Lermontov, Gogol and Turgenev, L. Tolstoy and Dostoevsky; to it belong Chaadaev, the Slavophils, Belinsky and Hertsen, Vl. Solov'ev, Russian philosophers, teachers and artists, all leaders of the nation in common for Russian culture, all the knowledgeable segments of the Russian societal aspect.

In this normal understanding regarding intelligentsia there is the best part of society, the most educated, the most developed, the most noble, the most talented and creative, it is the salt of the earth, the true proclaimer of the spirit of the people, the bearer of the people's ideals, and not special interests; its populism is not dependent upon prerogative of the gentry, nor upon prerogative of the intelligentsia. But in Russia there has been worked out an altogether different understanding of intelligentsia, and it has predominated among us. The intelligentsia in quotation-marks traces its origin to the decade of the 60's, it is not of so long a line of descent, not so old even, as the intelligentsia of the first and better sense; it possesses a strong social-class bent, rather than one common to all the people or all the nation; it is puffed up with a sense of its non-rank and democratic origin as a privilege, proud of its rebelliousness, and regards the absence of the traditions of spirit as a merit; it makes excessive pretensions for a decisive role in Russian history. This "intelligentsia" possesses its own small circles, trends of thought, party-members, almost its own classifications of great people, leaders, heroes, but to it remain foreign our heroes of thought and creativity common to all the people and mankind. For this "intelligentsia" the writers of illegal brochures and tedious speeches seem far closer, kindred and great, than do Vl. Solov'ev, Dostoevsky or Tiutchev. There has been worked out a type of "intelligentsia" writers, there has been formed an "intelligentsia" homespun philosophy, literature and journalism. Chernyshevsky, Dobroliubov, Pisarev, Mikhailovsky -- all these were talented people, they expressed often shrewd thoughts, but as writers often they were "intelligentsia", those of the small circles and trends of thought, they never could and cannot be common to all nations and peoples. There will never be enumerated to our great national literature the [Fyodor Mikhailovich] Reshetnikovs, the [Nikolai Nikolaevich] Zlatovratskys, the [Aleksandr Konstantinovich] Sheller-Mikhailovs, the [Pyotr Philippovich Yakubovich] L. Melshins, nor indeed the at the moment acclaimed Gorkys, etc; even the decadents, amidst all their being out of touch, receive moreso this right. All our "radical" journals, all the literature of these journals and the narrow circle of their officially-sanctioned ideas, have been a matter of intelligentsia clique, exclusively a matter of worth to the third element, conceited with itself as the saviour of the fatherland, the chosen spirit of the earth.

Even if the best leaders of the intelligentsia were gifted, and expressed ideas having general significance, then yet still the masses of the intelligentsia -- have been frighteningly ungifted, bereft of any creative idea relevant for all mankind, and banal to the point of nausea. The "intelligentsia" mistakes its own little world, its stuffy rooms, its small-circle disputes, for the world of being at large, for the life of the world soul. The current's jargon, quickly assimilated by students and circle-members, is assumed a language common to mankind, while at the same time in this jargon dissipate all the great problems. Most disagreeable of all is the self-smugness of this "intelligentsia", its noisiness, upon which is the basis of its pretentiousness, its absence of a becoming modesty. All the journals, the newspapers, the brochures, the meeting-prepared speeches in quite pervasively exorbitant a societal pretentiousness, with contempt for and denial of all the rest of the world, of all the "non-intelligentsia", and together with this the striking impression of spiritual wretchedness, despondency and dullness. The "intelligentsia" of the small-circles has spurned the whole of Russian great literature, it has not comprehended the religious thirst of the finest Russians and of the Russian people, it does not know Russian philosophy, and has rendered itself incapable of an organic societal developement. Our "intelligentsia" is conservative in the bad sense of this word and full of prejudices. Everything new, creative, truly radical scares our "intelligentsia", evokes within it suspicion and hostility. How has this "intelligentsia" met the new, the free currents in art, a philosophic work of thought, a searching for faith? A peculiar kind of departmental bureaucratism drives the intelligentsia souls, creates a stifling atmosphere, in which there is no stirring of thought, no free developement. This specific sort "intelligentsia", despite its pretensions, is very uncultured and little educated. A barbarian sort of insane impatience towards all the riches of culture, towards every thirsting of spirit, as is constantly inherent to the "intelligentsia", it does not recognise any thoughts otherwise, other than what it perceives. This characteristic intelligentsia stratum is an historical victim of the old regime, in it quaintly is reflected the slavery and darkness of the past, its ungrounded aspect has its grounds in the sins of the ruling powers and the upper strata of society. It seems to me, that the intelligentsia "third element" in large part is of the same decay, with an inward emptiness and incapacity for any sort of creativity, just the same as is our government bureaucracy -- the same kind of "third element", a wart outgrowth upon the organism of the people, not only conceited with itself as the salt of the earth, but also having received the power to cripple the life of the people.

The misfortune of the Russian state, is that within it the bureaucracy has governed, its own sort of "third element", foreign to the Russian people, often not even Russian by blood, apathetic to the faith and the hopes of the people. The misfortune of the Russian revolution, is that within it governs the "third element", its own sort of reverse bureaucracy, a stratum not organic, not connected with the fundamentals of the spirit of the people, and hostile to the faith of the people. The lack of success of the Russian revolution, its national lack of popularity to a significant degree ought to be chalked up to its being saturated in spirit with the intelligentsia philistinism, that of the small-circle "third element", of the group self-assertion. In the revolution malice towards the old life has prevailed too much over love for a new life, destruction prevailed over creation, the thirst for reward over thirst for creativity, the purely negative ideas over the positive. This malice and thirst for revenge, this anarchy of spirit and negative exclusiveness were nourished and have grown up in a psychological atmosphere of the "third element" (in the broad sense of the word), nervously unstrung, and in a majority of instances having lost the purpose and meaning of life.

This nihilistic spirit of the "third element", this intelligentsia emotional baggage has in fatal manner met up with the dark instincts of the masses of peasants and workers and has begotten something on the order of a Pugachevism, not purely a people's Pugachevism, but with a strong admixture of the "intelligentsia". And the "intelligentsia", blending itself with the people, has no other idea than this, that service to the people's *interests and instincts* is also a service to *the truth and the good.* For such woesome thoughts, that there exist interests and social particularities, the worship of which is very truth itself, -- is a condition that foremost of all requires doctoring.

The revolutionism, the "leftism" is chiefly a product for us of the "intelligentsia" in the small-circle sense, of people with disheveled senses, in its masses semi-cultured and semi-educated, without definite occupations, having found the power to wander amidst the colonies and exiles abroad. When among us they speak about a revolutionary seizure of power, about the acclaimed constituent assembly, about an interim governance etc, they then make their judgements too abstractly, they do not present themself concretely, as to whom it is that will comprise this interim governance and constituent assembly and what sort of psychological atmosphere would form around such. The interim revolutionary government, which is called for to save Russia, to forcibly direct it onto the path of a new, a free life, will be comprised of that same sort "third element", of intelligentsia-rebels, of statisticians, of small-time newspaper literary sorts, the members of the S-D and S-R committees and foreign colonies, and even then not of the best people of the "third element", but rather of the worst, the most self-conceited and ambitious in their pretensions and shouts. It is difficult to imagine, that suchlike a government would lead Russia out of its crisis of sickness. In accord with a fateful socio-psychological law, in the instance of a revolutionary seizure of power where the "maximalists" would win out and lead, very quickly both Social-Democrats and Social-Revolutionaries would be rendered into backward moderates. Now already they speak about how there exists more "leftist" a tendency than the maximalists, and this comic phenomenon threatens to be transformed into mass insanity, which only a new military dictator would have the powers to stop. The moreso cultural, more educated and responsibly aware segment of the revolutionaries would also now thus lose a guiding role, and not being popular it would not define the course of the revolution, and in a revolutionary seizure of power it would play no sort of role.[2] And nothing is said about this, that the [Pavel] Miliukovs, the [Ivan Ilich] Petrunkeviches etc would be eradicated from the face of the earth. Somehow the mighty absolute idea, the idea of God's just-truth ought to defeat the insane mania of "leftism", of "revolutionism", the temptation of naked negation.

All the unhappy, the jaded among the "third element" ought consequently to lighten up spiritually, to quiet down, to introduce light into their distraught soul, ulcered by nihilism, perishing from self-love, but not still to follow those, as would make for a power devoid of conscience and want to render reactionary a part of society,

---

[2] Plekhanov and the more reasonable "Mensheviks" are declared opportunists, to be defeated by the obsessed and demon-driven "Bolsheviks". The idealistic stratum of the Social-Revolutionaries would ultimately be dislodged crazy maximalists, having assumed the tactic of criminal anarchy.

and not worship them, as flatterers do. And also it is needful spiritually to contend against these misfits, in all senses, with the element, with its blind "leftism", with the destructive professional revolutionism. The black reaction feeds upon the aimless revolutionism of the "third element", the superficiality of its awareness, failing to comprehend the *end-purpose of life* and proposing all its radicalism only in the practice of forced *means*.

The peculiar little world of the intelligentsia has great positive merits regarding the societal developement of Russia: its finest representatives have selflessly served the welfare of the people, the Russian land, by much that is connected to the "third element". In its characteristics as doctor for our land and teacher of the people are to be encountered features of greatness of soul. But errors of moral judgement, the exalting of this means into a law of life, even amidst a moral outlook, leads to sad results.

It is impossible to pin one's hopes whether be it upon a particular social condition, or any one class, since every social condition and every class in its exclusive self-assertion and self-opinion begets evil, and not good, it destroys the idea of the nation, and of the people. The Russian revolution, certainly, cannot be called either that of the peasant, or the proletariat, or the bourgeoise, or of the nobility, lest class malice should poison the land. The "third element", itself per se having been derived extraneous to social condition and class, among us has been converted into a sort of special, self-affirming class, unknown in European lands, and it is neither of the nation nor of the people, it does not rise above class enmity but the rather rejoices in it, it bestowed upon the very idea of the people a social-class character, and expels from the nation whole segments of Russian society. But all the hope of the Russian liberation movement has been in this, that *the people* finally should have its own say, irregardless of social condition or class, the people and not the "third element", not the proletariat, not the peasantry, not the bourgeoise, not the nobility, not the bureaucracy, but rather the people, taken up with a singular great idea, the trans-human unity of the nation, always presupposing the self-sacrifice of the separate groups, the limitation of appetites. The hope is bound up with the overcoming of the social-group self-assertions, with getting above every limitedness of social method. There is very little of a populist, objective, higher humble truth in the bare appetites and greedy impulses of the peasantry, and still less such truth, objectivity and populism in the greed and appetites of the nobility.

There ought to appear *the select ones of the people* in the higher sense of this expression, leaders and those that inspire, keen towards the meaning of history, imbued with ideas embracing and encompassing all mankind. It is not upon individual social groups that there can be placed the hope, but only upon the people, having surmounted group self-assertion, from whence the people otherwise cannot escape. The nobility, in willingly repudiating its own social-condition self-interests in the name of a truth embracing all the people, would become therein an inherent part of the people, of the nation, it would be no less so of the people, than the peasantry or the proletariat, in the renouncing of their own class self-interests and struggling against unjust oppression, and indeed moreso of the people, than the peasantry or the proletariat, as asserted in their own exclusive class greed and self-smugness. It is time finally to be done with this false and exclusive connection of the idea identifying the people with the lower and oppressed classes of the population, time to unmask the lie of the intelligentsia democratic self-opinion, propping up the self-opinion of the nobility and the bourgeoise. For in truth it is a lie, that poverty, or oppression, malice, jealousy can become a source of just-truth, that they guarantee the justness of consciousness and nobility of sentiments. Something higher is begotten of a sense of guilt, and not outrage. The idea of the people and the just-truth of the people -- is objective, it does not depend upon any sort of human social conditions or social peculiarities, it cannot be defined by poverty, oppression, democratism of origin, just as neither by wealth, power or aristocratism of origin. In the people is included everyone, who has accepted within himself the objective, the non-avaricious truth, and herein it plays no sort of role, whether he be of the nobility, the proletariat or the intelligentsia. The pseudo-aristocratism of the proletariat or of the "third element" would be abhorrent the same, as is the pseudo-aristocratism of the nobility or the bourgeoise. The voluntary renunciation by the nobility from its privileges, from the land unjustly belonging to it in many an instance would be more noble, moreso objectively-right, than would be the exclusively avaricious attempt of the peasantry to take away the land by way of force. In the first instance in the world would be conquered a certain evil, an evil will would be humbled before the good, but in the second instance no sort of evil would be conquered, and there would be accomplished naught save only an outward preference, of doubtful felicity. Already certainly, such of the gentry, as the deceased Pr. S. N. Trubetskoy and Graf P. A. Geiden, were more of the people, national, more noble and for the realisation of the people's truth, moreso the select, than many of the intelligentsia from the "third element", or than a peasant, entering upon the path of Pugachevism, than a worker, with ease committing murder on partisan grounds.

The Russian nobility was once the vanguard class. It, chiefly, created Russian literature, and from its ranks once emerged the Decembrists and the vanguard people of the epoch of Alexander I, and then activists in the liberation of the peasants and the reforms of Alexander II, by it was created the rural liberation movement and from it through the present are still filled the ranks of the higher intelligentsia of the land. But the services rendered by the nobility were always connected with a self-sacrifice in social condition, subordinated to the idea of the people and mankind in common, these services rendered were put above the delimited lifestyle of their social condition, and with the surmounting of class avarice and interests. The nobility, in the self-assertion of their social condition with pretensions to privilege, not only do not have any sort of justification in the face of the entire people's just-truth, but it is also impossible from the point of view of social necessity. Aristocratism is not a privilege, aristocratism -- is a duty, an obligation of nobility, service, noblesse oblige. The aristocracy exists inwardly as a nobility by birth, as a chivalrous spirit. Such also were the finest of our gentry-humanists and from these finest, a yet not large portion of the nobility through the present have preserved certain features of the chivalrous nobility. In these finest one can moreso be confident, than with many of the "third element", one can trust on their sense of honour. An ignoble aristocrat, bereft of chivalrous sense of honour, full of a malicious greed and unbridled appetites, such an aristocrat -- is a boorish cad, and a thousand times moreso, than any non-aristocrat. Suchlike was the courtier cabal, the false abuses of power, the wild members of the last rural assembly etc. The greater mass of the nobility is uncultured, greedy, foreign to all ideas, of murky consciousness and wild in its sensitivities. The last rural assembly was such a spectacle of wildness, such greed and boorishness on the part of the nobility, that it has become terrible. What has become of the finest traditions of the Russian countryside? Not a single idea was expressed at the rural assembly, there was not a single noble stirring, no sparks of awareness of the importance of the proceedings, no signs of the comprehension of the historical tasks. Only in a small part of the nobility was evident signs of self-sacrifice and consciousness of the historical moment, yet in them still were evident features more lofty, than those born of the bourgeoise, than of those of the self-serving intelligentsia circles.

The countryside comprises an organic element of Russian society, and it has played already an historical role. In the countryside there is not such a rebelliousness, such an alienation from the life of the people, as there is in the revolutionary intelligentsia. The reactionary downturn in the Zemstvo is therefore terrible, in that from the countryside there ought to come forth the best people and act conjointly with the upper intelligentsia of the cities, with the select of the spirit. The staff of the party of the People's Freedom and Peaceful Restoration is most, it would seem, capable of leading the land out of its political crisis, most suited for governing, although in the masses of its people it is bereft of higher consciousness and calling. nonetheless, this is the most educated, cultural and in its psychology most responsible part of the populace, it is more suited than the "third element" for social upbuilding, for organic developement. Liberation however is an organic developement, whereas decay is not.

The black hundredists are likewise a product of the decay of the national organism of the people. In the black hundredists there is nothing positive, nor organic, this is its own kind of apostacy from the historical process, the offal of the people. A fatal chain of connection has been formed. The monstrous red hundredist aspect of the "third element", foreign to the faith and the will of the people, has been evoked by the sins of the ruling authority, with the crimes of the bureaucratic despotism, while the intelligentsia abomination in turn has evoked the vicious black-hundredism of the "Union of the Russian People". It is necessary to break out of this chain, to break out of the vicious circle of revolutionism and reactionism, yet anew both the red and the black hundredists need their baptism. The thirst for absolute truth among the best part of the intelligentsia can drown away therein the demonic apparition, by the instead really religious. And I believe: the select portion of the intelligentsia, having recognised the terror by way of human self-affirmation, will transcend and pass over to a meta-historical form of Christianity.

There will be manifest, sooner or later, a new chivalry, bearing within it the traditions of the old aristocratic nobility, there will be transformed within it the rebelliousness of the select into an higher deference to God, in Whose Name will begin the crusade against evil. Russia is in need of a knightly order, in need of a person of knightly a temperament.

REBELLION AND SUBMISSION IN THE PSYCHOLOGY OF THE MASSES [1]

I.

How do new ideas reflect in the masses, towards what do they lead in the process of democratisation, and is it possible to recognise these ideas, after they have become vulgarised? Here is a question, at each step posited by the Russian actuality. The result, to which a sacred revolt of spirit and a sacred vision about freedom and just-truth in the soul of the masses has already led, presents a quite gruesome nightmare. Never yet has it been so clear, that the mass of mankind can live only by *organic ideas*, that the critical ideas, the purely abstract, vulgarised, lead to dissolution, to hooliganism.

The peasantry, as an organic component of life, is based upon submission to an higher, -- aristocratically and nobly so, which senses its own more ancient, divine origin: to the latter the muzhik-peasant sensed his own connection with eternity and therefore could not become a philistine. Aristocratic was that human mass, which by a mystical impulse of submission to God was drawn to the crusades, and went off into the mysterious faraway to liberate the Sepulchre of the Lord. This latter became a knight of the Lord, a warrior of Christ, and scaled the heavens. The masses of the people, as a mystical organism, in which all the parts are subordinated to an higher centre and hierarchically co-subordinated to one another, never becomes vulgarised, always rises above the spirit of philistinism, is noble, striven afar and upwards. Suchlike a mass of the people -- is submissive in its relation to God, prayerful at its basis, but rebellious in its relation to the evil of the world, chivalrously brave and militant in its struggle with the slavery and the necessity of the natural order.

---

[1] Published in "Moskovskii Ezhenedel'nik", 18 December 1907.

But how dreadful is the mass anarchy, how foul the stench of the mass self-worship, how trite the mass decadence! The mass of the people, reverencing nothing, spurning everything sacred, worshipping and asserting only itself, inevitably disintegrates, becomes saturated by a spirit of philistinism, ignoble in its senses, insipid in its consciousness, trite in its expression. In it the One-Only Great God is replaced by a multitude of little deities, elements of selfishness, envy and malice enter into its rules. The rebellion of a sacred uprising against evil is transformed into the slave's malice against the absolute good, in the slave's submission to natural evil. In critical ideas there is part of a great truth and it is evident in the rebellion of the finest people, but in the masses the rebellion and these critical ideas are readily transformed into bare nihilism, the slave's swaggering, into triteness. The reactionary ideas are negative just the same, the same rot.

Everything critical, restless, refined, every revaluing of values -- is solitary, individual, tragic, receiving its significance from the experiencing of the best people, is justified by the personal drama. But the critical revaluations, gained by personal torments, can penetrate to the mass of mankind only still in connection with the affirmations, with organic ideas; thereupon only is there accomplished the creative and fruitful turnabout. When the individual rebelliousness, when the aristocratic negation is expanded into a bare and abstract view, it becomes vulgarised, and when the new only with its negative side passes over into general useage, then in a majority of cases, it results in something hideous, rotten and trite. The great within world history can be made only in the *name* of something great. The attractive power of the *name* has inspired not only positive creativity, but likewise revolt and critique, without which there could be no historical developement. The heroes of thoughts and deeds have always been rebels, they have criticised and negated in the name of positive values, either consciously or unconsciously they have cleansed mankind of every sort of defilement in the name of God. When however there has been revolt in the name of revolt, critique in the name of critique, negation in the name of negation, when there is no sort of "in the name of", when in the masses withers away every organic idea, when within them is made revolt not in the name of absolute truth, and the past is negated, then there is sensed the onset of non-being, there is revealed the empty abyss.

In the masses of the youth, impacted by anarchy of spirit, there is to be observed now a process of the vulgarisation of ideas, an adoption of quite the greatest of ideas only from their negative perspective. There is begotten a new psychological type, in which there intersect all the negative, disintegrative currents, there come together the ideas, which in the best are mighty and glorious, but in the worst become trite and weedy, and grow into something unrecognisable. And first of all grown out and become vulgarised have been the social-revolutionary ideas. The very idea of revolution has gone into decay and become trite, the very calling of the revolutionary has ceased to be honourable. The vulgar revolutionism of the new generation in accord with the law of mass psychology readily gets mixed up with modernism, with decadentism, even with mysticism. There obtains an unsightly mess, self-smugness and triteness. What attracts everyone is not the anguish of the search and the torment of a new complex experience among the finest, the old decadents and the mystics, but rather an anarchisation of spirit; what pleases one, is that "all is permissible". Freedom gets jumbled up and confused with licentiousness and capriciousness, honour -- with selfishness and vanity, the affirmation of person -- with self-worship and conceit, justice -- with greed and vengefulness. The individual torment of an anarchistic revolt in the nest people, with the aristocrats of spirit leads to a religious submission; in the anarchistically inclined mob there is not this religious torment, it is only the self-conceit of rebellious slaves. The finest have anguished not for an anarchisation of spirit, but rather in accord with an harmonisation of spirit, since the ultimate freedom and truth of anarchism, conquering force and compulsion, -- is in an organic ordering of life, submissive to absolute Meaning. The decadent "mystical anarchism", which now threatens to be transformed into a superficial, trite and dissolute fad, can be for the refined, the gifted, cultured, select people a bridge over to positive religion, to a new experience, which would posit new problems; but in its epidemic spread this most recent variety of anarchy of spirit leads to an ultimate nihilism, to an unbridled self-conceit. Indeed the exalted ideals of anarchism -- the ideals of limitless freedom and the abolition of every coercion over the person -- have led to our "anarchist-individualists", who are difficult to distinguish from simple robbers, and for whom the derivative formula appears to be in everything is permissible self-assertion. In anarchism there is a portion of truth, but it is impossible to jest with the elements of anarchy.

Among the youth are begotten new tendencies, organisations arise not political only, but quasi-mystical, they seize upon whatever some final word, the surface of ideas, they avidly pounce upon the negative inferences of ideas complex and misunderstood. There threatens a new woe: an epidemic of mystics after a whole series of other, altogether non-mystical epidemics. The very word "mysticism" has come to be a trifling matter happening in short order. Such a vulgar mysticism can but be a simulation of psychological refinement among the suchlike smug coarse people. Such a blind mysticism is an hodgepodge of what pleases one, not bound up with any sort of ideas, nothing compelling. The anarchy of spirit can just as readily assume the guise of mysticism, as it can the guise of a most extreme materialism and empiricism; the refusal of every absolute norm and absolute light can likewise appear as a mystical irrationalism, just like an irrational empiricism. Suchlike mystics are readily recognised by their disdain for religion and antipathy towards Christianity. People as it were value their own darkness, they are afraid of being blinded by the light, tempted by folly they spurn the religion of salvation. Those with a bent for everything the latest vogue don their mystical attire, but their souls remain without any change, they likewise affirm but themself, they worship but themself, they account themself mystical all the more in their self-assertion and self-worship. In the mysticism, in vogue at the present day, phantasms are jumbled up together with realities, such that there is lost the criteria for firmly establishing the difference. The pleasant giddiness from the overall confusion acts as an attraction towards an irrational, anarchistic mysticism. Of a sudden it seems, that it is possible to remain a Social-Democrat, to serve the coming kingdom of this world, it is possible also to be an anarchist, to assist in the chaotic falling-apart of this world, and amidst this to take delight in the elegant finery of mysticism. The mystical epidemic contains in itself nothing positive; it provides no organic sustenance to the masses, it alleviates not the spiritual hunger, it decides not the question about the meaning of life; it is a purely negative and destructive phenomenon. Mysticism, just like revolution, has imperceptibly become an everyday trite affair, and the mysticism has gotten mixed up with revolution in the element of dissolution. The religious consciousness ought however to be united with an honest liberation movement in building up, in the organising of a new spirit.

II.

It is impossible to imagine for oneself anything more tragic, more pitiful, more ludicrous than the solitary Nietzsche at the time of his death. This man all his life suffered from the anguish of solitude, misunderstood and unrecognised. In this, that Nietzsche was a solitary, having risen up over all the crowd, having hurled a challenge to all the world and by the world having been spurned, in this was all the meaning of the wrestling of his spirit, all the essence of his striking ideas. The success of Nietzsche posthumously is a great and terrible affront to his life of suffering, an outrage upon his torments. Nietzsche had basis to think, that almost no one would accept him, but almost everyone has acknowledged him, they have appropriated from him in parts, for everyone he has become in vogue, and all his ideas have become vulgarised and made trite. Nietzsche was a great manifestation of the world spirit, -- from Nietzscheanism however there comes an ugly stench, which becomes more stale with each passing day. Nietzscheans have started to go about in entire crowds, everyone suddenly is seized with the desire to become a superman, everyone is puffed up and bursting with self-conceit. Such a democratisation of the idea of the superman is not only a *contradictio in adjecto*, but also a moral and ethical bit of triteness. An herd of "supermen" would certainly be nowise distinct from a flock of sheep, since unknown to it would be the torment of the supra-human solitude and the whole inevitability of an egress into the God-manly communality of Sobornost'. Only a gloomy triteness can be happy with this solitude and alienation, as a pretty posturing: this solitude is a terrible torment, from which every deep soul seeks a religious egress. In the Nietzscheanising crowd of supermen however there is created a sort of vulgar, shallow, empty solitude spread out everywhere, the loneliness of the crowd. For Nietzsche there either opens up the path of an ultimate perishing and madness, or the God-manly path, drowning its thirst for the supra-human in God-manhood, whence all are filiated in sonship to God, where all are as gods, where all become victorious over the natural human condition and pass over to the supra-human. For the Nietzscheans, for the herds of the super-men, such a tragic dilemma does not present itself, within the natural and desolate mankind they attain to their supra-human triteness. Even the Social-Democrats have managed for themself to elaborate upon the democracy scorned by Nietzsche, they have drawn from him things useful for their own ends. And this is not so stupid, as it might seem, though for the hapless Nietzsche this inflicts mortal a wound. The socialist religion would as it were render all into supermen, small-time gods, true, though microscopically so and desolate as a result of being freed from everything higher, but themself still ultimately affirmed and made a god of. Hence there is no use for poor Nietzsche, plunged into madness over the religious idea of the super-man, and within this idea seeking God. For Nietzsche, true, the killing of God was a great torment, but for the adherents of the socialist religion this killing has become a great joy. For Nietzsche the visionary dream about the super-man was in contrast against the visionary dream of the happy socialist ant-hill, despised by him, but for the Social-Democrats the happy socialist ant-hill represents something instantly composed entirely of supermen. But indeed it is always possible to render Nietzsche harmless, to make him non-dangerous, to emasculate him, to prepare him for general consumption. A sort of Nietzschean Social-Democratic gruel would be the thing received, very tasty for the herd instincts. In swallowing this swill, certainly, no one would be rendered a superman in the Nietzschean sense, but many would feel themself supermen and in the end would bow down before one quite genuinely and likewise phantasmically supra-human, the enemy of the God-Man. So long as mankind does not recognise ultimately, that only the God-Man Christ was and is the sole Divinely Man -- the Supra-Man, until it accepts within itself His Spirit, until then it will not become godly, it will not pass over into a supra-human condition, it will remain the natural man, enslaved, limited and mortal, and God-manhood will fail to obtain. In God-manhood all are aristocrats, in it all are filiated into sonship to God, in it there are no slaves, in it even the least of people possess an absolute significance and destiny, nobility and comeliness, have a place within the Divine organism, in the Cosmos.

III.

The fate of "decadence" among the masses is just as instructive and just as pitiful, as is the fate of Nietzsche. The solitary decadents, the select natures, suddenly have begun to walk as crowds, and there has appeared the "modern" mass style, quite tasteless and trite. I say this, although I also recognise the great and worldwide significance behind decadentism as a crisis of spirit. But it is gruesome to see, when the refined, the cultured, the rebellious in the highest sense is transformed into everyday licentiousness and ignoble nihilism. Our decadent modernist journals present a pitiful picture of the rapid degeneration and vulgarity of our decadence and modernism: what strikes one in these journals is the small-circle pettiness, the mustiness and stuffiness of atmosphere, in which they find trifles to be of world significance. There is in them no genuine nobility, which would hold in check the slovenly brawling. The conceit of this cliquishness, rapidly coming into vogue, is insufferable, the pompousness and pretentiousness are glaringly apparent in each bibliographic notation. A stereotype has already been worked out, in accord with which all write in our new journals. Always and in everything by an immutable law the *negative* ideas become insipid, they decay and cause rot, when taken up by the herd. *Reverence* before the holy cannot become trite, cannot cause rot, when the human masses are caught up in this exalted feeling. The masses cannot live whether be it by decadence, or by Nietzscheanism, or anarchism, or purely negative revolutionary ideas, nor by just as negative reactionary outlooks. Mankind can be brought together and uplifted to the heights only by positive *organic* ideas, only by an absolute submission to God, which at various stages of developement has assumed various forms, all increasingly full. Only a voluntary submission to absolute sanctity renders slaves into aristocrats, into children of God, only this submission begets the very idea of mankind. Only a religious submission, reverence, a giving oneself over to the will of God provides a protection against that philistinism, to which the French Revolution led in the process of human self-assertion, and against that nihilistic hooliganism, to which the modern anarchy of spirit leads. In the reverent submission to God, in the uniting of one's human will with His holy will -- is an ultimate, an utmost, an absolutely-desirable freedom. An absolute affirmation of the human, of mankind and of man as God, of human freedom as the ultimate, is a terrible delusion from the spirit of evil, a greatest temptation, an ultimate slavery and non-being. Only a God-manly freedom is real, only a God-manly path to it is actualised. In Christ this path is pointed out for the world.

Revolutionary ideas, taken abstractly, and affirmed only on their negative side, lead to emptiness, they inwardly degenerate, if they do not pass over into the positive and the organic. In history we tend to see, that even the most justified revolt among the masses often leads in its results to evil. The sowings of Russian Marxism, though including certain healthy ideas, has come up thistles.

Decadence has been transformed into a trite and empty fad. The modern anarchism moreover has begotten hooliganism and decay.

IV.

When Dostoevsky wrote his "The Devils" [alt. English title, "The Possessed"], this novel did not correspond to reality, it produced an impression of being almost a lampoon. But the genius of the work of Dostoevsky has proven prophetic. For now the "devils" have settled in Russia, now there have appeared the people, of whom Dostoevsky had presentiment, not only the Verkhovenskys, but also the Kirillovs. The religious meaning of revolutionary demonic-obsession is now apparent. There appear now the actualised faces of "the Devils", and there has become clear not the political, but rather the religious character of the revolutionary thirst of our intelligentsia. The best of the revolutionaries have become disillusioned in the results of the revolution, they seek faith. And for us the salvation -- is in the collapse of the revolutionary ideas whilst preserving, connected with them, the thirst for just-truth upon the earth. Dostoevsky understood it more profoundly than others, what the revolutionary ideology would lead to, he understood both the truth and the lie of the revolutionary intelligentsia.

The fate of the new and emerging generation depends upon this, whether it accepts the sacred into its soul or whether it remains empty of soul; the fate of the generation, having come of age during the era of the revolution, in which negative ideas prevailed over the positive, inspires but apprehension, leads to somber considerations. The revolutionary ecstasy has already passed over into apathy. In this new generation there has been lost the centre of life, in it the past visionary dreaminess and craving for truth on earth has imperfectly passed over into emptiness, into naked negation. If indeed by way of purely negative a path there be stripped away from man the trappings of culture and also cast aside the customary general upbringing, then will be left but the primitive beast. Now already this beast often peers forth from the eyes. The Divine image in man, prevailing over every beast, cannot be made apparent by purely the negative path, for this there is needful a positive effort of spirit, a prayerful turning to God.

At present not a single young soul is taken up with the inexplicable anguish and deep disillusion in the very essence of the negative ideas: the best of the youth are tormented with the results of the long desired revolution. This anguish and torment however will increase, and lead to a great crisis. The tendency towards suicide increases, alongside with an insensitivity towards murder. To live for nothing, only destruction, rebellion without any sort of "in the name of" has led to emptiness, to meaninglessness and beastly chaos, and has shewn nothing positive nor organic. Never yet, it would seem, has there been born a generation with such a grievous sickness of spirit, with such dissatisfaction and groaning. The demands have become enormous, the conceit puffed up to incredible proportions, and man draws back with terror before the abyss of emptiness. The old hindrances have fallen into ruin, and no sort of new ones have appeared. The fetters of spirit have been taken off, but the spirit itself would sooner go to pieces, than get itself organised and strengthened. The anguish, which manifests itself at the end of rebellion, is an harbinger of an higher submission, a languishing for submission before the Absolute. Faith in earthly idols is replaced by a lack of faith and disillusion in the natural human ideals, dreams that result in emptiness. Therein is begotten faith in the Good as an absolute power, in Meaning as absolute being. The elements of the Russian revolution, having concentrated in itself all the negative ideas, dissolves everything into the component parts, the primal and extreme elements and by this it destroys all the illusions, it lays bare genuine realities, and by this it serves indirectly for the rebirth of the religious. Never yet has it been so clear, that mankind on its own cannot arrange itself happily and freely, it cannot save itself by its own powers alone.

To believe in the mass of mankind, in the multitude of people, in the crowd, in the herd -- is impossible, history teaches otherwise than to believe. But this by no means is indicative of a pseudo-aristocratism, a contempt towards people, it is not a sanctioning of an alienated and solitary individualism. It is possible to have a fiery faith in mankind, to unite one's will with the will of God, it is possible to love this mankind, it is possible to connect the messianic idea with faith in the people, having accepted Christ in one's soul. God-manhood is not the crowd, the herd, it cannot be made vulgar and trite, for this is a supra-human and organic unity, the theosis-deification of mankind, the descent upon it of the Holy Spirit. Before the God-manly will of the people we would be inclined to be heedful and reverent, since this would be the will of God. Everything, that was suffered for and dreamt out individually in quiet and solitude, everything would be realised in the God-manly life of the people, in the life of mankind, conjoined with God and through the God-Man.

The truth of democratism -- is in that communality of Sobornost', in the conjoining into unifying an organism, in which each has an absolute significance before God. But the religious idea of mankind and of the Cosmos -- is hierarchic. There can be and there ought to be destroyed the false hierarchy of this world, to rebel against it, but for this reason only -- in order to submit to the true and authentically Divine hierarchy, in which for each is destined a place. Only in this hierarchism is there the salvation from triteness, vulgarity, impersonality and the herd. And then let all submit to the free hierarchy of the Divine Cosmos.

A SICK RUSSIA [1]

Wherefore Jesus commanded the unclean spirit to come out from this man; since that for a long time it had tormented him, such that they bound him with chains and fetters for to safeguard him; but he brake the fetters, and was driven by the devil into the wilderness. And Jesus asked him: What is thine name? And he said: "Legion", since that many a devil was entered into him. And they besought Jesus, that He command them not to go into the abyss. And here upon that mountain was feeding a great herd of swine; and the devils besought Him, that He should suffer them to enter into them. And He so suffered them. The devils, having come out from the man, entered into the swine; and the herd ran violently down off a steep place into a lake, and was drowned.

from Lk. VIII, 29-33.

The devilishness of the revolution has ceased, the revolution has not succeeded, it has played itself out and there begin all the signs of a new devilishness, the devilishness of reaction. A failed revolution always has grievous consequences, in consequence of which is the revenge of those, which nearly for one mere moment experienced the sense of loss of their position in life. The devils have settled themselves into the sick body and the sick soul of Russia and they migrate from reaction into revolution, and from revolution into reaction. These -- are all the selfsame devils, assuming at one point a reactionary guise, and at another a revolutionary guise. At the second Duma there was the devilish left, at the third Duma there has begun the devilishness of the right. Both there and here is the same grip of obsession: people situated precisely under the grip of some sort of extra-human power, distorting their human features. Those ruling and

[1] Published in "Slovo", 23 February 1908.

those struggling against the rule in society, the reactionary part of the people and its revolutionary part -- are in the grip of possession by an unclean spirit, which torments and fetters.

The vicious circle of reaction and revolution -- here is a nightmare of human life, here is the repayment for the grievous sins of the past. Both the reaction and the revolution are sent from above in chastisement for transgressions committed, for the sins of the rulers and the sins of the people. Over the unworthy and sinful rulers, having betrayed their task, bursts forth the thunder of revolution, and over the unworthy and sinful society, having betrayed its worthiness, there bursts forth the muddying rain of reaction. Healthy organic growth is served only by the pure heart of the people and the crystal-clear consciousness of the difference between good and evil. Once the unclean spirit has found itself a start in the body and soul of Russia, then the lacerations from reaction and revolution are inevitable and inevitably necessary is a repentance by all the nation. For the averting of the devilishness of revolution, the ruling power and the governing classes of society ought to repent of their sins; for the averting of the devilishness of reaction the intelligentsia and society ought to repent of their sins.

The Russian revolution did not long continue and it finished tragically. By precious a price was bought from those days of drunkenness and revolutionary debauchery. Too quickly has begun the reaction in the government, which still is half bad enough, but also in society itself, in the very cells of the organism of the people, which is downright bad. There were days, when much might have been gained, when it seemed, almost that it might have been possible to outpace Europe, but now with ease are swept away even the crumbs received, with quick steps we march backwards, and now it is difficult to gain even the smallest, the most indubitable and needful. Monstrous mistakes were made, ruinous for Russian freedom, but these mistakes were connected not only with a false consciousness, they lay also in the depths of the element, defiled by the unclean spirit. The revolution suffered therefore the wreck with suchlike a failure, that within it obtained no organic constructive forces. Within

Russian society the long series of decades has sprouted a sick apostacy, a rupturing off from the mystical foundations of the people's organism, negative feelings have been amassed, and fighters have become inspired by hostility and discord, and not by love or creative idea. The historical ruling powers have committed great crimes, having devoted itself to the idol of imperialism, and has served the instincts of the governing classes, with rare exceptions it was not of the people. Society together with the Russian intelligentsia has lost its sense of Russian citizenship, in its apostacising rebelliousness it would see as its own honour and worth. The *people* however have remained even up til now an enigma. The Russian intelligent would sooner sense himself a citizen of the planet Mars, but in no way of Russia, he is bereft of conservative feeling as regards the organism of the Russian people. In a very backward society this intelligent is wont to confess the most extreme socialistic and anarchistic ideals, totally abstract, lacking in historical flesh and blood. An obligatory break with the fathers, with everything past, with history, has become the norm of life of the Russian intelligent. And the Russian intelligentsia has rendered itself rebellious not only in regard to the ruling powers, in which was its truth, but also in regard to Russian literature, to Russian philosophic thought, to the faith of the people, to the sense of nation, and in this has been its great lie. With us much has been written and been spoken on the theme about the split between the intelligentsia and the people, but in viewing this theme exclusively from a sociological point of view, it is impossible either to understand or to resolve anything in it; this theme remains unfathomably deep.

We have amassed a century of negative consciousness, intensified with atheistic and nihilistic ideas. The latest results of European developement are reflected in Russia in a most extreme and limitless form. If a Russian -- be a socialist, then he is not such a socialist as they have in the West, he is a socialist most extreme and fanatical, his socialism extends beyond time and space, his socialism is a religion. If a Russian -- be an anarchist, then it is a most limitless rebelling against the primal foundations of being. If a Russian -- be a materialist, then materialism is for him -- a theology; if he be an atheist, then his atheism -- is religiously so. If -- a decadent, then he is disintegrated into his component parts. Radicalism -- is for us a national trait, this trait has begotten much that is bad, but it can however be a source of the greatest good, this trait can avert the philistinism.

The Slavophils sensed the bad, with organic ideas they sought to halt the growth of negative and apostacising rebellious ideas, but they proved powerless. The conservatism of the Slavophils, on the one hand, was but romantic, and on the other hand, it made too much a concession to official Russia in the teaching about the ruling powers and nationality, and contains within itself the conceptions of reactionary nationalism and coercion. The split of the generation of the 60's from the generation of the 40's marked with it a great step forward in the growth of the apostacy and the strengthening of the negative consciousness. If within the generation of the 40's Westernisers and Slavophils all still belonged to one family, and represented the blossoming of Russian culture, then during the generation of the 60's there begins a final split and division: Westernism in its radical part is transformed into the revolutionary apostacising rebelliousness, into nihilism, lowering the level of culture, and Slavophilism gradually is decayed into a reactionism as clear as water, into an hatred for mankind and national conceit. The Eastern savagery is to be sensed in both the one and the other. The discord and hostility grow with each passing year, there is lost the common language and any possibility of mutual understanding. To the revolutionary apostacy, all the people of the other circle hostile to them represent a different race, a lower variant, relative to which there exists a different ethics, than that, operative in their own circle. In completely the same way for the reactionary apostacy, all the people of the other circle hostile to them represent a different race, relative to which anything is permissible. There is lost not only the awareness of a national oneness, but also even the awareness of an human oneness. The abyss, which all more and more separates the two ideologies, corresponds to the abyss, which separates society from the ruling powers.

With Hertsen there was still a sense of Russian citizenship, an instinct for all the people, in Chernyshevsky there is no longer this; Hertsen was the bearer of an higher and refined culture, whereas Chernyshevsky is already the bearer of a lower culture, a culture of diminished capacities. In Khomyakov there was an all-human idealism, a consciousness of universal ideas; in the successive reactionary nationalists the universal ideas common to all mankind vanish and there instead govern the instincts and interests, finding expression in the black hundredist pogroms. The idealistic conservatism and liberalism sought to uphold for us an oneness both human and national, to stand forth for an higher culture, but they did not possess that energy and enthusiasm, which could outstrip the march of history. [Boris Nikolaevich] Chicherin was the bearer of an higher culture and the consciousness of the universal, but he was a rationalist, wanting for the vital fire, he was afraid of everything new and could do nothing to change the fatal course of Russian life. The split, the apostacy, the mutual lack of understanding and hostility grew. The ruling powers and society despised each the other. Everything reactionary had success on the one side, and everything revolutionary -- on the other side. The intelligentsia was sundered off from the people, from the life of all the people, and it lived a life of the small circles, suffocatingly stuffy, mistaking its narrow rooms for entire worlds. Moreover, the intelligentsia lacerated itself for the people, it thirsted to unite with it, but united only on the grounds of the people's instincts and interests, not the people's soul nor the great idea lodged within it. the intelligentsia began to worship the people as an idol, and it understood as people exclusively the common-people, the peasants and the workers. And together with this, the intelligentsia became sundered off from the traditions of world culture, from the world and from national developement of faith, literature, art, philosophy, science. The greatest results of national creativity seem to it just as foreign, as is also the historical ruling powers. the great Russian writers it does not regard as its own, and has rather its own sort of writers from the circles. With world knowledge our intelligentsia likewise has little in common. The populist intelligentsia of the decade of the 70's began even to assert, that it is not necessary to study and read books, since this is a sin against the people, and this mindset has remained with us into the present. And from the "scientific" they have created for themself an idol, they worship scientific knowledge as one might an idol. the ruling powers and the reactionary part of society have persecuted the intelligentsia with an unlimited cruelty, they have driven it underground, and strengthened its feeling of apostacy and the consciousness of its being sundered off from the unity of the nation.

Dostoevsky understood the sickness of Russia most deeply of all the Russian writers, although he did not always prescribe the correct means of treatment. In "The Devils", one of the most valuable and perceptive of Dostoevsky's novels, he grasps with a prophetic gift the religious drama of the Russian intelligentsia and the limitations of the revolutionary element. Dostoevsky with the touch of genius caught the feel of demonic-possession, the obsessiveness of the revolutionary intelligentsia, and that, about which he wrote in "The Devils", in his own time little corresponded to reality, but did find its justification after the passage of many years, when the Russian revolution broke out. Dostoevsky inadequately understood however, that *the revolutionary devilishness is but the reverse side of reactionary devilishness*, that in our reactionism was expressed that selfsame infirmity, which is also in the revolutionism. the revolutionary element goes to extreme limits, and the reactionary element but pushes these extreme limits. And so one is given to ponder over whether Russia is condemned to experience the terror of a most extreme evil. The chronic sickness of Russian national developement, in which has all intensified the ruptures within all the parts of the organism of the people, has found its expression in the course of the Russian revolution, and has led to all its failures.

Only now has there been uncovered the bankruptcy of all the intelligentsia world-view, the inner inconsistency and emptiness of the foundations of our traditional radical ideas. This intelligentsia world-view was fed by reaction and it feeds the reaction, it was conceived in the grievous sickness of our national organism and the sickness only but intensifies. Russia -- is a land so enormous, so mysterious in its bosom, that it least of all can be an object of experiments. This is not France, in which life moves along on orders from Paris and which would be adjudged to be the object of the spirit of a social experimentalism and demonstrate obviously the sickness of certain sides of European developement. If all the powers were directed at an inward overcoming of the dissension among us, then it might be possible to weaken the consequences of the sickness, but for this first of all there has to be a breaking down and sweeping away of all the entire basis of the traditional intelligentsia world-view, there has to occur a radical turnabout of ideas. And such a turnabout is already being prepared for us, imperceptibly it is being readied in the various ends of life. The Russian revolution and reaction have revealed a deep antinomy of human existence and they ready a turnabout of spirit. The gentry Russia and the intelligentsia Russia -- these inveterate enemies have been rocked to their foundations, there has crumbled the power of the first within life and the power of the second within ideas. the gentry way of life and the intelligentsia mind-set are closely connected between them, and it was foreordained for them to have fallen simultaneously. The nihilism from above and the nihilism from below, the nihilism of the nobility and the bureaucracy and the nihilism of the intelligentsia and the people have given forth with their own fruits in life, and the crisis of ideas can now only be concluded in the surmounting of every nihilism. The crisis of ideas, which also will have its own social consequences, will lead to a new consciousness of the idea of the people as an higher reality. And on the other side, this crisis ought to rock to its foundation the pagan cult of power, which inspires both the ruling powers, and the revolution, and the bureaucracy, and the intelligentsia.

For a long time already with us in Russia they tend to seek for the *people* as a certain sort of reality, and in accord with its will and its spirit they wanted as though to harmonise the social order. But the people is not something empirically given for us as a reality, such a fact is not apperceived within experience, this is a fact grasped but mentally. The people -- is a mystical reality, and this reality -- is an object of faith, "of things in the guise of the invisible, known of in hopes". Nominalistic positivism does not believe in the reality of the general and therefore it denies the reality of the people, it annuls the very idea of the people as a mysteried organism. But this nominalistic positivism by a roundabout path produces a whole series of general realities under various guises. The Russian intelligentsia, poisoned by positivism, has renounced the idea of the people as a mystical idea, but it believes in the reality of its own particular people whether as the common-people, the oppressed classes of society, the peasantry or the proletariat. Marxism is fully nominalistic as regards its philosophic world-view; and in the people-proletariat it believes as a reality. But indeed this proletariat never and by no one empirically could have been apperceived, as a fact as such it does not exist; this is a reality likewise of a mystical order, and it is accepted on faith, under the guise of something invisible. The Social-Democrats believe in a mentally posited proletariat, since the empirical proletariat either does not at all exist, or it exists in very varied forms, having little in common with the "idea" of the fourth estate. Where is the empirical, the experiential proletariat in England? The Social-Democrats believe in the proletariat contrary to the experience in England, and will believe contrary to everything empirical. And if so, then why however is faith in the people absurd, in the genuine people, in this mysterious reality, in this mentally-grasped fact? If faith in the people be superstition, then a superstition also is faith in the proletariat, and also faith in the people as the working class, and every roundabout allowance of general realities.

The will of the Russian people and the idea of the Russian people have not found themself an adequate reflection, neither in our ruling powers, nor in our intelligentsia. The bureaucracy has maimed the people's life, and the intelligentsia has maimed the people's thought. And with all ever newer and newer acuteness is put the question about the relationship between the intelligentsia and the people, about the origins of the sick sundering and about the paths for treating it. With us the intelligentsia has become s special social group, caught up in its circles, and membership in it is determined not by capacities of intellect nor by talents, but by a special social-moral outlook. Mediocrity and lack of talent find inclusion amongst the intelligentsia, at the same whilst Pushkin and Lev Tolstoy are excluded from it. But to make history and create culture requires people with genius, people with talent, the people and an intelligentsia of an higher intellect and higher consciousness. That stratum, which among us is wont to be called the intelligentsia, is sundered off from the people and in opposition to it, but together with this it has not a modicum of genius or talent, of higher intellect and higher consciousness. The true intelligentsia involves the gift of expressing the will of all the people and the idea of all the people, the genius of the people, its intellect. If there exists the people in general and the Russian people in particular as a general and mysteried reality, then it ought to have its own mysteried representation, an adequate reflection of its spirit. We believe, that the spirit of the Russian people is reflected in the Russian great literature, in the unique character of our genius and talents. we believe, that the will of the people was reflected in suchlike a titan, as Peter the Great. The soul of the people was expressed in St. Sergei of Radonezh, in the Russian popular piety and some sides of our sectarian movements, full of mystical thirstings. If the organic spirit of the people be seen in Russian literature, then the starts of an organic sociability are provided for in the agrarian setting, but they demand further developement on the basis of an higher consciousness. The historical bodies have been created over thousands of years, and in a few years it is impossible either to destroy them, or to re-root them. Russia has to grow with an inward growth, or it will be threatened with ruin from philistine reactions and revolutions. Only an organic character of developement gets beyond the inescapable vicious circle of the reactionary and revolutionary demonic grip.

But developement never happens without problems, and all peoples pass through reactions and revolutions. Every revolution is a reaction against a reaction, after which there ensues also a reaction against the revolution. And both the one and the other point to the sickness in the organism of the people, and unmask the devils, that have taken up their abode in the soul of the people. The people disintegrates into "leftists" and "rightists", into two races, from which each reckons that everything is permissible relatively against the other. The "leftists" regard the "rightists" almost as not being human, and the "rightists" relate the same way towards the "leftists". In actuality for both the one and the other in their masses they are -- average people, with deficiencies, but also with abilities, and everything human is possible for both the one and the other. But the elements under the demonic grip hinder seeing the actual man, everything transpires not as though by ordinary people, but by hostile races. And indeed this horror is occurring in a Christian society. It is evident from afar that society has forsaken Christ, and that the unclean spirit is strongly settled within it. The unclean spirit instigates both the ruling power and the revolution, both the "rightists" and the "leftists". But in order to gain victory over the evil, it is needful to be aware of the source of the evil, of what is changed at the very foundation. And the source of evil is not outside of us, not in a power thrust upon us, not in this or some other social order, not in the oppressions by these or other classes of society, but the rather is within, in the sin, for which we all are responsible. The victory over evil, a real and radical victory, is a victory over sin, the redemption from sin, a birth into new life. Sick Russia ought to become conscious of its sins and be redeemed from them, and therein the devils lacerating it would be banished. The basis of sin however is in an inward apostacy from God. Both the "rightists" and the "leftists" ought to repent; the former ought to become aware of the inevitability of radical changes, of a profound turnabout, oriented towards new life, and the latter -- to become aware of the inevitability of conservatism, of the profound preservation of what is found to be of eternal value in history and revealing its absolute basis. Then only will the devils of revolution cease to threaten the "right", and the devils of reaction -- the "left". As long as the ruling power remains unaware, that its forcibly maintained presentday state, law, economy, family, morals -- are not Christian, up til then God will threaten it with the punishment of revolution. As long as revolution does not renounce its self-smugness and self-interests, until then it will find itself threatened by reaction. A communing with higher being ought always to be preceded by repentance, and repentance up til now has not been evident either in the one or the other side, and it is all the same self-smugness and unbridled instincts. The crisis, which Russia is now experiencing, ought to lead to a final break with the traditions of a reactionary rule and reactionary nobility, just as it ought equally with the traditions of the revolutionary intelligentsia and revolutionary "people". It ought instead to lead to the idea of the people as a mystical organism, in the name of the idea of all the people, possessing a great destiny in the world.

To the cult of power there will be always opposed another cult of power, and the one power will be forced to yield before the other power. In the clash with one beast there comes another like beast. And where is the truth, conquering the beastly power, the truth, more powerful, than every power? Truth is born in the victory over sin and the raging of beastly powers.

It is untrue, that the elements of revolution can nourish anyone, that the raging of revolution can provide bread. In this regard it is necessary for us first of all to sober up, to be aware, that bread is provided by a laborious social developement, by a constructive economic process, always appearing too slow for the starving. Our productive workers movement should come out of its primary social cells and it ought to bypass the illusions of political alchemy towards an healthy economism, towards a socio-cultural creativity. Only a culturally creative work is able to disarm the devils of reaction and weaken the devils within the liberation movement itself.

Man cannot be free, while there is a devil within him, he is held down with chains and fetters. The vicious circle of reaction and revolution is a fettering, an enslavement. It is possible to escape this nightmarish circle, only by a casting out of the unclean spirit, only by being freed from the demons. Who then can be the deliverer, who has the power to order the devils out? The reaction does not have the powers to cast out the devils of revolution, and revolution does not have the powers to cast out the devils of reaction, the devils alike support and feed the others, these are all one and the same devils. The governing powers do not possess the power of spirit for a victory over the chaotic anarchy, and the revolutionary intelligentsia and revolutionary people do not possess the power of spirit for a victory over the devilish reactionary power and the reactionary part of society. Russia is breaking its bonds and is driven by the devils into the wilderness, into the wilderness of chaotic reaction and chaotic revolution. Only Jesus can order the unclean spirit to go out from the body of Russia. Only Christ can be the deliverer. but for this it is needful inwardly to return to Christ, to seek in Him the quenching of one's thirst and the abating of one's torments. We believe, that suchlike a crisis now transpires within the broken hearts of the finest of the revolutionaries. Among the sick and the obsessed there are many worthy of the finest and highest lot. The body of many of the presently demon-possessed can become repository of a clean spirit. While many there be among the obsessed and demon-possessed, amongst the revolutionaries there be also seekers of truth and seekers of God. And perhaps they are also to be found amongst the reactionaries. When the unclean spirit shall have been cast out, then only will people appear in their true nature, and with the authentic will of the Russian people, then will become conscious the idea of Russia. And the unclean spirit will enter in thither, where it becometh it to dwell, -- in the herd of swine. To be demon-possessed is to become swinish, piggishly boorish. And its ranks are recruited from both reactionaries, and from revolutionaries, and from the moderates. The Gospel herd of swine is a symbol of swinishness, of boorishness, which itself attracts to itself the devils, and in which the devils ought to pass out from a body, destined to be the abode of the clean spirit. how large this herd be, we cannot know. In the devilishness of the reaction at present is sensed an almost total swinishness. It cannot be overcome empirically, it cannot prevail quantitatively, we know only one path of treatment, and this path -- is Christ, an inner self-denial in

His name, an inward orientation to Him. Disintegration and ruin await Russia, if the question about its societal existence be posited upon the basis of godless powers. Only in the truth of Christ -- is the power of salvation.

AGAINST "MAXIMALISM" [1]

The question concerning the essence of "maximalism" is born of the loins of life. The Russian revolution has endowed this question with an especial acuteness. I speak not about the specific maximalism, which is connected with the expropriations, the killings, etc. I have in view rather the principle of maximalism, which has taken hold with a large portion of the Russian intelligentsia, which was lodged within the basis of the Russian revolution, and which has led already to fatal consequences, to the black and ugly reaction. What interests me is not so much the political and social maximalism, as rather the religious psychology of maximalism. The article by V[alentin Pavlovich] Sventsitsky, "In Defense of the 'Maximalism' of Brand" [cf. Hendrik Ibsen's play, "Brand"], and certain of his former articles tend to evoke a vital protest against religious maximalism. The danger lies hidden not only in the socio-political maximalism, but also in the religious. Maximalism all too readily can get mixed up in a demonic volitional self-assertion, and this demonic bent is seen foremost in the acclaimed Brand. The religious psychology of maximalism is an extortion from God of that which still is not merited, it is a demanding of the miraculous. This extortion, this demanding not for oneself only, but also for other people and for all the world seems to me not good. The preaching of maximalism, whether the social, and so also the religious, too often begets hatred in place of love, it ultimately disunites all and everything, it cuts off all the paths. The preaching of "all or nothing" can readily prove itself immoral, since it can encourage a do-nothing attitude in the consciousness of the masses of weak people. To attain "all" is not possible to attain by inexorable toil, and will gain "nothing".

---

[1] Published in "Moskovskii Ezhenedel'nik", 6 September 1909.

The question concerning maximalism is posited in radical form and falsely, when they set in opposition to it the compromise, the middle ground, opportunism, etc. The question is too much simplified, when maximalism is characterised by the formula "all", and every other trend and frame of mind by the formula "some but little". They presuppose, that only maximalism is principled, has ideas, and everything, that is not maximalism, is a compromise of principle, a bargaining with the idea, i.e. the selfsame principle, but not taken to its end, the selfsame idea, but halted half-way. Sventsitsky also holds to this false positing of the question. To maximalism there can be opposed another and non-maximalistic principle, another and no less powerful idea. Non-maximalism and anti-maximalism can be just as principled, be just as endowed with idea, be just as radical and heated, as is maximalism. A non-maximalistic principle can be just as consequential, just as extreme, as is the maximalistic. The "moderate" current can be just as principled and just as radical, as is the maximalistic current. In essence, every mindset of idea and current of principle sincerely desires to attain the maximum, and not the minimum, it strives for the "all", and not for "some but little", and the question is merely in this, how to attain the maximum, and what is to be said about the maximum. If I differ in opinion from Sventsitsky, then it is not because that he desires the maximum, the "all", and I the minimum, the "some but little". I likewise want the "all", the maximum, but we can strive ether towards a different maximum, and in different things see the "all", or otherwise variously understand the means and paths of attaining the all.

In general they tend to forget, that the revolutionary-maximalist tactic can be condemned on the grounds, that with it there is attained the minimum, less, and not more, than they desire. At the climax of the Russian revolution many were aware and sensed, that the revolutionary-maximalist tactic leads to bitter reaction, that the tactic hinders the making of the gains, which might have been made in the conditions of the historical moment. Were these presentiments opportune? The course of the Russian revolution and its pitiful results give sufficient justification to this truth, that not every maximalist tactic leads to maximum results, that too often it leads to an extreme minimum. The generally widespread opinion, that revolutionary maximalism is always the true radicalism, the true path of principle, the true possessing of idea, is a coarse mistake, a vulgar opinion. There is this bias, that in politics it is always necessary to choose between the widely held extremes: the extreme herein can prove itself to be a very vile middle ground. I can on principle spurn both the colours black and red, I can deny the necessity of having to choose between these colours and be fond of the colour green, or violet or yet some other. there is a third principle, simultaneously distinct from both the left and from the right maximalism, and it is not a middle ground, not a compromise, but rather a third different idea, profound and radical.

This question is very complex. Every believing, sincere man of ideas always desires the maximum, but can differently understand the pathway towards this maximum. In the fundamentals of every "maximalist" tactic there lies an immense human conceit, hysterical pretension and often obsession, a demonic-possession. The psychology of "maximalism" in a majority of cases is connected with a maniac-like obsession by a single idea, not very encompassing, and there is seen a single point, and towards this point is taken a straight line. Along it moves the maximalist, taking note of nothing around, unreceptive to all the richness of existence. The whole breadth of life is hidden for such a type of maximalist, he is incapable of sensing his selfsame idea in all the manifestations of life, in the whole of culture. The point, towards which the maximalist goes in a straight line, taking note of nothing and no one, can readily prove empty, while the line of his movement bypasses existence. There obtains something like a nightmare in the psychology of maximalism, there is no sense of the expanse of soul, of spaciousness, the divine gift to understand and feel much. Maximalism imposes upon life an heavy burden, it recoils from the ideal of sanctity, in it there is that moral fanaticism, which is in essence deeply contrary to the religion of Christ. The maximalist-revolutionary esteems himself a saviour of the world and regards himself a judge of the world. But in the world there was only one Saviour, and no one man can have pretensions to this, that he himself will save the world. And the judge of the world can only but be not human. The maximalist sees the source of evil outside himself, in other people, in external forces, in these or those layers of society, and so passionately does he wish to pronounce judgement over this evil, that he is already incapable of seeing the evil within himself, as would be were he humble to that without. Maximalism therefore is deeply contrary to Christianity, in that all confessing maximalism presuppose the world abiding in evil, and themselves the saviours of the world, and dwelling outside this evil. But the fundamental sin of maximalism is however in this, that it is anti-cultural and anti-historical.

Maximalism, consequently, taken to its end, is thought which is merely individualistic. A person reaches maximalism by way of an exiting from history, by way of defiance of history, a denial of history. And L. Tolstoy manifests the typical maximalist. This maximalism also sins, in that it strives towards the attainment not of an universal maximum, but rather an individual maximum, it thinks more about itself, than about the world. Our revolutionary intelligentsia has always striven not so much towards the attainment of illustrious results for Russia and for the Russian people, as rather for the preservation of its own purity. Maximalism is compelled to deny the meaning of world history and its stages, and it lacks the capacity to find justification for the creativity of culture. Maximalism is incompatible with the religious consciousness of the truth, that the deed of salvation is wrought by *history*, and that this deed is universal. In the sins of the world, in the bonds of each with all and to all, in the mutual responsibility for evil are set limits to every historical action. The maximum of historical activity is always connected with the degree of victory over sin, and every attempt to attain the maximum apart from this inner victory over sin is itself sinful. The victory indeed over sin is not attained by outward social turnabouts, it is not attained by constituent assembly, nor by nationalisation of the land, nor by collectivisation of the means of production, nor by anything similar. What is needful is inner revolution, a conscious denial of the human will in the name of the will of God, then only will a social turnabout give birth to a new life. Maximalism is connected with a false understanding of developement, it does not see, that absolute principles lie at the basis of every developement, and not only at the end, and not the goals which should be attained. In conservatism as a guarding of the eternal within the past there is likewise indeed an healthy grain of truth, an absolute basis of history and culture. Maximalism does not want to see these absolute groundings, it denies the eternal within history and in its striving to realise an absolute tomorrow it readily passes over into nihilism.

Sventsitsky in his defense of maximalism stands upon an individual-moral point of view, all his arguments bear an individual-moral character. When he suggests to Prince E. N. Trubetskoy to distribute off his substance to the poor and in this he sees maximalism, for which he is prepared to forgive Trubetskoy, in that this latter does not demand a constituent assembly, then it clearly becomes evident, that on this question he does not stand upon an universal-religious point of view. The religious meaning of history is realised not by this merely individualistic path. Sventsitsky -- is a believing Christian, and his maximalism is distinct from the maximalism of the Social-Revolutionaries and the Social-Democrats. But I fear, that his psychology is too close to the old social revolutionism, and he too much adapts his Christianity to it.

I believe, that the world is moving towards a most profound religious revolution, and perhaps the world will come fully towards it, but this faith of mine is not bound up with any maximalist principle and maximalist tactic. I believe, that into the world is entering a new religious principle, still not revealed, that a new religious idea will produce a turnaround in the world, but this principle itself is not at all maximalist and has nothing in common with a maximalist tactic. But there arises the question: was not all the great within history, every developement within it, all the creativity within it -- maximalist? I think however, that history works religiously and not by the maximalist principle. Can one say, that the greatest religious genius -- the Apostle Paul -- was a maximalist from the point of view of Sventsitsky? Certainly not, and especially since there was in him no false maximalism, and he brought the religion of Christ into world history. With the Apostle Paul, as with every genius, as with every God-inspired man there was a sense of times and seasons, a religio-cosmic sense of history, of breadth and spaciousness of soul. In the situation of the Apostle Paul, a "maximalist" would ultimately have led the Christians out of history. Certainly, not everything connected with history is good. Constantine the Great was in the same measure an evil genius for Christianity, in which the Apostle Paul was its good genius. Paul was a new principle in the world, whereas Constantine -- was a compromise. Howsoever one regard the Reformation, it is impossible not to admit, that Luther and his work possesses not only a cultural-historical, but also religious significance. The Lutheran Reformation signified a turnabout in history. Was Luther a maximalist? everyone knows, that Luther was no maximalist, whereas various revolutionary sects from the era of the Reformation were maximalist. This extreme revolutionary movement of the Reformation had little significance: the religious maximalists exultantly awaited the onset of the thousand-year kingdom, they established a city of God, in which was created devilishness, but they nonetheless remained outside the realisation of the meaning of history. The "maximalism" of this sort of movement made them anti-historical and anti-cultural, almost darkly-demonic. Not without foundation did [Ferdinand] Lassal regard as reactionary the peasant revolutionary-religious movement of the Reformation. The non-maximalist, the "moderate" Luther was many a time more progressive both from a religious and from a culturo-historical point of view. And all the social figures of genius, as Cromwell, Mirabeau, Bismarck, were not maximalists, the maximalists were rather moreso limited people. The pity is in this, that in religion "maximalism" leads to sectarianism, to a false exultancy, almost pathological, and often ends with a fanatical frenzy. The universality of spirit is always contrary to sectarian maximalism. In politics maximalism is either anti-religious or conversely religious, since it deifies social objects, external things, this or some other societal order, it desires paradise on earth against or alongside the heavenly paradise and it always ends up idolatrous. Social maximalism wants to attain its own paradise, its own maximum, independently of changing the essence of things, innate to human nature, indeed not only without a victory over sin, but even without a consciousness of sin. In the elements of revolutionary maximalism there is always begotten a *reverse apocalypsis*, an anti-Christian apocalypsis: a thirst for the Kingdom of god upon earth, but without God, a kingdom inwardly unmerited, and a foretaste of the coming earthly power.

It is needful religiously to become free of this maximalism, to be rendered more modest and humble, with all one's essence to sense the human frailty and the inevitability of giving oneself over to an higher will. It is necessary to be aware, that salvation is a matter of a world-historical task and that the path of this task is complex and manifold, that the growth in life is organic and slow. And first of all and most of all it is necessary to realise, that a religious turnabout in the world occurs from within, and not from outside, from an inner turnabout in the hearts of men, from an inward conversion to Christ, and all else, everything external, is an addendum. Social maximalism and pseudo-religious maximalism sows hatred and malice in place of love, it curses all and everything, it separates and sunders apart, it is contrary to the spirit of Christ, to the spirit of love and meekness. The maximalistic character of our revolution, seeking to extort from God that which we have not merited inwardly, has filled Russia with malice. The defense of the maximalism of Brand at present is a surrender to malice and discord. To the question of Sventsitsky, -- whether it is necessary to be a maximalist and whether it be possible anywhere not to be such, -- I answer: it is necessary nowhere to be a maximalist, if the very principle of maximalism, if its fundamental mindset be false; but always and in all to be radical, to look to the root of a thing, to think about everything and sense it in essence, to change that which is primary and not merely derivative and secondary, to know the outward value, the outward successes in life, to sense the illusoriness of the constituent assembly, of the democratic republics, the nationalisation and socialisation, taken abstractly, to understand the demonic danger of every false exultancy, of every enthusiasm, of every arrogance and presumption.

MEREZHKOVSKY CONCERNING THE REVOLUTION [1]

The new book by D. S. Merezhkovsky, "Not Peace, but the Sword" [cf. Mt. X, 34], as regards its style it is brilliant, like almost everything written by this writer. As regards the content of this book it is interesting, it posits themes both great and vital, but it suffers a lack of clarity of thought, with a philosophic muddledness and an atrophied sense of actuality. In the fundamentals of his book Merezhkovsky lays down an explicit religious schema, but the revealing of this schema in its application to life is not always clear. The skillful repetition of a single idea often substitutes for the developement of the ideas, the revealing of their content. This most recent book of Merezhkovsky discloses great changes in him: the book is devoted to an investigation of the revolution from a religious point of view, and concerning the revolution the author earlier either thought little, or thought otherwise. Here in the attitude of Merezhkovsky towards the revolution is also a great lack of clarity, there is the sense of a great lack of experience. Concerning the revolution, Merezhkovsky speaks too often from the sidelines, he did live in it, and theoretically and practically he looks upon it from afar, as one might at a certain gorgeous lady. It seems to me, that for Merezhkovsky generally there has not taken hold the realistic acceptance of actuality, there is for him no direct feeling of what is happening at present in Russia. This deficiency of realism in the acceptance of actuality for Merezhkovsky is connected with his romantic-artistic temperament, with his literary aspect. Merezhkovsky is a realist as regards his religious ideas, but his literary romanticism always is expressed in an insuppressible inclination towards the extreme, towards the grandiose, the

[1] Published in "Moskovskii Ezhenedel'nik", 25 June 1908.

catastrophic, towards the tragic, towards the limit. He sees only the extremities, only the polarities, evil itself is assumed by him as something grandiose, he does not at all want to take note of the middle, the dullness of life, the triteness and nothingness of evil. In his brilliance of style Merezhkovsky has a tendency towards dramatic effect. Merezhkovsky tends to think with great antitheses, he aesthetically accepts only the limit points, whereas actuality however in its concreteness and individuality, all the jumbled middle of life, is neither accepted nor reproduced by him. In this what seems the power of his religious insights is also the weakness of his evaluation of reality, his sense of living people. He is religiously caught up with an interest in revolution, but that prosaic aspect of life, which feeds and sustains people, does not interest him, for him it does not exist. Societal evolution, social reforms -- all this is aesthetically unacceptable to Merezhkovsky, for him are necessary geological upheavals, cosmic catastrophes, and he impatiently thirsts to see them in something historically that already was or is being incarnated. several years back Merezhkovsky sought to see in the Russian autocracy a religious core, as the potential for a religious sociability, by which he justified the autocracy religiously. He is quick to become enchanted. Now Merezhkovsky attempts to see in revolution a religious core, as the potential all of that selfsame religious sociability, by which he justifies the revolution religiously. Autocracy and revolution -- are extreme limits and opposite poles, which Merezhkovsky accepts not so much really, as rather aesthetically. He did not sense the actuality of the autocracy and he does not sense the actuality of the revolution, in politics he remains abstractly literary. The mystical idea of autocracy had too little in common with the factual reality of the autocracy, and likewise remote is the mystical idea of revolution from the factual reality of revolution. Merezhkovsky as it were catches sight of the mystical fundamentals of the historical empirical, but the historical empirical itself he does not see. The empirical actuality remains in his consciousness as it were sundered off from its mysterious primal-origins. The religious justification of the empirical autocracy and the religious justification of the empirical revolution -- are two very simultaneous temptations, two temptations from the prince of this world. But this temptation is very understandable, since it is burdensome to sense one's alienation from historical flesh. There is a deep need to connect one's faith with the empirical. As a romantic and an aesthetic, Merezhkovsky can choose only the extremities, only the limit points, but within the empirical limits of the revolution he is as little able to find sacred flesh, as he was in the empirical limits of autocracy.

Merezhkovsky not so long ago, together with [Zinaida Nikolaevna] Gippius and [Dmitry Vladimirovich] Philosophov, brought out a book in the French language, "Le Tsar et la Revolution", in which he defended his attitude towards the Russian revolution and expressed his search for sacred flesh within the revolution. In the Russian anthology there came out by way of a preface to the French book also an article entitled, "Revolution and Religion". Merezhkovsky makes a tremendous effort to defend religion from being suspect of reactionism, he asserts, that religion and revolution -- are one and the same thing. But the very setting of the question concerning this, whether the religion of Christ be reactionary or revolutionary, seems to me a misunderstanding. To believe in Christ -- means to acknowledge, that He -- is the supreme criterion of life. The religion of Christ and every religion is a supreme measure of progressivity, of true value, and cannot be judged merely from the perspective of revolution or reaction. All ought to be subordinated to religion, and to nothing can religion be subordinated. For Merezhkovsky, certainly, religion stands higher than revolution, but after him might come people, for whom revolution stands higher than religion, and religion be rendered merely a means of struggle against the absolute, one of the methods in the attainment of purely social aims. Merezhkovsky in his attempt to unite religion and revolution can give rise to misunderstandings: the very desire that religion should prove revolutionary is as tempting, as the desire to prove it reactionary. Revolution will only then become religious, when it consciously renounces the revolutionary criterion as being supreme, i.e. when it ceases to see in the revolution itself a religion and senses the need to revalue the revolutionary values, subordinating them to the religious criterion. It is impossible to imagine for oneself anything more dangerous and contrary, than the transforming of religion into an utilitarian tool of politics. And amidst the current anarchy of spirit it would be very easy to render religion into a new tactical tool. Our intelligentsia always valued religion from the point of view of progressiveness and revolutionariness and therefore they bypassed the religious searchings of the greatest of Russian people.

The first article of the new anthology of Merezhkovsky is very fine. "The Sword" -- is one of the best articles of Merezhkovsky, and this is a very much needed article, very helpful for surviving the crisis. "Every life suffers defeat by death. In order to give life meaning, we ought in love to affirm the eternal existence of the person; but death, in annihilating the person, annihilates also love, the sole possible meaning of life for man. In order to comprehend the irresistible force of this antinomy, it is necessary to experience love and death. For every man it was or will be so. Every man at a certain moment of his conscious life is led by two of the greatest realities of existence -- love and death -- led to the need for religion". But how to conquer death by love? The solution can only be religious, and all the other solutions illusory. Merezhkovsky rightly rejects a whole series of false escapes by modern man from the tragedy of life and death. Suchlike pseudo-religious escapes as: art as religion, science as religion, the family, the race as religion, the social aspect as religion. The real victory of love over death is given only in the resurrection of Christ. "If Christ was not resurrected, then our faith is in vain. And not only faith, but also hope and love. If Christ was not resurrected, then He was worthily crucified, since then He would have deceived mankind with the greatest of all deceits, asserting, that God is the Heavenly Father: a God, in permitting the annihilation and death of such as is the person, which the whole world would not tolerate -- would not be Father, but rather executioner, not God, but rather the devil, and the whole world, -- a joke of this devil upon man, and the whole of nature -- madness, a curse and chaos". The real resurrection of Christ[2] is not only the essence of Christianity, its central point, but it is also the principle of a new religious process within the world, awaited by all those, who have strong expectations for the realisation of the Christian prophecies concerning the Kingdom of Christ upon earth and concerning the general resurrection. With Merezhkovsky these expectations are very strong, and he preaches a religion of the Holy Spirit, which is called to realise the prophecies of Christianity, similar to how the New Testament realised the prophecies of the Old Testament. In the old Church life has halted, wherein the Church bestows blessing upon reaction and sanctions against the movement towards freedom. But in the world itself there has begun a new religious life, in it there is the potential for sanctity. "The Spirit breathes, whence it will" [Jn. III, 8]. And Merezhkovsky has caught sight of the breathing of the Spirit in the world liberation movement. In socialism and anarchism are given conflicting nuances of truth, which can be realised and united as one only on the religious plane.[3] "The Sword" article approaches the question concerning the relationship of religion and revolution. But generally also, the negative setting of the question by Merezhkovsky is stronger, than in any concrete application to historical actuality.

With Merezhkovsky there is a romantic thirst for the grandiose, the unprecedented, exceeding all bounds, a thirst for the materialisation of the mystical. And here the Russian revolution, which he has observed at great distance, is perceived by him as suchlike a trans-historical manifestation. In the opinion of Merezhkovsky, revolution "will remove for Russia all its historical shore-lines". within it as it were will begin a trans-historical,

---

[2] Merezhkovsky employs the philosophically imprecise term "physical" resurrection. He is not at all a philosopher, and he weakens his religious teaching in that he combines it with a falsely conceived philosophic criticism, whist ignoring the higher forms of philosophy.

[3] This thought I developed in my book, "The New Religious Consciousness and the Societal Aspect" [1907].

apocalyptic process. The Russian revolution will prove "the final act in the tragedy of world liberation". In the struggle of the Russian revolution with the Russian autocracy, Merezhkovsky ascribes an apocalyptic character. For him the autocracy -- is the manifestation of a mystical order, connected with Orthodoxy. Merezhkovsky asserted this then already, when he hoped to catch sight within autocracy of a core of holy societal flesh. Back then in the autocracy he saw Christ, now -- the Anti-Christ, now he sees Christ in the revolution. But the struggle of Merezhkovsky with autocracy is, chiefly, his own mental struggle with himself, with his past, his own particular temptation, and this form of struggle involves no one, who never ascribed to autocracy a religious significance. The theoretical position of Merezhkovsky is an inverted inside-out revolutionary Slavophilism, which at present sees in the Russian revolution those same lofty traits of the Russian spirit, which the old Russian Slavophilism had seen in the Russian autocracy. This revolutionary neo-Slavophilism has found itself brilliant expression in the preface to the French book. This preface ends with the words: "Such singular, precocious anarchists, as Bakunin, Tolstoy, [Max] Stirner, Nietzsche[4], -- were at the mountainous summits, shining the first rays of day; and below, where it was still dark night, -- our innumerable unknowable brethren, the working people of the world, this great army of the coming world revolution. We believe, that sooner or later there will arrive also for them the thundering voice of the Russian revolution, in which will resound over the old European graveyard this trumpet of the archangel, announcing the dread last judgement and the resurrection of the dead". These words resonate unpleasantly, they grate upon the ears. There is too little in the Russian revolution of resurrection, too much of death, and in the revolution there is not this resounding trumpet of the archangel, announcing the end of history. I stand with Merezhkovsky, it would seem, on the grounds of some of the same beliefs, I esteem him highly, but to me particularly onerous

---

[4] Merezhkovsky makes a great mistake, including Nietzsche amongst the anarchists.

are his mistakes, his inaccurate sense of reality, his terrible exaggerations. Combining the Russian autocracy and the Russian revolution with the apocalyptic I regard as a dangerous mistake. With the apocalyptic is connected the whole of world history, and the Russian revolution has also a connection with it, but least of all does our pitiful revolution announce the end and resurrection. The struggle with autocracy for us is very long overdue, and our political turnabout is of a very elemental sort. Russia now ought to bring to completion the work of Peter the Great, it ought ultimately to be part of world culture, and cease to be an Asiatic land. This, it would seem, modest deed, possesses a religious meaning, but a world-wide religious turnabout from it will never happen. The Russian revolution is not religious, and that anarchistic savagery, which transpired at the end of the revolution, is very akin to that anarchistic savagery, upon which was long ago built our old statecraft.

Russia is filled with great possibilities, and Merezhkovsky is right in his characterisation of Russia as the antipode of Europe. But it is full all the same with savagery and lack of culture. In it there is not the elementary developement of human self-initiative, there is not the elementary sense of personal responsibility for one's own fate and the fate of one's native land. Within the revolution was reflected the higher sides of our spirit, but so also our savagery, the incapacity for creativity and an inner slavery. Merezhkovsky by his nature is a cultured Westerniser, preserving under this guise the missionary expectations of our national spirit. Why then does he not see, that this cultural Western flesh is needful for all the Russian people, that without a minimum of Western culture Russia will perish? This is explicable in that Merezhkovsky has a weak sense of the people as a whole, he senses only the select, only from the circles, and almost has no sense of Russia as a single organism, and the responsibility for it does not torment him. and about the revolution Merezhkovsky judges as regards individual persons, and not as regards the masses.

Merezhkovsky is tempted by the scheme, regarding which a new religious epoch, an epoch of the Holy Spirit will begin in the world, in world revolution, in the religion of mankind, which also would be a subconscious religion of the Spirit. In humanism there is a subconscious religious truth, bound up with the religion of Christ; this is indisputable, and I least of all would want to deny it. But, when humanism during the XIX Century passed over into a religion of mankind, it clearly went astray upon a path not only anti-Christian, but also godless. In the "Declaration of the Rights of Man and Citizen" can be sensed a breathing of the Spirit, and indeed the historical origin of this Declaration of Rights -- was religious.[5] The rights of man not only are not a religion of mankind, but even are opposed to this pseudo-religion. The rights of man possess a source supra-human, divine, and therefore in them obtains a God-manly truth; revolution however, based upon a religion of mankind, rejects everything supra-human; only then will there be the breath of the Spirit in it, when it repudiates making a god of the human and insofar as it repudiates it. In a certain sense fire-worship is religiously higher than the worshipping of man. Merezhkovsky seeks a sacred flesh of the world, which would appear in the coming Church, in which there would be elements of the new Revelation. His search itself is just and holy, but he goes off upon a mistaken and illusory path. The problem is in this, that at the basis of revolutionary maximalism lies a world-negation, and not world-affirmation, that within social revolutionism we meet not with sacred flesh, but with an ascetic denying of flesh. In the Russian revolution this asceticism, this turned inside-out sort of Orthodox Christian world-denial was expressed with particular force. Expressed rather vividly, and taken to its logical end, the type of the Russian revolutionary is a type of ascetic. The revolutionary psychology is a break with historical flesh. Upon the life of some of the revolutionaries lies a glint of Christian holiness, but the Christian saints themself were incomparably loftier and more profound. The

---

[5] Vide the fine book of [Hermann] Weingarten, "The People's Reformation in XVII Century England" [German Title: "Zeittafeln Und Uberblicke Zur Kirchengeschichte"]. In this book Merezhkovsky could quote many an idea of his, about the Third Testament, about the religion of the Holy Spirit, about the Communion of Saints, about a mystical revolution upon the soil of chiliasm.

revolutionary ascetics deny this world, but another world they do not admit. And this new asceticism at times produces an impression of non-being. The strangest thing of all in the ascetic revolutionary psychology -- is the preaching of the poverty of life and a poverty in the name of an unknown what. The Christian ascetic denied one world, he renounced the false blessings of the world, but in him there already lived another world, a world endlessly rich. In the new asceticism there are not the riches of other worlds. In the average fellow off the street, loving his native land, attached to it by historical flesh and blood, taken up with interests towards the concrete aspects of life, there is moreso flesh, moreso the world, than in the revolutionary maximalist. The flesh of the world was strong in Goethe, this antipode to the hero of revolutionary maximalism. The flesh is in the creativity of culture, which revolutionary maximalism subjects to doubt and limits in its rights. Our revolutionaries, the old populists, the People's Will movement, and indeed the modern revolutionaries regard as the riches in life, the assertion of flesh in history and in the person, -- of sin afront the people, of sin afront a future mankind. The sacrifice of the whole of modern life in the name of the future is elevated into a principle. Where indeed is this flesh, which Merezhkovsky seeks? He has hit upon a new form of asceticism, but bereft of religious realities, severed off from any faith in another world.

Once upon a time, upon the standards of the Roman legions was set the sign of the Cross, and this was a fateful fact in Christian history. A Christian flesh from this was not formed. The new religious consciousness faces the danger of setting its own sign of the cross upon the legions of revolutionary socialism. All the same blunder is repeated. The flesh of revolution, just like the flesh of autocracy, is not sacred Christian flesh. The sacred flesh, which Merezhkovsky awaits, only then will be formed within history, when the new religious movement creates its own legions, and not set its sign of the cross upon foreign legions. In the world are sown everywhere the seeds of a new religious life, they need to sprout and grow. Within history is being formed flesh, which has not yet been sanctified by the visible Church and it demands its own consecration, -- this flesh is in all the creative values of culture, in philosophy, in science, in art, it is in love both humanistic and erotic, it is in the Declaration of the Rights of Man and Citizen and in the creativity of social justice. But revolutionary maximalism, just like reactionary maximalism, is per se instead fleshless and in it is not born the new flesh of history. The religious movement ought to be combined with the elemental truth of life, which mustneeds be sought not there, where the official marker of revolutionism has been raised, but in the organic, the often still secret sproutings of life, in the experiences of the soul of the people. Both in the Russian and in the world liberation movements there is a genuine breath of the Spirit, there is the truth of God, but it is impossible to consider it identical with maximalistic revolutionism or with a given revolution, as Merezhkovsky tends to do. Superficial maximalism sooner enslaves, than liberates; all the jacobinism and demagoguery are directly opposite to what is sacred in the Declaration of Rights, in jacobinism and demagoguery there is instead the spirit of a reactionary coerciveness. Merezhkovsky simplifies too much the question and insufficiently considers both history in its concreteness and reality in its living complexity. The breath of the Holy Spirit is within everything, that liberates man, but it mustneeds be known not in mere words, not in formulas and shoutings, but in the deed, in the depth of one's being, if indeed it is human freedom which is desired by all these maximalists, jacobins, etc. I tend to think, that some of the revolutionary maximalists desire enslavement, and not liberation, and they act in a spirit of enslavement, whereas some of the moderates and minimalists do sincerely desire liberation. The breath of the Spirit is in each one, who sincerely and with all his being thirsts for freedom, the victory over slavery, the uplifting of man to an higher degree of being, howsoever he understand the path towards liberation, whatever the tactics he engages. Revolutionary maximalism however is usually defined not by its goals, but by its means. It often even becomes difficult to say, to what sort of maximum the revolutionaries strive, but it is possible always to say, that they practise on the outside extreme means of struggle and that this practise of extreme means also renders them maximalists.

Merezhkovsky is insufficiently familiar with the psychology of the revolutionaries, he has insufficiently examined their practise and therefore does not distinguish the nuances, he does not see the inner emptiness of the revolutionary maximalism, the inconsistency of the maximalist ideal. He will not find herein the sacred flesh of the world and history, he will find only tragedy, from which he ought to help people emerge from. Many a revolutionary maximalist, with a broken heart, with shattered hope, might seek an egress from the terror of life in the new religious consciousness. But the new religious consciousness cannot be subordinated to the revolutionary maximalism, because it is something even more maximal. At present there is occurring a profound crisis of spirit in the revolution itself, within the soul of the revolutionary intelligentsia: there has been lost the faith that revolutionary socialism can serve as a religion. Many seek for faith. To assist in the emergence from this crisis is a deed for Merezhkovsky and all the people of the new consciousness. But for this it is necessary to deal otherwise with this crisis, not to become subordinated to the revolution, but rather to subordinate it to oneself. Merezhkovsky however would rather doctor his own wounds with a touch to the truth of revolution and therein he weakens his religious activity. Another weakness of Merezhkovsky, which is rooted in his past, in his temperament, in his individuality and specialty, -- is in the total ignoring of the realistic side of social life, the total contempt for social science, which is called to guide the technical aspects of social life. The agrarian question is impossible to be decided mystically, it is impossible mystically to improve the lot of the workers, just as it is impossible mystically to decide questions of physics and chemistry. The believing Christian nonetheless can and ought to resort to the assists of medicine. The new religious consciousness posits the religious question concerning the sacredness of work, concerning the holy matter of life. But the creation within concrete history of this holy societal corporeality possesses its own socio-technical side, which ought to be subject to the dictates of social science and which cannot be annulled mystically. Herein Merezhkovsky is too much the artist, and in this is his weakness, since artistic criteria in politics do not suffice. A political mysticism in general seems to me dangerous from both a religious and a societal point of view. A political mysticism would weaken the genuine mysticism, -- the contact of other worlds, -- the sense of eternity, and together with this it would weaken the societal-political creativity, the necessary sustainance of people and ordering of their lives, since it would await a societal miracle. real politics, social building on the plane of the empirical ought not to be arranged as a great tragedy of human life, it cannot decide the question about the meaning of life and cannot conquer death, but it supports life, culture and history, without which there cannot be realised the religious meaning of the world. It is needful, that there not be starving people and slaves, that the demands and rights of man have an elemental affirmation, but not in the name of the ideal of gluttony and an ultimate earthly ordering, but rather in the name of the transcendent emergence from the tragedy of life. A minimum of satiated fullness and order only but sharpen the search for the religious meaning of life. Man senses the inescapable emptiness of all the earthly ideals, whilst severed from heaven. But the minimum of free life-affirmation and life-ordering ought to be realised for all people, so that each man can assume all his growth and can choose his ultimate path. Mysticism in politics, which not only in Merezhkovsky, but also in all the maximalists, though in primitive form, kills the sense of responsibility for the fate of people and of peoples, for their hunger and suffering; it preaches increase of suffering and torments, and without which they should but attain dullness and non-being.

Just like the revolutionaries and reactionaries, Merezhkovsky maintains the connection of Orthodoxy with autocracy. For him, the Orthodox metaphysics is conjoined with a reactionary statecraft, and within the bounds of the Orthodox Church it is impossible to surmount the absolutism, to escape the vicious circle of reactionism. I tend to think, that this is one of the engrained mistakes of Merezhkovsky, which he committed then already, when he mystically justified the autocracy, and from which he is unable to free himself even at the present time. With far greater religious and historical basis it is possible to defend this thought, that Russian absolutism, just like every state, -- is of pagan derivation, whereas Orthodoxy, just like the whole of historical Christianity, though still not societally, has not fully disclosed its ideal of society and in its essence it is external to the state. To assign an apocalyptic aspect to the struggle with autocracy, to the old forms of a pagan state, to see the Anti-Christ behind and connected with the remnants of primordial evil, seems to me an enormous religious and historical mistake. The apocalyptic struggle of the Church of Christ against the church of the Anti-Christ cannot have any direct connection with the autocracy and with stage of mankind, in which courses the Russian revolution. The Universal Church will contend against the church of the Anti-Christ, but the church of the Anti-Christ lies forward and not behind, and its historical embodiment might the rather be connected with the ultimate triumph of socialism, in which intersect all the Christian and anti-Christian forces of history. It is with socialism, and not with autocracy, that there is bound up the resolution of the fate of mankind, in socialism there is great truth, and in it also is the possibility of great falsehood. Socialism heightens the eschatological problem, in it there is a chiliastic expectation, with it can be connected both the Christian apocalyptic and also the opposite apocalyptic; in autocracy there is no such eschatology, this -- is a remnant of the past, and the evil of the autocracy -- is a legacy of savagery. Merezhkovsky evidently thinks, that autocracy can be defeated only on the apocalyptic plane, that the victory over the beast of absolutism will already be a beginning of the end of history. But the apocalyptic victory over the beast will only then have begun, when mankind has become free and cultured, when it will have passed through all the tests and all the human constructs of the societal aspect. The boundary limits of the socialistic and even the anarchistic paths have to be lived out first of all, whereof mankind will enter upon a path trans-historical. Otherwise it is impossible to explain the apocalyptic prophecies. An intensified sense of the end of history is very dangerous, since none of us knows the day nor hour. The concrete nearness of this hour in the imagination can readily lead to a denial for the developing of labour, to an ignoring of the duty for historical work. In accord with the Christian prophecies, the Universal Church, the Bride of Christ, will appear in the flesh and unite with its Bridegroom Christ at the end of history. Within it will be the fullness of being, the fullness of everything, that within history has been won and created. But while the Universal Church materially still is insufficiently visible and its voice not heard, it is indeed impossible to deny politics, philosophy, science, art, love, all the life and creativity of mankind, which would seem yet external to churchliness. Such a denial would lead to fanaticism and darkness. There is still many a deed also yet to be within the sphere of secular politics, philosophy, art etc, although I believe, that everything "secular" ultimately will be rendered churchly, will enter into the Universal Church. Merezhkovsky in his striving to render churchly all the flesh of the world along the way negates all this flesh, in intellect certainly, but not in life. He falls into the new asceticism of the religious narrow-circle.

Merezhkovsky reckons too little with individuality, he does not want to recognise, that each man has his own path and that it is impossible to impose upon all the one and same path. The old Church did not demand from all people, that they should all go off into the wilderness and thus become saints, it understood, that suchlike sanctity is the lot of but few. Merezhkovsky demands a new sanctity from all people, although he himself does not know, how to realise this sanctity. But with each man there is his own vocation, his own destiny, his own relationship to God and his own path to Him. The Universal Church admits this, since it does not kill life, it does not annihilate that which is most dear in life. It is impossible to take upon oneself a burden beyond one's strength, which should overstrain and destroy one. It is necessary to show a bit of humility, to be aware of one's weakness and limitation. When we take on too heavy a load, we want to jump higher ahead, and sometimes it seems, that in this there is something demonic. To me it seems a terrible mistake -- these expectations of a religious maximalism, of an heightened religious activity based upon an intensification of the outward sense of tragedy in life, of outward terrors, of hunger, oppression and blood. In a bloody delirium and chaos there cannot be born new religious activity. And I do not believe in that religious maximalism, which appears as a result of terror and delirium. With the growth of culture the tragedy of life is conveyed from outside inwards for man. The bloody terrors might yet not be, but life might become yet still more intolerable, and anguish take hold in the affairs of people, and a sense of emptiness engulf their souls. Then will begin a final religious process.

No sort of social order can be an end, it is always only a *means* for higher ends, above and external to the social ends. Strictly speaking, there cannot even be talk about a societal ideal as a limited aim, every outward community is but a means. Social maximalism is based upon a jumbling together of means and ends, upon a substitution, upon a transforming of societal means into ideals. Towards sociality, towards community there cannot be a maximalistic, i.e. a religious relationship, since all sociality, all community relates wholly to the category of means, and not the ends of life. There can be a religious relationship only towards the ends of life, but nowise to its subservient means. I cannot have a religious attitude towards the fork, with which I eat, but outward community, social matter is also like the fork. The idea of religious community, of the Kingdom of God upon earth, in a strict sense is not a social ideal, with it we do not connect anything concretely of the social, this is an ideal of a religious communion of people, and not of any sort of a social organisation. The religious maximum is already a finish of this world. But the revolutionary maximalism, in which Merezhkovsky seeks for sacred flesh, is always connected either with certain means of struggle (terror, insurrection etc) or with certain social objects (socialisation of the means of production, etc). Social maximalism -- is either subconsciously religious, based on an error of consciousness, which ought to be set right, or it is anti-religious or religious in reverse, i.e. it confesses a religion, contrary to

Merezhkovsky's. Upon this basis and within the bosom of the revolution there is occurring a crisis, which inwardly ought to be resolved. Inwardly there ought to be surmounted the sins of the revolution. Social-revolutionary maximalism therefore is not uniteable with religious maximalism, since they compete, and since social-revolutionary maximalism seeks to substitute for religion. Maximalism outside the religious and outside the churchly is something unworthy and inadmissible, outside of religious perspectives there is possible only evolution and reforms. Religious revolution is not at all that, which usually is called "revolution", it approaches it neither in its ends, nor in its means. Merezhkovsky in his striving for sacred flesh is too much tempted by the externals, the outer appearances. For him the flesh is as it were identical with the empirical, whilst its religious meaning is altogether otherwise. Merezhkovsky mistakenly identifies the spiritualistic and the spiritual with the heavenly realm, the other side, but the material and the fleshly -- with this world, with the earth. But the world also is spiritualistic, in it also there is much of spiritual richness, which nowise comes under any schema of ascetic world-denial. At the basis of the schema of Merezhkovsky concerning spirit and flesh lies a profound and true religious perplexity and expectation, but it is bound up with a false philosophic theory (the anti-spiritualistic), or more accurately, with an extreme lack of clarity of philosophic awareness. I attempted several years back to sort out the metaphysical tangle, connected with "flesh" and "spirit" in the consciousness of Merezhkovsky.[6] A muddled and mistaken metaphysics, the confusion of flesh in a religious sense jumbling it up with the empirical world and the matter of this world leads Merezhkovsky both to an exaggerated denial of Christian asceticism, and to an exaggerated expansion of the ascetic principle itself, after which almost all the creative values of spirit fall into the category of asceticism and world-denial. In this schema of flesh and spirit there is not met with

---

[6] Vide my book, "Sub specie aeternitatis".

that spiritualism, which occupies a visible place within history and which cannot be delegated to an ascetic metaphysics.[7]

The article, "The Last Saint", -- is interesting, and in it there is much that is true. But this article clearly shows, how risky it is to write literary works about the Christian saints. The ideas of Merezhkovsky are true, with questioning and perplexity, focused by him towards historical Christianity, deep and penetrating, but in the tone of his article there is that which is unacceptable, there is a lack of appreciation for Christian sanctity. With Isaac the Syrian it is impossible to polemicise, and Merezhkovsky not only polemicises, but even in a very harsh and unjust form. He makes suchlike a selection of citations from Isaac the Syrian, as to depict the great Christian saint as some sort of fanatic. But indeed many another place from that selfsame Isaac the Syrian might be quoted, and then would be evident the positive meaning of his ascetic exploit, his thirst to fling off from himself the old man. It is unclear, in what for Merezhkovsky Christian sanctity consists: an evil, a misunderstanding or truth, but already outmoded? The reading of his "Last Saint" might also indicate, that Christian sanctity is hateful for Merezhkovsky, that in it he sees evil. The image of St. Seraphim of Sarov for him comes out almost demonic, he even failed aesthetically to sense the beauty of St. Seraphim, he did not comprehend, how much in him there was of the new, the white light. I concur with the questionings of Merezhkovsky relative to the Church, I concur with his positing of certain themes, and concur that the old type of Christian sanctity has grown stale and that there mustneeds be sought the new. But his attitude towards the Christian saints evokes protest within me. It is incomprehensible, how Merezhkovsky for himself can make the connection between the religious past and the religious future, how he can carry over the sanctity of the past into the future. Does Merezhkovsky sense himself dwelling in the Church of the

[7] The history of world culture is filled with spiritualness, with creative spirituality, and the greatest philosophies, in affirming rather than denying life, were spiritualistic.

saints? The sanctity of Isaac the Syrian and of Seraphim ought to be somehow united with the sanctities of world history and culture -- here is the theme of a new religious consciousness. Merezhkovsky has done quite much for a new setting of religious themes, but he provides no clear solutions and he often goes astray upon false a path. Concerning the positive merits of Merezhkovsky I have already much spoken, but in this article I have chiefly set myself the purpose to point out his mistakes. Merezhkovsky has received wide reknown and popularity in the capacity of novelist-artist and literary critic, but his religious ideas are insufficiently familiar and little understood. Merezhkovsky merits quite more serious attention.

The religious ideas, which not long ago seemed the individually-derived experiences of artistic and romantic natures, have become vital matters, connected with the crisis, transpiring within the bosom of life itself. The book of Merezhkovsky can much help the seeking, but it can also mislead. And from this misleading I should want to safeguard to the extent of my abilities. Merezhkovsky wants to subsume the revolution to his own religious consciousness, but he himself imperceptibly is subsumed to the revolution as a fact, since with too great an haste he seeks uniting with the prevailing worldly power (earlier -- with the idea of autocracy). It is necessary to be more astute, more patient and humble, to await the coming, holding to one's own to the end. The "revolution" readily might prove but lentil soup. I am not at all wont to deny, that in the revolution there is a great truth and that in many of the revolutionaries there is a subconscious religiosity. But in the revolution and in the revolutionaries there is also a reverse principle, and it is not so easy to distinguish from the positive truth. The revolutionary consciousness does not sense and does not conceive of sin as the source of evil in the world, the source of evil for it -- is in the outward ruling powers, in the government, in this or that class of society. Therefore revolutionism in its extreme forms preaches hatred and extermination of societal enemies, as bearers of evil. This is incompatible with Christ. It seems to me, that Merezhkovsky is insufficiently aware, how impossible it is for religious people to tolerate the perspective of class struggle, the struggle of two seemingly different races. But revolutionary maximalism always is connected with this division of mankind into two parts as regards social standards. with hatred of one part towards the other. The struggle of societal groups possesses its own relative truth within existence. The defense of the interests of the oppressed classes, of the peasants and workers, is a matter of elementary justice and moreover a duty of love. But a mysticism of class, set at the basis of social maximalism, cannot be united with a Christian mysticism. And I am convinced, that amidst a close contact with actual life, that Merezhkovsky himself would sense the literary aspect of his "maximalism". I speak, certainly, not about a religious maximalism, since without the ideal of a religious maximum it would be impossible to live worthily and preserve in oneself the image and likeness of God. But it is time to free religion from literary schemae.

RUSSIA AND THE WEST [1]

Thoughts, Evoked by the Article of P. V. Struve, "Great Russia"

After the upheaval of our revolution, after all its lack of success, the Russian intelligentsia acutely faces many a new problem, there is now much that seriously needs to be thought about, and much now seems not so clear and simple, as formerly it seemed. The revolution has posited with an especial poignancy the problem of the state and the ruling powers. The inveterate hatred towards the historical authorities, towards a given form of governance and a given government has muddled a clear setting of the problem of the state and the ruling power within the consciousness of the intelligentsia. Struve makes an effort to get free from the traditional impediments in the resolution of this problem, but out of a spirit of opposition, out of a psychological reaction he bends the bow the other way and provides a completely abstract apology to the idea of the state as something self-sufficing, as a certain sort of absolute. The article of Struve is abstracted from every sort of historical flesh and blood. This -- is a publicist's approach via the method of "abstract principles", a sort of artificial experiment, by which is an attempt to demonstrate for us, what ought to be, if the absolute self-sufficiency of the state be acknowledged, -- what there ought to be with this that might apply for Russia. The suspicion, that Struve is meeting halfway the existing powers in Russia, that he is putting together some sort of opportunistic-diplomatic combinations, -- seems to me unjust and without foundation. Struve -- is one of the bravest, and as regards his character one of the least opportunistic writers in Russia. He might

---

[1] Published in "Slovo", 11 July 1908.

the sooner be accused of this, that he wants to heal the Russian intelligentsia of traditional sins with the help of office-cabinet experiments, by way of abstract thought, concerning an isolated part of the whole living organism. The article of Struve is little understood, since it is built upon foundations of a complex and intricate philosophic methodology. He declares very concrete things, he gives advice to the ministry of foreign affairs, and to naval and commerce and industry, but his article essentially is outside the historical. In it is expressed all the difficulty of adaption to life by a publicist from the methods of German philosophic criticism, dissecting everything alive. The Westerniser-rationalist Struve has insufficient a sense of the mysterious soul of Russia. And to him is foreign any mystical sense of history.

The method of Struve is critical-analytic, very modern, but his philosophic pathos at present is very close to that of Hegel, to the Hegelian apotheosis of the state as an adequate expression of the absolute spirit, the absolute idea. This spirit leads Strove to an apology for a modernised imperialism and it cannot tempt those, who morally and religiously have overcome the temptation towards every imperialism. To separate the problem of the majesty and might of the state apart from the moral and cultural problem is possible only within an intellectual abstraction, -- in life they are inseparable. Within the historical life of peoples the problem of the state and its grandeur is ultimately always posited and resolved religiously, within a synthetic wholeness of this or that other-world sense. The ancient, the pagan deification of the state, which in history led to the creation of the Roman Empire, -- to this limit of a greatest stately might, was a matter fully religious. I do not think, that Struve would be content with this pagan religiosity: too acute for him is the question concerning the person, the question of Christian culture. Russian absolutism likewise has affirmed itself religiously (or more accurately, pseudo-religiously). Russian religious statecraft is completely foreign to Struve. If his apology for the state be not only a methodological mode and pedagogic means of influence upon intelligentsia craniums, if we meet here with his faith, as he declared in his reply to D. S. Merezhkovsky, then it would be interesting and important to know: with what faith? Struve as regards his moral-philosophic and indeed religious convictions is an extreme individualist, and it is very unclear, how he combines his individualistic faith with the Hegelian apotheosis of the state. He once wrote an excellent article, "What is True Nationalism", which even now he has not disclaimed. What sort of connection is there of this article with "Great Russia"? Struve, evidently, by methodologically-conscious means has separated the question concerning the state from the question concerning the nation and has found himself face to face with a fictitious "collective person", which he has prepared for himself in the office laboratory. The nation -- is a collective person, the state however, -- is merely a subsumed function of this collective person. The nation -- is a living organism, an extant being; the state - is a function of the extant, its composite form, or idol, a false god. Struve has flooded off the great idea of nation into the state, he has subordinated his own nationalness to the state, and has rendered it a tool of Leviathan. And all this happened not from evil an intent, but from the tendency for a methodology of isolation, for "abstract principles".

The state cannot in any sense be asserted as an extant being: the people is an extant being, and the existence of this being is fully conceivable without the state, with the abolition of this function, which is wholly dependent upon historical times and seasons. The state is a sovereign subject only for juridical thinking, when intellectually taken as an abstract principle. In the actuality of life, not only empirical, but also mentally-posited, such a subject does not exist, and from a living, organic, religious perspective suchlike a subject possesses no sort of rights to existence. The people, the nation, some ernstwhile collective person, obtains for us not empirically, but mentally-posited, -- here is a subject, but likewise not sovereign, since everything alive in the world bears within itself one sole sovereign being -- God. The nation, and not the state, makes revolution, dethrones the government, and it likewise dethrones the revolutions, if they run contrary to the supreme law of its existence, if they impede its organic perfecting. The people it is which dethrones the historical forms of the state, when such are no longer in accord with its conscience and its reasoning, and it abolishes every state, when it matures for new life, for an higher and ultimate freedom. The state can be appreciated only historically as a subordinate and temporal function of the living organism of the nation, and it is impossible to appreciate it as an absolute. Absolutism was possible for as long as it served the nation, and defended it from disintegration. The state is a coercive form of rule, the obverse side of the evil will of the people and a form of defense an enemy of the people. The nation affirms itself like a person, it defends itself from death and from being swallowed up by others, this -- is a sacred self-affirmation, an instinct of life, given from above, and for this defense itself is the fact of its existence, as something unique in the world, necessitating the external power of the nation, as long as the various peoples have not attained to brotherhood in the world. The slogan of Great Russia, which Struve wants to promote, ought to be a slogan patriotic and national, and not simply for the state. A land has become great, when the state power -- is the humble servant of the nation; when however the national and patriotic feeling has become a servant of the state, then there erupt shameful military disasters as at Tsusima and Mukden in the Russo-Japanese war. We ought to be not statists, not imperialists, but rather patriots, we ought to discern the national feeling in the higher sense of this word.

The thesis of Struve concerning the prevailing of external politics over the inner includes within it an indisputable truth, although not quite successfully expressed. This thesis means, that Russia, as with every nation, ought first of all to exist, to affirm and protect itself as a collective person, as an individuality, having its own destiny in the world. Only in nationality does man realise himself and will mankind realise itself, outside of nationality there are no living organisms, --in cosmopolitanism all are rendered into dead abstractions. On the outside politics the nation appears as a single one, on the inside it is fragmented. The paradoxical and at first glance repulsive assertion of Struve I would tend to express in suchlike a concrete form: towards absolutism, towards the state despotism I react not only negatively, but also with aversion and disgust, I love freedom infinitely, but at that moment, when I shall have assuredly recognised, that only an absolute state can save Russia as a single nation, can safeguard it from being swallowed up and enslaved by other nations, only at such a moment I shall have become a passionate adherent of absolutism, even though I shall have comprehended its ultimate lie. This is first of all -- a spontaneous feeling, but this is also the awareness of the impossibility of an outwardly-national assertion of one's being. In the era of the Russo-Japanese war, in all regards meaningless, amoral and not of the people, I nonetheless fervently desired victory for the Russian forces, since I cannot sunder within consciousness the unity of my existence and the existence of the nation. The Russo-Japanese war best of all has demonstrated, that the old statecraft is unable to safeguard its native-land, it betrays the fatherland. Struve was right in his assertion, that the reactionaries and the revolutionaries are alike in their anti-patriotism. Merezhkovsky in his reply to Struve did not sense the religious importance of the defense of one's native-land, in him there has been lost as it were the national sense together with the sense of the state.

But in the name of what is it that Russia ought to affirm and safeguard itself as some sort of person? In the name of the might of the state, in the name of imperialistic politics, in the name of nationalistic self-conceit? Vl. Solov'ev provided a deep and original resolution for the national question, remote alike both from nationalism, and from cosmopolitanism, -- a resolution, transforming all that was said about the West. To this same religious resolution of the national question Dostoevsky strove and with a power of genius expressed his expectations. In the capacity of an extreme Westerniser, Struve goes alongside Dostoevsky and Solov'ev, and he is inclined towards a Westerniser nationalism. The English, the Germans, the French, all the cultured Europeans -- are nationalists, they all have no strong consciousness of their mission to mankind in general within world history, but rather a national self-conceit and national rapaciousness. Can it be desired, that this bourgeois nationalism should enter into the flesh and blood of the Russian people? The finest of Russian people have always dreamt, that Russia would never become a bourgeois land in the European manner, that within it is lodged the potential for an higher life, that it should never forsake its spirit. We call to mind, how Hertsen felt in Western Europe, and that he wrote his "From the Other Shore": the Westerniser Hertsen despised the Western philistinism and in the West he found his own Slavophil soul. Many Russian people have experienced this Slavic anguish in the West and variously have expressed it. The Slavophil bacillus lives within us and it cannot and ought not to be eradicated. There can and ought to be a freeing from the old sins of Slavophilism, but not from their faith in the great mission of Russia and in the uniqueness of its soul, antagonistic towards the Western bourgeois philistinism.

We all want to become Westernisers in one only sense: Russia ought to become adjoined to world civilisation, ought to get to an higher degree of world culture, and the human element within it ought to be freed from slavery and in the Western manner become self-activating. But we will never be fond of a bourgeois state, brazenly asserting itself, and we will not be transformed into bourgeois nationalists and chauvinists. Vl. Solov'ev well understood the truth of Westernism and with an extraordinary power he revolted against our Asiatic savagery, but he did not lose the mystical feeling for Russia, for Great Russia. We ought to be civilised and irreversibly conjoined to cultural mankind, we ought to conquer the Asiatic savagery and backwardness. The deed of Peter the Great is still not finished in Russia, and only by having become an European cultural land, will Russia be able to contend against the worldwide bourgeois philistinism. The Asiatic lack of culture and inward savagery are expressed both in the character of Russian rule, and in the character of the Russian intelligentsia, in both the black hundredists, and in the red hundredists. The Tatar still sits within us, and this Tatar ought to be expelled from Russia. But besides the Tatarism, the wildness and unculturedness in Russia, there is indeed also something else, and this other and higher is expressed in the finest Russian people, in those select ones of spirit in the Russian land. The Slavophils of the decade of the 40's were people of high culture, no less high than the Westernisers, and their feeling of Russian messianism was not an expression of backwardness. The Slavophils did defend the backward forms of the state, in this was their fatal mistake, but they however dreamt of freeing the people from the oppression of political philistinism. It was the same with Dostoevsky, with Vl. Solov'ev, with all the Russian seekers of the Kingdom of God. But it mustneeds not be forgotten, that the Pugachevism and hooliganism are no less dangerous for the great task of Russia, no less corrosive for the soul of the people, than the philistinism and aridity of positivism. With people like me, and perhaps with Struve, as with him and Merezhkovsky, it is a mere matter of plotting in defense of culture, and of the civilising of Russia, the common struggle against reaction and against its reverse reflection in revolution. But this is a temporary bloc. It remains unclear: what is the attitude of Struve towards the final goals, what is his faith, for him is it a bourgeois state on the basis of world culture and the Western assertion of person -- ultimately? We mustneeds forsake the idol-worship, but so as to be subject to God and not become drunken anew.

Russia stands at the centre of West and East, as though conjoining two worlds, two various orientations, two forms of religiosity. The West -- is humanised, anthropologic, in it the human element is set free and exalted, and the culture of man attains to an higher emphasis. The East -- is both super and sub humanised, in it is little of anthropology, in it the human element is dissolved away into the Divinity and into nature. The East has prostrated itself before the Divinity, whereas the West makes an intense effort to lift itself up to the Divinity. Within the bounds of Christianity this has expressed itself in the deep difference between Catholicism and Orthodoxy. Catholicism is anthropologic, in it there is much of the human, of the human effort to lift itself upwards, to stretch upwards. Orthodoxy, preserving the sacred, -- is godly, in it God has come down for mankind, but the human activity in it has always been insignificant.

This difference has likewise been expressed in the architectural style of temple for the Western Catholic and the Eastern Orthodox. The gothic is an aspiring upwards, of an upwards stretching, and in the gothic temple there is not the feeling of the descent of Christ, it is cold in it, but there is the human effort to lift oneself up from the earth to Him. In the Orthodox temple Christ is as it were having come down upon the earth, in it there is warmth, in it man stretches in prostration before God, but the human nature is constricted.

In the non-Christian East, in India and even further, human nature ultimately is constricted by divine forces, where almost nothing of the human remains, no world culture and no human stirrings upwards and forward, all instead goes into the depths, within. In the Christian East -- Christ is the subject, Christ is within: He -- is the foundation of life, and not the object of aspiration. In Eastern Christian mysticism human nature is deified by an inner acceptance of Christ. In the Christian West, Christ -- is an object, an object of imitation and love, and towards Him strives the human element, but it does not accept Him within itself. In Catholicism, Christ remains all the time outside of man, remains in the objective realm, and not the subjective. Here is a source of the religious difference of East and West and a religious cause for the high culture of the West and the lower culture of the East.

But the West at the heights of its culture approaches an awareness of the emptiness of the human, in its separation apart from God. The East approaches an awareness of the emptiness of God, as separate from the human. When the awareness becomes acute and this rift becomes intolerable, then there begins the religious striving of East towards West, and of the West -- towards the East, of the reuniting of the Divine and the human, of the mystical and the cultural. Vl. Solov'ev conceived of this movement for himself in terms of a re-uniting of the churches, the confluence of Orthodoxy and Catholicism into the Church Universal. Whether it is enough, it is still needful. We think, that this would be an emergence from historical Christianity into the supra-historical Church. But only Russia can be the connecting link between West and East, in it only can there begin the God-manly process. For the fulfilling of its mission Russia ought to become a land cultural and free, civilised like the West, wherein the human element in it should be set free and orient itself towards independent life. But also so as inwardly not to lose its uniqueness and not perish, Russia needs to preserve its Divine basis, given within Orthodoxy, with its visionary dream about the Kingdom of God upon earth in opposition to the idea of the human kingdom, the bourgeois state in the Western sense. Constitutionalism appears at present to be a civilising force, liberating from the Asiatic aspect and moreover asserting state power in forms, most corresponding to the given maturity of the Russian people. But we are hardly capable to be pervaded by the pathos of an abstract constitutionalism. The Russian state ought to become a tractable tool for higher ends. The old theocracy lies in ruins: only in being set free from false theocracies can there be cleared the grounds for theocratic truth. Within Russia beats the pulse of the religious life of the world, in it are being undone the old, the false connections of the Church with the state and new God-manly connections are being made.

When the Russian intelligentsia conquers within itself the elements of Eastern-Asiatic wildness, and also in its consciousness the superficial Westernism, then within it will be cut the pattern of a truly Russian and truly universal vocation. The fate of world history depends upon the conjoining of East and West, but for this conjoining East and West also is the need to renounce their limiting parochialism, they need to learn from each other, each of these parts of the world ought to realise its own calling within the whole. Then only will Russia be Great, when it fulfills its vocation as intermediary between East and West, an uniter of the cultures of God and of man. The acceptance of a nationalist-state ideology would render Russia a second-rate bourgeois land, and would disfigure and degrade its collective person.

Russia has repelled Tatarism and saved Europe and world culture, therein having been drenched in blood, and having sacrificed its own cultural developement. But now a new task faces us.

THE QUESTION CONCERNING THE INTELLIGENTSIA AND THE NATION [1]

I.

In the "Slovo" gazette was published an article by P. B. Struve, "The People's Economy and the Intelligentsia". In this article, Struve has managed to formulate a characteristic peculiar to the Russian intelligentsia -- the idea of personal irresponsibility, combined with the idea of equality. The thought in the article is closely bound up with the intellectual crisis, which Russia is experiencing. If there is a word which would express a modern moral turnabout, then this word -- is *responsibility*, the personal responsibility for one's own fate, and for the fate of the people and of society. History has accustomed us to irresponsibility. The Russian bureaucratic state has killed the feeling for personal responsibility, and the Russian radical intelligentsia has come to reflect traits in itself similar to the historical ruling authority, whereas the responsibility for the evil has tended to reside exclusively in this ruling authority. The moral irresponsibility, humiliating for the very idea of person, has triumphed along all lines, and it has found expression in the levity, with which are confessed and preached the most droll socialistic and anarchistic teachings. The sense of Russia as a whole, as a national organism has been lost, its splintering is considered a lofty trait, and not a misfortune. Responsibility for oneself and responsibility for one's native-land have one and the same moral grounding. P. B. Struve in his Marxist book, "Critical Notes" [1894], said the same thing that he says now, but the Russian Marxist-intelligentsia do not understand this and shout about Struve being a renegade, since he has not adopted Marxism exclusively in

---

[1] Published in "Slovo", 30 November 1908.

the sense of an "irresponsible equality". In the creative social process we have always had in view the impoverished, the down-trodden by fate, the spurned of the fatherland. But indeed beyond the ruling power itself, which rules in our fatherland, we ourself also are responsible, and in it are reflected our historical sins. To portray oneself as down-trodden by fate and to demand an "irresponsible equality" -- is a profound moral mistake. The qualities of person underlie the basis of society. And in order to prevail over reaction, it is needful to think about the sins of society.

At the core of Christianity is lodged a sense of personal and collective responsibility. responsibility is least of all a bourgeois and materialistic idea, this idea at root is religious. With materialism is connected the idea of "irresponsible equality", the salve's envy of person out of mediocrity and the victory of quantities over quality. They say: Struve wants to make Russia bourgeois, to inculcate the Russian intelligentsia with bourgeois virtues. And Russia mustneeds "be made bourgeois", if by this there be understood a call for social creativity, the passing over to higher forms of a people's economy and the negation of aspirations for mere equality, with its complete disregard for the degree of wealth of the nation. Capitalism itself per se is a category of production, and the economic necessity of a transition over to a capitalist economy does not mean the necessity of a bourgeois spirit and a bourgeois form of exploitation for our land. The bourgeois or non-bourgeois aspect of spirit cannot be seen to be dependent upon materialist principles and forms of economy. Moreso the contrary. The very problem of distribution is first of all a moral problem, and it should be decided upon the basis of an ethical, not materialistic, socialism. The very idea of personal responsibility is in spirit profoundly anti-bourgeois, with it is bound up the ideal dignity of man, the image of God in him. The idea of an irresponsible equality is a bourgeois idea in the spirit of the ant-hill, and of the realm of compulsory virtue. The Russian maximalists -- are fanatics for compulsory virtue, coerced equality, the collective oversight of everything qualitative. Upon this basis creativity is impossible, the building up of culture whether material or spiritual is impossible;

there is possible only the social and spiritual reaction, to which we have come nigh. This intelligentsia mindset denies the Christian ascetic effort, it confesses utilitarianism and hedonism, but it leads to a societal asceticism, as expressed in all the forms of populism. The intellectual crisis ought first of all to find expression in the surmounting of the *populist* frame of mind and in the formation of a consciousness *national*.

The people has been understood almost always by the Russian intelligentsia in the context of a social and class sense, and herein the people -- this is the common people, the peasants and the workers. The populist mindset has been bound up with a nominalistic and atomising idea of nation, with a loss of the sense of the people as an integrally whole organism, as fatherland. The people-nation is a living organism, a living reality, active within history, accomplishing great deeds, striking fear and terror into the hearts of mankind. The living whole is higher than the parts, and the feelings, evoked by it, are more sacred than the feelings, evoked by the parts. And therefore the nation is higher than the peasantry, than the proletariat, the intelligentsia, the bureaucracy, the bourgeoise and the nobility. At the basis of the attitude towards social community ought to sit the idea of *nation* at the right hand of the idea of *person*. Having lost the sense of nation, the intelligentsia has transformed itself into a renegade class, into an isolated social group, at the very time when it ought to be but an higher organ of national life, a blossoming of its native-land, the bearer of its intellect and higher qualities. The intelligentsia as a special social group, isolating itself from "the people" and at the same time idol-worshipping before this selfsame "people", would then cease to exist and it ought altogether to cease to exist. It is the offspring of the old Russian history and it cannot create the new within Russian history. But every people-nation ought to have its own intelligentsia, the bearer of their higher qualities, their higher moral consciousness, their own intellect, their own giftedness and insight, their own prophecy and search for truth. Such an intelligentsia could be formed and take root only upon the soil of a new and ideal national awareness.

Belonging to the intelligentsia ought to be determined only by the *qualities of person.* Members of the intelligentsia ought deliberately to transition over into the "everyday life", into the "people", so that the people's everyday life might be lifted to higher a stage. Participation in economic production ought to become an intellectual deed, a national service.

II.

I have always thought and I tend to think, that the intellectual crisis of the intelligentsia, the forming of a new awareness, a new attitude towards the people and towards the fatherland, -- all this has intimate a religious root. Only a religious consciousness can be at the basis of that national-liberating consciousness of the intelligentsia, and one such as would worship neither the ideal of imperialism nor pagan nationalism.

But, sad to say, I see indeed that a whole series of representatives of "the new religious consciousness" move rather to the side directly opposite, they cleave to the old biases and idols of the intelligentsia, they but augment the apostacy, and paralyse the sense of responsibility. There tend to prevail negative and irresponsible tendencies, long since already holding sway in the ranks of the Russian intelligentsia. There is engendered a mystical populism, a mystical maximalism arises in place of the materialistic. And I refuse to understand, why the new Christianity, whether in the person of Merezhkovsky, D. Philosophov, Z. Gippius, A. Bely,[2] -- why it is that they regard it religiously possible to veil over with new

---

[2] I have in view the book of Merezhkovsky, "Not Peace, but the Sword", his articles subsequently in "Rech" and "Obrazovanie", the articles against me, of Philosophov (in "Tovarisch") and of A. Bely (in "Obrazovanie"), and likewise the articles of Philosophov, in which he propounds his view on the tasks of the religio-Philosophic Society (in "Slovo"). My article is a reply to the sharp attacks made against me, but it is also relevant concerning the article of P. B. Struve.

words the old mindset of "irresponsible equality", to provide a mystical sanction to a false populism, a false social maximalism, always bound up with idolatry, with an attitude towards the people (or the proletariat and towards mankind as towards an idol? The religious consciousness in particular is obliged to unmask the tempting lie of that love for man and worship of man, which obscures the love for truth and of worship of God. It is time to stop playing with words and seeing religion there, where there is no positive relationship to the Divinity. Just as with the old populism, Marxism and other intelligentsia ideologies, these representatives of the new religious consciousness get into the preaching of a social asceticism, on the one hand, and a social idolatry -- on the other hand, in which they deny personal responsibility, they uphold the old attitude of the intelligentsia towards the idea of nation, towards its concrete historical tasks, but with an irresponsible levity they deny the necessity of economic production, of statecraft,[3] and of other functions of the historical life of peoples. The old Christianity was less ascetic, it moreso acknowledged history, it was more reconciled to love for one's native-land and with responsibility for its earthly fate. For Merezhkovsky and his like-minded ilk, why has Russia suddenly been transformed on the one hand into intelligentsia maximalism, and black hundredists -- on the other; why does he reckon it possible to assert, that one, who relates with criticism both against the maximalism of the left, and the maximalism of the right, -- how can he assert that such an one is situated on the outside of life, on the outside of Russia, on the outside of society? Is it not more accurate to think, that both the intelligentsia maximalism, and the black hundreds -- are but superficial fringes of life, only small circles in conceit considering themself the nation, -- whereas the great and immeasurable life of all the people's life possesses a different and

[3] Or if they avow it, then all the same they purport, that it does not become them to participate in such a dirty business. Life itself has taught me this, that a similar kind of "boycott" on mystical grounds, to which I myself was once inclined, does not hold up under moral criticism and leads to a denial of history.

organic depth. The intense and searching life of spirit always is expressed in separate persons, at the summits of an authentic intelligentsia, in thinkers, artists, in prophets, in people gifted and of genius, of knowledge and moral attainment; and the organic fundamentals of life obtain within the people, to which cannot be attached an official label of the extreme left or the extreme right. If I were to have proved to Merezhkovsky, that Russia is comprised exclusively of maximalist-revolutionaries, on the one hand, and on the other hand -- by the demonically-dark black hundreds, I would then be considered madly to be out of my mind. But there is no sort of basis to have faith in the terrors and harmful extremes, the illusions begotten of an overheated imagination, bereft of historical and national sensibilities. Life does not flow its way in accord with schemes, howsoever capacious, poetic and mystical be the schemes. I see regretably with Merezhkovsky an aesthetic and irresponsible misuse of apocalyptic prophecies. Likewise dear to me is the matter of the new Christianity, I believe in the Christian prophecies concerning the Kingdom of God; but I think, that the historical path to the God-manly goal is a path of positive societal creativity, of constructive work, and not an irresponsible negativity and exaltative expectation of an as yet unwarranted Kingdom of God. I fear, that Merezhkovsky and others are tempted by the easy way out, they seek to go the way of least resistance. Merezhkovsky thirsts impatiently to foist his religious consciousness onto societal life, to receive power over the hearts of mankind. Everyone incredulously asks, where are the deeds, where are the exploits of the representatives of the new religious consciousness? And here Merezhkovsky answers, that the deeds and exploits of the revolutionary intelligentsia are also the deeds and exploits of the new religious consciousness, that in it lives subconsciously the Coming Christ... In that the revolutionary intelligentsia make heroic efforts, this is something that even the public prosecutors and gendarmes admit, this was something obvious to me even at the age of twelve, and even up to the present day I am wont to esteem the figures of some as heroes. But can every revolutionary exploit be called Christian? Does Christ live in every exploit, can a revolutionary deed be already termed a Christian deed? I tend to think, that an exploit per se possesses as yet no religious significance, the readiness to devote one's life to something still of itself proves nothing. The officer devotes his life to a sense of honour, and the thief to thievery, and the lover to his beloved wife, and the revolutionary to the struggle against despotism, and the Christian-martyr, and the suicide -- to everything in life that has wearied him, and even the pogromist to his Jewish pogrom. Here the relevant thing is not in that a man devotes his life to something, but is rather in the name of what he makes his exploit and what inwardly amidst this that he experiences. The value of an exploit is indeterminable by external empirical facts, whereas an exploit can also be unseen. And only that exploit can be called Christian, which is made in the Name of Christ, though even without remembrance of His Name, i.e. that it be accompanied by a sense of self-denial and inward humility afront an higher truth. An exploit, committed in the name of idols and bound up with self-assertion and pride, cannot be termed Christian. But the revolutionary psychology in this regard is convoluted and duplicious. Striving itself as such to make effort and sacrifice is not automatically a Christian striving, -- herein lies a great temptation to confuse oneself and one's sacrifice with the Saviour of the world and His sacrifice. One ought to strive towards the truth of God, and not after exploits and sacrifices per se. If one mustneeds sacrifice one's life in the name of truth, if the evil of the world demands this, then one simply dies and would suffer not to see in this an especially titanic result. And thus all the Christian martyrs accepted death, never having striven after titanic efforts, therein becoming titans in the Kingdom of God. It is sometimes a greater exploit to bear the burden of life, each day its cross, than to go out dying with affectations.

About exploits one mustneeds speak with alacrity and appeal only to those with a sharp sense of responsibility. The words of the prayer, said with all one's being: "Lord Jesus Christ, have mercy on me a sinner" [the Orthodox "Prayer of the Heart, the Jesus Prayer"], for a modern member of the intelligentsia might prove a greater exploit, than participation in armed uprising. From the most recent preachings of Merezhkovsky against me wafts forth human pride. He mixes up the Coming City of God with earthly human ruling powers, and his psychology itself appears a jumble of Catholicism twisted up with Judaism. With the Christian consciousness it is easier instead to conjoin the preachings of Struve, in promoting both a sense of responsibility and love for one's native-land.

D. V. Philosophov, a very sincere man of public spirit and a radical, proposes for the new religious consciousness to adopt the social ideas of the radical intelligentsia, to sanction its social mindset, so that the intelligentsia in gratitude for this might come to follow the religious preachers. Such a method is called demagoguery, and it is hardly just only the reactionaries that also term demagoguery the attempts to present incompatible hues of religio-social thought. It is only possible to sympathise with those social ideals, which one acknowledges as just and true, independent of whomever it be that bears them: the value of an ideal is not determined by whom it is that confesses it. The new religious consciousness ought resolutely to stand up for the side of freedom and the friends of freedom against every sort of slavery and coercion, but the freedom is the essential thing. Insofar as the Russian intelligentsia are for freedom, it is necessary to be with them, insofar however it harms the cause of freedom, it is necessary to be against them. The question is quite more complex, than Philosophov think it to be. In the traditional psychology of the intelligentsia I see little of the love for freedom, the "irresponsible equality" for it is always more dear than is freedom. Philosophov says, and even has already said, that from my point of view and my mindset, the only appeal would be to the rightist Cadets party, or indeed the peace-reform Oktobrists. I first of all do not understand, upon what Philosophov bases his conviction, wherein that every SD or SR moreso actually desires the liberation of Russia, than does every Cadet or peace-reformist. I tend to think, that Pr. E. Trubetskoy or P. Struve moreso desires freedom, than do some of the maximalists. I likewise do not understand, why Philosophov is not interested in the truth or falsehood of my opinions, but rather by whether they please the extreme left. Truth loses nothing by being pleasing to no one, and it does not cease to be true even in the sad instance, that it not please Purishkevich himself.

Merezhkovsky, Philosophov and others deny the creative effort, they yield before the inert psychology of the intelligentsia, they subconsciously flatter it in its prejudices, they demonstrate themself opportunists on the left and they stand up for a course of life, already forced out by the intelligentsia from the stuffy atmosphere of the maximalist small-circles into the expanse of historical life. With Merezhkovsky and the others, at present tactics has won out over intellectual radicalism, at that very time when tactics ought to know its place and ought to be subsumed to essential ideas. In the tactical fervour to show, that religion is not reactionary but rather revolutionary, -- it can only lead to this, that religion be suppressed altogether. To Merezhkovsky and his school has remained foreign and little familiar that complex philosophic work, which ultimately has explained, that every societal community is but a temporal means and that extra-temporal values cannot be made subordinate to the community. Merezhkovsky and those like him are sundered off from the organic flesh of history and they are therefore fatally doomed to mere mechanical unions with exclusively negative tendencies. Merezhkovsky does not want to participate in the constructive work of history, he wants only to delimit himself with the sanctioning of negative work. For A. Bely it remains only to make a play on words with a theme on this, that the mechanical and the mystical intersect and coalesce. But the mystical always is bound up not with the mechanical, but rather with the organic. To the fleshlessness of the new religion can be opposed the fleshliness of Vl. Solov'ev, in whom the religious mysticism was combined with a sober realism, with a powerful sense of history and with an affirmation of historical flesh in its dynamism. The political and economic ideas of Vl. Solov'ev were naive and not entirely thought out, but he was an implacable foe of every demonic obscurity and every reaction, howsoever they be veiled over with revolutionary words. He always posited the "Jewish-Christian Question": is a given mental phenomenon useful or harmful for the God-manly *deed* upon earth *at a given historical moment*?[4] For the God-manly deed upon earth in the given historical moment, harmful is that mental phenomenon, which -- though unconsciously -- would transform religion into a tool of the community, and in the community sustain that inert prejudice, whereof only the negatively-irresponsible path be seen as progressive and radical. It is time to stop foisting off the human as the Divine.

[4] Vide "Letters of Vl. Solov'ev".

CONCERNING "LITERARY DISINTEGRATION" [1]

Still not so long ago they were wont to ignore the "new tendencies" in art, in philosophy, in religion. But at present these themes have come into vogue, they are written about in the newspapers, and these themes do enjoy pitiful a success. In that the literary-artistic and philosophic trends have become fashionable, this is half woeful, but that the religious themes have become fashionable, this is genuinely woeful. Matters intimately experienced and thought through have wound up out on the street and have become fatally vulgarised. With us everything becomes in vogue, nothing takes root deeply. Thus the so-called "new" ideas prove of no genuine influence, the new consciousness does not solidify for us, and only the soil is loosened, only the anarchy of spirit intensifies. It has become terrible for the rising new generation. It has become accustomed to a levity of attitude towards all ideas and to all values, in it there is no tradition, there is nothing stable and strong. The very religious ideas themself, called forth to halt this anarchy of spirit, to fortify, to construct a new tradition and connect it with the old, are perceived as but one of the manifestations of this anarchy, of this unprincipled epoch. One might console oneself in this, that revolutionary epochs are always accompanied by an anarchy of ideas, and the old values wither, while the new values are still as yet uncreated. But we have too quickly entered into a reactionary epoch, which does not create, but rather destroys, and this transition from a negation revolutionary to a negation reactionary suggests serious dangers for our future. The old, the rotten, the false still is not finally destroyed, and the new, the vital, the true is still not fashioned.

---

[1] Published in "Moskovskii Ezhenedel'nik", 12 December 1908.

The epoch that is being lived through by us is so complicated, that no simplistic scheme can explain it. The attempts of the Marxists to make sense of our troubles, with the help of economic materialism, by class theory and every sort of materialistic rubbish, begets at times the results of high comedy. To be dauntless afront the comic -- is a venerable touch, but all the same it sometimes becomes awkward for these dauntless people. There are things, which do not allow of the instinct for eternal the aesthetic. But this healthy instinct has not held in check the pen of Mr. Lunacharsky at that moment, when he wrote, that the Old Testament prophets were ideologues of the petite bourgeoise, he vulgarised the great names and great beliefs of the past with a Marxist jargon, and making the leap from "the ideology of the petty land-owners" in the Old Testament to parallels in a similar alike ideology of contemporary Socialist-Revolutionaries, etc, etc.[2] Nor has this instinct held in check the authors also of the anthology, "Literary Disintegration" ["Literaturnyi Raspad"], when they recognised the whole new literature, as something artistic, so also the religio-philosophic, and they recognised at once therein also the ideology of the petite bourgeoise, and of the big bourgeoise, and the feudal nobility, and the proletarian intelligentsia, and I know not still what else. Here it is not only aesthetics that suffers, but logic also. A certain Mr. Steklov had the audacity to write the following: "In place of Lavrov, Mikhailovsky, Eliseev and Schedrin, the law-givers of mental a mode have become Dostoevsky, L. Tolstoy and Vl. Solov'ev. There has vanished the great Patrokles and in place of him upon the throne of public opinion has arisen the stuttering and grotesque Thersites of petty triteness and mysticism".[3] In his being dauntless afront the comic, Mr. Steklov is truly one of the foremost, one of the boldest. Not everyone is wont to say, that the replacing of Lavrov, Mikhailovsky, [Grigorii Zakharovich] Eliseev, and [M. Saltykov-]Schedrin by Dostoevsky, by L. Tolstoy and Vl. Solov'ev,

---

[2] Vide Lunacharsky, "Religion and Socialism".

[3] Vide Literaturnyi Raspad", p. 41.

singular geniuses of their epoch, the pride of Russia, is a replacing of Patrokles by Thersites, is a literary decline and decay. Eliseev being replaced by Vl. Solov'ev -- here is what presents itself to Mr. Steklov as the triumph of petty triteness. Schedrin was a remarkable writer, but suddenly this certain fellow Dostoevsky and that certain fellow Tolstoy have become the rulers of minds, herein is such decay, herein is such decadence! This demands no commentary. And the selfsame Mr. Steklov numbered Ibsen amongst the psychopaths and degenerates and in this he even outdid Max Nordau -- that narrow-minded ideologue of philistine health.

They go on to critique quite strangely the religio-philosophic searchings: they criticise not the ideas, but rather the persons. Concerning the ideas per se, about their value, about their veracity they say nothing, they do not even try to enter the world of religious realities. There transpires a search either sociological or psychological, they explain away everything either as reaction or by class psychology, or by insincerity and pathology. Of all these class, pathological and other explanations is produced such a stench of philistine limitedness, that it becomes chokingly foul. It becomes necessary to either open the windows or break them open. The remarkable American psychologist and philosopher James in his book, "The Varieties of Religious Experience", starts with this, he establishes a connection of mysticism with pathological conditions. Does he thence make deductions in the spirit of Max Nordau and the other philistines? No. James is a very precise thinker, very reflective. He says: granted that mystical experience is connected with conditions, which within science it is accepted to term pathological, yet by this in no way is decided the question about the *value* of the mystical experience, about its significance: the question concerning value and truthfulness is not to be decided by empirical origin or other empirical connections. This -- is a philosophic axiom. James appraises mystical and religious experience as something positive, as a broadening of human experience, as an enrichment. And James is no mystic, he is not a religious thinker. James -- is a representative of scientific philosophy, very outstanding amongst modern psychologists. Certainly, Messrs. Steklov, [Nikolai Aleksandrovich] Morozov etc, know how to see in James an ideologue of the petite bourgeoise or big bourgeoise, or even feudal nobility, which in this case would have been somehow especially transported to America, but the value of James himself is not shaken by these trifles. I offer the example of James here for a reason. Howsoever they might explain at present the rise in Russia of religious experiences and religious searchings, this does not resolve nor even posit the question concerning the value and the veracity of religious faith. Granted that from the point of view of Marxism and other more moderate currents, the signs of a religious renewal ought to be relegated to a societal pathology, and not physiology. But what of it? I tend to think, that at present within Russia the societal pathology is quite stronger, than the societal physiology, and I think, that this but renders acute the religious problem within human consciousness. Religion always is connected with the pathology of the world (the fact of the existence of evil), and this pathology is untreatable by any means, except the religious. The antinomies underlying the ills of life focus the religious consciousness, beget the thirst for a religious way out. But the value of religion is no wise shaken by this, quite the contrary. And indeed who is it by way of judge in the deciding of the question, that it is pathological, and not healthy? The scientific definition of the "pathological" is always something relative, conditional and with reservations, it neither decides nor tackles the question about ultimate *value*. The unreservedness, the self-persuadedness and absoluteness of Marxism in the deciding of the question about the pathology of societal phenomena has nothing in common with real science, and this is a primitive self-conceit, a narrow view, deriving from its own surrogate religious faith.

The "Literary Disintegration" anthology is interesting concerning the reaction of Marxism regarding the new currents, regarding the modern searchings. The Marxists have become afraid, that the ideational grounds are receding from beneathe their feet, and they have rushed out to compromise any attempts to strengthen the new consciousness. "In the breakdown of society they have resurrected various forms of a mystical idealism. There has been renewed an interest in religious questions, -- a sure sign of moral collapse and political reaction. The revolutionaries and atheists of yesterday in crowds have begun to throng to the sessions of the "Religio-Philosophic Society" and there with popes and jesuits acting the fool in Christ they lead endless and absurd discussions about all possible kinds of "religio-moral" questions."[4] Wild words these, in which the interest for religious questions is equated with a moral collapse, religio-moral questions openly are acknowledged as absurd, and they witness to one thing only: the Social-Democrats have begun to sense, that things are going badly. Hence it was necessary to take measures. "Literary Disintegration" is thus an administrative taking of measures by our literary Social-Democrats. This collaborative anthology is impersonal, everyone speaks one and the same thing with all the same words, it is impossible to recognise the author, they could all be undersigned by the collective pseudonyms Ivanov, Petrov or Semenov. There is, otherwise, the already quite weak articles by Messrs. Steklov and Morozov and more decent, more intelligent articles by Messrs. Bazarov and Yushkevich. The Marxist anthology -- is a brilliant illustration not only of weakness, but even a comic and absurd Marxist explanation of "ideology". The new currents in art, in philosophy, the new positing of religious themes -- all this is explained away, ultimately, as reactionary and bourgeois. But "bourgeois", "reactionary" -- this is all a matter of sweeping generalisations and empty words, and all their concretisation and detailisation, all their approach to actuality begets but contradictions, lack of clarity, and ends as comedy. The literary disintegration -- the phrase, by which are characterised phenomena very varied and even contradictory, is the product of a social breakdown. But what is it with us that is breaking down? The Marxists connect this "breakdown" with the "bourgeoise", and according to Marxism at present every aspect of the breakdown ought to be imputed to the bourgeoise. But shame on the actuality, and let history beware! The

---

[4] p. 49.

bourgeoise in Russia is not suffering a breakdown and its breakdown is not transpiring even in accord with any Marxist schematic. With us there is only just beginning a capitalistic era, the bourgeoise are only just forming, it is still in its diapers, and if the Marxist schema were accurate, then it faces still a long process of developement and its blossoming forth lies still ahead. Why however is it being proposed, and full of hopes, that the bourgeoise should prove suddenly to be of a decadent ideology, from whence the bourgeois collapse and the disintegration literary, philosophic, religious? What emerges is nonsense, and neither by scheme, nor by design. The authors of the anthology themself sense, that there is something wrong here, and in their elucidations they constantly flit about from the bourgeoise to philistinism, from philistinism to the feudal nobility, from the nobility to the intelligentsia. For us here the nobility as a class actually is in collapse, with it everything is in the past, and not in the future, thus so it is in reality, and thus so in accord with the Marxist schema. But to regard our modern literature, philosophy, mysticism as being from the nobility -- this is already an herculean height of absurdity. What is relevant concerning our urban philistinism, our petite bourgeoise, is that it abundantly comprises members of the "Union of Russian People", and its ideology is defined by black-hundredist instincts. Perhaps according to the Marxist schema the philistinism is deemed to be revolutionary democracy, but in actuality it turns out otherwise, and this will do you nothing. Individualism, according to the Marxist schema, is a trait characteristic to the petite bourgeoise, to the small land-owners. But if the Old Testament prophets proved themself already to be ideologues of the small land-owners, then I should willingly agree to be an ideologue of this stratum. The difficulty however consists in this, that I am not an individualist and I contend against individualism. For the Marxists, classes do not exist as they are in actuality, in all their complexity and concreteness, it is only the "ideas" of classes that exist (almost in the Platonic sense). The classes -- are as it were intelligible essences, which can be operative even distantly remote from reality.

Concerning the intelligentsia there has to be a special discussion. This stratum causes the Marxists many an unpleasantness, they can no wise sort out, what it is behind this strange social form. Our Social-Democrat intelligentsia deny and even swear against it, but they themself are typical of the intelligentsia, infected by the spirit of intelligentsianism and quicker than anyone can they be acknowledged as ideologues from the intelligentsia small-circles. The Social-Democrats are far off and even foreign from the workers, from the broad circles of the people. Intelligentsia down to the very marrow of their bones -- they are all in a quandary to find a place for the intelligentsia in their scheme, here accounting the intelligentsia to the bourgeoise, while yet there to a special aspect of the proletariat. The authors of "Literary Disintegration" impute the literary collapse to the fault of the intelligentsia, to the fault of the intelligentsia helplessness before the terrors of life and death, the intelligentsia want for strength. But the authors of the anthology themself are moreso naught else than hapless Russian intelligentsia, frightened by the inner crash of the revolution and the outward might of the reaction, all agitated by this selfsame terror of life and death and clutching at the "proletariat", at a bit of comforting Marxist terminology for self-consolation, in order to create for oneself an illusion of strength, of stability, of hopes for a tremendous future.

They have found a new slogan by way of an explanation for all these unbearable, disturbing, distressing new tendencies -- *urbanism*. The Big City (with capital letters, its specific atmosphere, its alienation from nature, its rattling effects upon the nervous system -- here is what begets "modernism", and evokes the attraction for mysticism, for the replacing of real unity with an entirely fictitious mystical unity. In all these discussions concerning urbanism there is something of a true insight, but this true insight is not the monopoly of Marxism. And the "mystics" could say much about the modern city, about the alienation from nature, about the pressure of city capitalism upon the person; and they would say all this no worse than the Marxists, but what of it?

We admit, that the tendency towards (modern) mysticism is engendered in the atmosphere of the big city. Perhaps the inclination is compromised by this? It is possible even to assert, that the inclination towards "mysticism", begotten upon the soil of urbanism, is an healthy instinct, an healthy thirst for reuniting with the Cosmos, an healthy thirst for the liberating of the person from the oppression of city capitalism. The striving to transform the city into a village, to transform all the world into a big village -- is an healthy striving. The building up of a world and cosmic village upon the soil of an higher culture is also a task of world history. But is this aim permissible upon grounds positivist and empirical? Would not all the world then be transformed into a factory?

All the new creativity, all the new searchings are explained away by the Marxists as the sense of an impending ruination. But where then is the genuine new creativity, the creativity of the future? A proletarian creativity we do not see, the whole value of life, all the life of spirit is borrowed by the proletariat and its ideologues from the bourgeoise and from bourgeois culture. The values of materialist philosophy, of utilitarian morals and naturalistic art, the values of economic productivity, the values of a negative faith and vision -- all these are bourgeois values, created by the bourgeois period of history. Proletarian socialism has not advanced one step further beyond the bourgeois-enlightenment ideas, it has created nothing of its own, all are dependent like slaves upon that selfsame accursed bourgeois world. I speak about the "socialistic ideologues" of the proletariat, since the proletariat themself, the working people themself live a different life, and in their masses all still live a life religious and without religious values it is impossible to live. The workers in their masses are all still Christians, Catholics, Orthodox or Protestants, Christians of little awareness and yet of the old consciousness. But this Christian blood is a great hindrance upon the path of a Social-Democrat "enlightenment" of the masses. And never will the Social-Democrats rouse the masses of the people to great a deed in the name of certain class interests of materialistic "enlightenment". Instincts can be fired up, but without certain instincts man cannot live, nor any people live.

The authors of "Literary Disintegration" toss all and everything into a single heap, they sort out nothing, they do not get down to the essence of anything and evidently, they even sense themself incapable to sort out, that what is the genuinely important is not "modernism", not "mysticism", not some sort of indefinable new searchings and currents, but that the important is Christianity and Christ. It is only with Christianity that they have to reckon, only on the Christian question depends also the fate of the world, and not on modernism, nor an indefinable mysticism etc. If the authors of "Literary Disintegration" were more given to insight, more perspicacious, less hemmed in with all the "class" terminology, they would then have focused their especial attention on the rebirth of the Christian faith and would not have jumbled it up into the same heap with decadence, mystical anarchy and even pornography. Then, perhaps, the anthology "Literary Disintegration" would not be so exclusively a book for children of a tender age, it would not be so childish and laughable.

The method to jumble everything into a single heap, to combine together with the negative things of the most positive, is very coarse and primitive an approach. If this hodgepodge is made intentionally, then it is unscrupulous, if unintentionally, then it witnesses to such a lack of talent, such a weakness of consciousness, that better it were not to have slithered out from the cracks with suchlike a criticism. When whatever some wild-eyed reactionary were to jumble up into a single heap not only such nuances as "Bolsheviks" and "Mensheviks", or Social-Democrats and Social-Revolutionaries, but also combines into one the liberals and the maximalists, the socialists and the anarchists, and indeed lumps them all as "anarchists", then everyone would laugh at such an uncouth fellow and adjudge him no one to be taken seriously. But do the Marxists fare any better, do they come across any more intelligently or more cleverly, in having undertaken a matter beyond their wont? With them the new art gets thrown together with pornography, the religio-philosophic searchings together with decadence, Christianity with mystical anarchism, [Georgii Ivanovich] Chulkov with [Sergei Nikolaevich] Bulgakov, [Kornei Ivanovich] Chukovsky with D. S. Merezhkovsky, [Petr Moiseevich] Pil'sky with Vl. Solov'ev, [Frank] Wedekind with Dostoevsky and etc. In modern life there does reign a terrible anarchy of spirit, but the Marxists in their blindness have espied unity in this anarchy.

Much is accurately said in the anthology concerning the "modern press", concerning the new type of impressionist writers, concerning the street modernism. But the truth is, this "modern press, this street modernism and impressionism is a residue of revolution and democratisation, and all this is characteristic to a transitional era of revolutionary democratisation, when ideas hit out upon the street. And here amidst this is nothing whether of the new art, or philosophy, or religion, particularly with religion there is nothing here. There is indeed actual anarchy of spirit, the actual literary disintegration, reflecting this anarchy, as the residue of revolution. By revolution has been set loose chaos. Even the collective eroticism, which has threatened to turn into a dangerous epidemic, is a by-product of the revolutionary era, of the revolution, having negated the old norms and values whilst not having created new norms and values. This anarchy of spirit, this disintegration is essentially anti-religious, and religiously one ought to contend against these phenomena. Religion is the wellspring of positive norms and values, the cessation of the anarchy of spirit, the surmounting of the disintegration. Materialism cannot overcome the disintegration, it cannot halt the growth of anarchy, it but intensifies all this, and gives birth to a debauchery of instincts.

It is impossible not to admit, that our modernistic literature is beginning to become vulgar and to deteriorate, our decadence all more and more is showing its inward emptiness. But all the so-called decadents -- almost all our sole talents, in its camp at present, represents almost all our only literature. This might seem pathetic, but it is so. In "Russian Riches" ["Russkii Bogatstvo"] and others in the literary sense *conservative* journals there is nothing of a literature there, and the literary there is of no interest, since it is impossible to term literary some tale about how a district police inspector was a bad man, whereas a teacher of the people was a fine fellow. The *freedom of art*, an appreciation of artistic values, it would seem, is an advance within our awareness, and in this mustneeds be acknowledged a positive service behind decadence, as a protest against our barbarity. But against which there has to be a decisive struggle also, just as against the connecting of decadence and modernism with religious currents. This connection is empirically fortuitous and is situated within the sphere of external culture. The journals, which served to express our religio-philosophic searchings, first also provided an asylum for the then hounded decadents, since they acknowledged them as talents, they acknowledged their original significance as art and were in a cultural regard more free and in the vanguard. Individual representatives of religious tendencies in their own past were connected with decadentism, but this proves precisely nothing: indeed, other representatives of religious tendencies in the past were connected with Marxism. Inward decadence and religion, just like Marxism and religion, are profound contraries, they are mutually exclusive and in the last resort can only be enemies. The confusing of a religious setting however with the problem of sex, lumping it together with pornography -- this is already a vile polemical method or else a stupid lack of understanding, something here beyond all question. It is difficult to discuss the problem of pornography with people, -- for whom the question itself about sex is something dirty. The sick and degenerate eroticism, so tormentive for modern man, can only be overcome upon the grounds of a religious setting and a religious resolution of the problem of sex. No one can be freed from such an eroticism by the likes of materialism, by biology, by hygienic norms and philistine morals. Our youth has long ago already outgrown the Bazarovism, it haplessly thirsts for something other, and Mr. Bazarov cannot return it back. Youth is tormented by the moral question concerning sex and cannot force its way out from the contradictions, which already lead to the question of a religious context.

The authors of the anthology hold forth upon the view, that they stand on firm and solid ground, which nowise and by no one can be shaken. What however is under this ground? As firm ground they reckon every materialistic bit of rubbish, with which no man skilled in philosophy would even begin to bother with. Materialism is a schoolboy philosophy for children of a tender age, and concerning materialism in philosophy it is impossible seriously to discourse.[5] This question gets itself resolved by references in school-books on philosophy. Against dangerous innovations, against all these searchings, against the "disintegration" the Marxist Messrs come out with a socio-biological idea of *form of race*, into which the person ought ultimately to be subordinated and enslaved. A form of sanctity very old, and very conservative! It would seem, that this appealing to race, to the ancient source of "necessity" and the slavery of man, no longer can make one captive and is no longer to be guarded against. The proletariat has already grown out of its diapers, within it likewise the awareness of person has awakened, with the sense of human worth and the thirst to comprehend the meaning of one's life and one's destiny in the world. If one fell back only upon conscience, upon reason, upon the instincts of mankind, but this is instead race, biology, conformity to the average etc. The very idea of mankind is not identical with race in the biological and sociological sense of the word; this idea presupposes instead a religious norm.

The authors of the anthology play most of all upon a suspicion of insincerity in the religio-philosophic searchings. This facile method of refutation is widely employed not only by the Marxists, but also by many other critics, and this is a method very much in vogue. But the accusation of insincerity possesses this defect, that it can be with equal success turned back upon the accusers themself. I do not know Mr. Yushkevich, and I do not know,

---

[5] The materialism revised and renewed by [Ernst] Mach and [Richard] Avenarius in the externals hardly can be more improved upon. This -- is a materialised empiricism, and to it are applicable all the objections against materialism and empiricism in general.

what he does in life, just as he does not know me and the other targets of his criticism. The articles themself per se of Mr. Yushkevich do not witness to any correlation between word and deed, and since the literature itself per se cannot witness concerning this, then other sources for making a judgement are needful here. The writings of Mr. Yushkevich are of the same sort of literature, as that of all of us sinners, and are perhaps only insufficiently a literary literature. The word "literature" I employ not in view of derision, I would even want to protest against the in-vogue despising and deriding of literature, would want as it were the more loudly to say, that thought and writing is a deed, that literature possesses a great significance and great meaning, that the writer ought the moreso to respect himself. As regards to sincerity, it ought to be said to Mr. Yushkevich, that at all times and with all people, under sincerity has been understood a correlation between word and experience, between the literary and the life experience, between that, what a man says, and that, what transpires inwardly with him. Under this criterion namely, Nietzsche was an extraordinarily sincere writer, but in terms of his outward actions and dealings he had almost none. And consequently Lev Tolstoy also was sincere, although his words were quite divergent from his deeds. And indeed there has been many an extraordinarily sincere writer, acknowledged as sincere by all, yet bereft of outward deeds, quite many of them were not endowed with an active and willful nature, and indeed not in suchlike activity was the meaning of what was transpiring within them. Everyone is familiar with the precept, that there ought to be a correlation between word and deed, but with this precept one comes nowise nigh to so subtle an object, as sincerity of search. In order to catch sight of the document of the human soul within literary works, there is necessary such a subtleness, such a co-feeling of experience, such a desire to see whatever it be,

while that all the Messrs Yushkeviches with their class manias ponder nothing about this. I quite well know, how little activity there is in our religious movement, how little there is of deeds, and I know, how people suffer from this sincerity. But this movement is in its very first initial stage, indeed not even a movement, but only a prelude to it. And the searchings themself present here an already great activity, already a deed. For the time being this is still only a crisis of consciousness, connected with anguish of heart and dissatisfaction of will. We live in a transitional era, victims of a transitory condition of spirit. At present it is a time not so much of outward deeds, as rather of inward work, the time of a readying of a new consciousness, of a cleansing from the old idols. When Marxism started up, it likewise was a legacy of the circles, it was literary and became a deed in life only afterwards, only when the Marxist consciousness had gained ground amidst the broad masses. Our religious movement has not yet emerged beyond its condition amongst the circles, from the literary, it is being wrought within persons, and not in the masses.[6] Thus begins every movement. But we are all aware, that then only will it be an authentic, vital, impressive religious movement, when it shall have become of the people and emerge beyond the phase of a literary expression of the religious experiences and searchings of individual persons and circles. And in this matter the religio-philosophic literature plays its own genuine and preparatory role. As individual persons, other individual thinkers earlier perceived much and they then hammer out the new consciousness, needful for the masses. And in that enemies are suspicious of insincerity, thus it has always been, and the Marxists themself were suspected of insincerity by their enemies, as tends to happen with sinful man.

That we are moving towards a religious turnabout with the people, towards a religious renewal of life for the masses, this can only be an object of faith and hope, here there cannot be precise knowledge and scientific foresight. But we know, we know assuredly, that our people, and indeed every people amongst its masses has never lived and cannot live otherwise, than religiously,

---

[6] I speak, obviously, not about Christianity in its world-historical significance, but about our current searchings.

that no sort of materialism can satisfy its needs in the supreme basics of life, the utmost sanctions. The preaching of class interests, with which the Social-Democrats have gone to the people, and indeed other revolutionaries too, standing upon materialist grounding, has not been accepted by the religious instinct of the people, it has begotten only a wild unruliness and ultimately it has led to reaction, to disenchantment with the idea of liberation. The people cannot experience that complex drama, which individual persons experience, of the upper culture, which is reflected in literature. The people in its masses passes over from the old form of religiosity to a new, more full, more conscious form, not having experienced the many tribulations, the many doubts, experienced by individual seekers. The people will build a new religious life,[7] and therein will be pronounced the judgement of history over the religio-philosophic searchings of our transitional era. These searchings are however not afraid of being adjudged "literary". They but desire, that they should be perceived and sensed by all: that this trend of religious thought, which is closely bound up with Christianity, should not create its own sort of new closet-religion in being a literary path merely, but the rather firmly stand upon the soil of the people's and the world-historical religion, issuing from it and heading towards the future, foretold by the prophecies of this religion.

If would be good, were the authors of "Literary Disintegration" to admit, that new themes face the Russian intelligentsia and that a serious crisis is transpiring within it. The whole traditional world-view and traditional psychology of the Russian intelligentsia has collapsed with a crash. Our revolutionary intelligentsia has become bankrupt not only outwardly and materially, but also inwardly and spiritually. Ideas, the positive points of departure at the basis of our revolutionary movement, have been undermined by doubt, have not held up under the testings of life.

[7] In the avoidance of misunderstanding it ought to be noted: the sources of religious life mustneeds be sought not in the "people", and not in the intelligentsia, but the rather in God, in the Divine revelation.

New ideas, a new faith and a new disposition of soul are necessary. With the old means there is nothing to be gained. A new intelligentsia ought to spring forth to life for us, taking up the old thirst for truth upon earth, but upon the grounds of a new consciousness and a different disposition of soul. To halt this crisis is impossible with the experience of the Marxists having things backward. The old materialism no longer still captivates, it nowise saves from a complete crash, since this crash was set up by the materialistic Marxism itself. In vain do the Marxists swagger, in vain do they get themself all artificially excited and pluck up their courage. No one believes them. In consequence of all the experiencing of almost shameful projections with pathetic words concerning the might of the proletariat, and about class psychology, the future society etc. Marxism has tried within Russian life to carry over its word into flesh, and this has proven so unsuccessful, so pitiful in results, so ruinous for the cause of Russian freedom, that Marxism in its flesh has vanished from Russian life, and now anew it wants to rise up, as word, to be transformed into a shabby word, and this crash of Marxism -- is not a temporary by-product of reaction, for its cause is far deeper and inward. Indeed, according to the teaching of the Marxist church the gates of hell will not prevail over the proletariat. The proletariat, as a word, all still holds sway over the minds and the hearts of the intelligentsia, but as flesh, it lies wounded and its might is alive only in Marxist words. Why has it all transpired thus? More intelligent, more honourable and more brave it would be to be conscious of its fatal mistakes and ponder over the cleansing of its awareness. The religious movement has still not passed over into flesh, it is in the future, it is in hope, and to it will come those intelligentsia, thirsting for liberation.

THE OVERCOMING OF DECADENCE [1]

Anton the Extreme [Krainy] (he is Z. Gippius) has published his "Literary Diary", a collection of articles from eight years back. I should like to say some several words in defense of this writer, towards whom has formed an unjust and erroneous attitude. Anton the Extreme has the reputation of being a very extreme decadent, and his writings it is accepted to regard as neither for anyone without understanding nor for which there is no need. All the same everyone knows, that Anton the Extreme, daring to write about questions serious and deep, is naught other than a woman-poetess. And no one has read Anton the Extreme outside of an exclusive small circle of people, no common journal up to the present time has wanted to publish him. But everyone, who attentively and without prejudice peruses the "Literary Diary" of A. Krainy, has to acknowledge, that this is a very cerebral a writer, sharp of thought, full of faith in an higher meaning of life, incessantly aspiring upwards. The identification of Anton Krainy with Z. Gippius not only does not compromise him, it even elevates him. Z. Gippius is our very talented poetess, very original and moreover little appreciated. Gippius it is proper to regard as one of the first in the Russian decadent movement. This is true only in part. Gippius has had an undoubtable relationship to decadence, but she has occupied there an altogether special place, since within her was already markedly the possibility of the overcoming of all the decadence. In the prayerful poetry of Gippius has been alive an intense sense of person and an intense seeking of God. There was sensed in this poetry also something dark, a certain demonic mysticism, a dangerous dividedness, but hope also never disappeared. In her decadent period she overstepped the bounds of person, beyond which is lost the distinction between the "I" and

---

[1] Published in "Moskovskii Ezhenedel'nik", 16 May 1909.

the "not-I", she tried to love herself, as God, but never did she get mixed up with the decadent impressionism, with the decadent aridity of ideas. Gippius is first of all a writer very much of ideas, at times even too ideational, to the impairment of artistic inspiration: she seeks all after the "meaning", and sometimes it would seem, that she loves "life" less than she does "meaning". In her writing of prose Gippius is many times weaker than in her poetry, and her penchant for ideas assumes the form of tendentiousness, many an account and narration is written as though on an assigned theme. There is the feeling, that Gippius is incessantly waging a struggle against some sort of dark element within her, she does not to have her person destroyed, and she opposes to the dark powers a norm. The remarkable aspect of this inner struggle within herself in the name of her own salvation sets Gippius apart from those decadents, for which might be said: "the small bird walks merrily the footsteps of hardship, not anticipating any consequences from it". The decadence of Gippius herself and the decadence of, for example, [Konstantin Dmitrievich] Balmont -- is at opposite poles. For Gippius life is madly difficult, and not madly easy. She is altogether not an aesthete. She cannot live elementally, with subtle impressions, with pretty dabblings and whimsical lines. This is fine, certainly, but sometimes it seems, that the remarkable poetess does not sufficiently love aesthetics. Within her there is little of an elemental inspiration. The path of a religion of aestheticism seems hidden for Gippius, it cannot satisfy her, and she always had little in common with that aesthetic decadence, which planted itself into our "World of Art". Her surviving of decadence had a great deal more in common with certain of the heroes of Dostoevsky, than it had with the superficial aesthetic decadence. The experience of such a sort of decadence with an inner inevitability leads up to a religious path, it permits only of a religious overcoming. As a poetess and decadent Z. Gippius was little bestown a direct grace, life was difficult for her, in the art itself per se she did not find meaning, paths seemed hidden, and she went on to seek grace in the new religious consciousness.

Anton Krainy overcomes both the past decadence of Z. Gippius and decadence in general. Indeed, the "Literary Diary" of A. Krainy is none other, than suchlike an overcoming. Many of the ideas of A. Krainy, possessing general and broad a significance, would seem too intimate and particular to the small circles, yet especially adapted towards the overcoming of decadence. The book itself of A. Krainy is pervaded by an already positive religious world-concept, which the author applies very originally to all the phenomena of life and of literature. A. Krainy was a chief figure of "Novyi Put'". "Novyi Put'" -- was a whole era of our literary religious searchings, a bright era, but already past. The significance of "Novyi Put'" is beyond doubt. But this journal was not successful in fulfilling the task, about which A. Krainy speaks: "to demonstrate, that 'religious' and 'reaction' are not synonymous". The unrest of the liberation movement was then growing and the revolution was immanent, but the societal ideas of "N.P." were too indefinite and inconstant, and the figures of this journal in mindset were insufficiently socially involved. "Novyi Put'" was but a tortuous state of perplexity afront the problem of religious societal aspect.

A. Krainy strikes some strong blows upon our decadence, its dearth of idea, its superficial aestheticism, he accurately focuses in on the decadent aspect of decadence. These blows are stronger than those, inflicted by our literary old-believers. A. Krainy knows the secrets of decadence, knows its weak sides and does not deny its strong points, its merits. The central question, which A. Krainy raises in his surmounting of decadence, -- is the question concerning person and its boundaries, a very complex and difficult metaphysical question. A. Krainy is no philosopher, has no philosophic background, and indeed, is little familiar with philosophic resolutions of the question about person. The explanation of A. Krainy bears a strong newspaper-criticism sort of character. But the innate mind of this writer and the strong sense of person assist him in sorting out the complex philosophic question and prompt his resolution, which can be strongly justified philosophically. A. Krainy subtly understands, that the basis of person perishes on the soil of an extreme individualism hemmed in by nothing, that decadence in its perview is the ruination, and not the triumph of individuality. The consciousness of one's "I" is bound up with the consciousness of the "not-I", with the consciousness and acknowledgement of all the other "I's". Herein is an undoubtable psychological and gnosseological truth, which A. Krainy well understands and senses, but which the decadents neither understand nor sense. With the decadents there is no awareness of the difference between the "I" and the "not-I", there is no acknowledgement of the other "I's", with them everything is mixed up and tangled, the "I" extends to all-engulfing proportions and is therefore lost, becomes indistinct, wherein the consciousness of the "I" is absent.

As regards the question concerning the relationship between decadence and individualism, there reigns confusion. Decadence has come to be regarded as an extreme individualism. In a certain sense this is true, but together with this also not true. The consciousness of the person and its affirmation presupposes a norm, the realisation of individuality presupposes its gathering and concentration around some certain centre. In the decadent psychology there is no sort of centre, every norm is denied and therefore the person becomes indistinct, individuality perishes, disintegrates into disjointed and fleeting experiences of the moment. In this sense decadence is anti-individualistic, it reflects in itself the loss of person and the vanity of searches for it. The hypertrophy of individuality, a sick "I-ness" is nowise different than the perishing and disintegration of individuality. In Ibsen's "Peer Gynt" is magnificently portrayed the anti-individualistic character of such an hypertrophy of individuality. Peer Gynt has lost his "I", he sickly seeks for and does not find it. On the other hand, true individualism -- is an individualism, subjecting the person to a norm, and not only is this not opposed to universalism, but it even inevitably presupposes universalism and in universalism only is it realised. But the great service of this writer -- a former decadent, is that he so well understood, in what was the sick spot in the decadent world-sense, and thus subtly sorts matters out in the question concerning the person and individualism.

A. Krainy speaks about the most difficult metaphysical problems in a simple and conversational language, and decides these problems unceremoniously, without regard for philosophic traditions. In a certain sense this is a merit, since metaphysical problems cease to be the provenance of specialists, and instead become matters vital and accessible for every seeker and thinker. With A. Krainy, it would seem, there is also a clarity, an avidness for thought and simplicity, for an all-humanness of language. But this clarity and simplicity are deceptive, and herein there is a certain optical illusion. The generally understandable words of A. Krainy frequently become understandable only for but the very few, only for a select few. A. Krainy writes intimately and remains all still a writer of the small circles. He wants to get out beyond the shut-in circle of intimates, wants to turn to everyone, but does not always succeed in this, and chiefly he remains fully comprehensible only for the few. A. Krainy overcomes decadence and struggles against decadence, but he overcomes it intimately, in the shut-in circle, and his sharp struggle with decadence is understandable only for those, involved in this circle. These peculiarities bestow an acuteness to the writings of A. Krainy, make them interesting, but these peculiarities however can also evoke perplexity. A. Krainy is too assured of the singular veracity of his path and is insufficiently sympathetic to other paths, leading to this selfsame Rome. "Novyi Put'" was one of the episodes of our religio-philosophic quests, an episode, true, and vivid and valuable. But "Novyi Put'" indeed is not the sole motherland of these quests, is not the sole path and is not the solely new. This new path has to enter into the main current, and then only will it result that, what should be of value to it. A. Krainy is inclined to invoke only the "Novyi Put'" source. This -- is a view proper to the circles, and it is necessary to free oneself from it, if one desires the spreading about of one's influence of idea and community with ideas, having other sources. It is an hindrance moreover in getting close to A. Krainy and appreciating the thorniness of this writer and that chill, which remained in consequence of the former decadence. A. Krainy masterfully pricks an opponent, but does not inspire, acts little upon the senses, and without any sense of animation and enthusiasm.

The basic religious idea of A. Krainy is the same, as with Merezhkovsky: the uniting of soul and body, of heaven and earth, of religion and life, and an awareness of the insufficiency of Christianity for this synthesis. This does not means, that A. Krainy is only a follower of Merezhkovsky, since this idea belongs to him no less, than it does to Merezhkovsky. And indeed these ideas, as with all the ideas of a religious nature, cannot be the mental work of one man, they always presuppose a certain collective consciousness. The individual product of thought, it is true, comes into play also for religious ideas, since the life of an idea transpires within the human element, but there ought to be a supra-personal ground, in order that this idea should have some sort of pretense to veracity. A. Krainy makes pretense to the supra-personal as his grounding, but there remains the question, can this ground be acknowledged as sufficiently universal in its significance and sufficiently bound up with the successive traditions of church and culture.

In other articles of the anthology is sensed a grumbling against the young literary generation. A. Krainy does say honest things about this young generation, he well understands its ailment, but it would be more pleasant, if there were less a sense of guarding his own generation, his own circle. Always and in everything A. Krainy is for consciousness and against elementalness, he leads a struggle against the modern trend towards thoughtlessness and lack of awareness. A. Krainy -- is a man of acute awareness, even of the hypertrophy of consciousness. His struggle against elementalness bereft of idea, such as is vogue with our chaotic epoch, mustneeds be acknowledged an undoubtable merit. But his properly just struggle against the chaotic and unaware elements leads A. Krainy to a lowering of the significance of the *immediate sense*, to which belongs a visible place in religious life. A. Krainy falls into a *rationalisation* of human nature.

We take note especially of the article concerning "Being in Love". The dreams about an higher sort of love -- are very hallowed dreams of A. Krainy, the thoughts about love -- the most intimate of his thoughts. A. Krainy came to an idea of love, very akin to the genius-endowed teachings about love by Vl. Solov'ev, but came to it independently, deriving this idea from within, pondering its experience. And most hostile of all is A. Krainy to Rozanov and Rozanovism, to the natal birth love, the impersonal instincts in sex. The intimate sense of person is expressed most of all in the article about being in love. And A. Krainy cherishes a dream about a transfiguration of sex, which is already altogether inexpressible and ought to seem folly to the "reason" of this age. The most original and strongest aspect with A. Krainy, Z. Gippius -- is a critique of the old love, the acute awareness of the perishing of person on the grounds of the impersonal physiology and psychology of love, the acute awareness of this, that only personal love, connected with Christ, proves saving of person. In his writings, evidently, A. Krainy has not expressed his experiences and thoughts fully enough -- he has presentiment of more, than he is able to express philosophically. If the dreams about a new sense of being in love constitute the soul of A. Krainy, then the thoughts about *lifestyle existence* and *events* constitute as it were his body. A. Krainy does not love lifestyle existence, is sundered off from every mode of lifestyle existence. Lifestyle existence for him is static, the remnants of movement, mere fallow repose. Lifestyle is in opposition to events, motion, dynamics. True life is revealed not in lifestyle, but in events. The confusing of life with lifestyle -- is a ruinous confusion. A. Krainy thirsts for new life, the old life with its everyday concerns is unbearably wearisome, and only events bear with them the new life. Love for A. Krainy is a forward dashing journey, the rapidity of its motion intensifies the hope to catch sight of new life, of new frontiers. All this is true, and at present many speak about the death of lifestyle. But herein arises a not so small difficulty with the philosophy of developement, which the author of "lifestyle and events", quite likely, is not aware of. How does the author conceive of the nature of the movement of the world forwards, and is there realised within history anything real and of value? If so, if the movement becomes also an attainment -- in part, certainly, -- then the attainment of the value and the realisation of the real is already an authentic existence, extra-temporal in its significance. Outside of lifestyle and event there is still *existence* in the history of the world, and existence ought to be safeguarded. One mustneeds be firm upon this, in order to move on further and create events. The very opposition between the static and the dynamic is relative, and everything extra-temporal is already an overcoming of this opposition. But our Anton is very much the Extreme, he comes out with the bias, that truth and beauty are only within the most extreme extremities. Imposing upon himself an obligation of extremity does not permit him to appreciate the conservative element of movement and developement within the world. A. Krainy is very much taken with that historicity, which hints to him of the instinct of motion, but there is another historicity, hinting of the instinct for eternity, which he insufficiently esteems. He is unaware of the religious bond with those the deceased, who for us are as alive and dear, as are all the generations to come.

The article concerning the anthology, "Questions of Religion", which is quite strongly entitled "Worldless" ["Bez mira"], touches directly upon the question about the old and the new within Christianity. The article is very sharp, the characterising of certain authors from the anthology is on target and caustic, the basic objection also as it were is accurate. But in the article there is something unclear, and unclear first of all is the attitude of A. Krainy to Christianity, to the *eternal* within Christianity, and most of all unclear is how he would overcome that insufficiency of sobornost'-communality, which he discerns in the anthology, whether he himself knows an unmistakably sure path to religious sociability in community. The authors of the anthology did not come up with a religious sociability, they contradict one another, but all the same it is apparent, that they are people involved in the societal aspect by instinct and by their past. In what measure Krainy himself is of the societal aspect, is not apparent, and his sharp article -- is entirely negative. The deficiency of A. Krainy generally -- is an excessive self-assertion, too great an assuredness that by him and by his associates will be found the sole path, as also an insufficient valuing of the positive in others.

A. Krainy is on principle correct, profoundly correct in his polemics against decadentism. Upon Russian soil, culturally immature and backward, possessing not even a genuine cultural medium nor cultural tradition, there cannot sprout up that type of hypercultural decadent, so extraordinarily refined, so extraordinarily cultural, so extraordinarily beautiful in its withering type, as for example, Huysmans.[2] Hypercultural and refined among us is Vyacheslav Ivanov perhaps, but he is no decadent, but a mystic rather. A. Krainy is disenchanted with contemporary art and has seen in its final extent all the same positivism. In modern art there is a taking to flight, it beckoned up mystical hopes, but it has all ended up with pretty trifles. There is occurring at present a deep crisis in art. There is nothing large scale, great, eternal. The "new" art quickly grows stale, and in literature they again await the latest word. This new word cannot be the abstract, self-sufficing art, but should open out into the sphere of religious experiences. But God preserve art from its tendentiousness.

Most valuable of all in A. Krainy is his incessant struggle against the triteness, the prosaity, the everydayness of life, with its grey day to day matters. Within him there is a striving forward, of winged flight, faith in the meaning of life and hope in the celebration of life. If to Checkhov himself A. Krainy is not always just, then nonetheless the severe judgement of Checkhovism, the engulfing grey melancholy, that hopelessness, the foretaste of non-being, -- is also just, and true, and of value. A. Krainy does not himself undergo hopelessness, he does not want to whine and languish about, he eternally finds and inspires hope for others. He is unable to be reconciled with the meaninglessness of life, and it is in this very irreconcilability that there is already great meaning. I should like, that there be established a just attitude towards A. Krainy - Z. Gippius,

[2] Huysmans -- is the greatest writer of France of the last era, so unjustly unappreciated and overlooked.

and that there be acknowledged the merits of this interesting writer and man, a visible participant in our religious searchings. But I would also like, that he should emerge out from the stuffy small circle setting, and moreso value the values of the world, won not by a "new pathway".

* * *

My article was long already completed, when I read in in the journal "Rech'" the article of Anton Krainy, entitled "The White Arrow". This article produced upon me such a grievous impression, that there has become apparent a need to add some several words more. With sorrow I have been given to feel, that A. Krainy has still not overcome the decadence, has not yet conquered in himself the decadent conceit and scorn for the world, has not yet emerged out from the decadent small circle setting into the expanse of world life. The article is devoted to a praise of A. Bely, a promotion of sorts going about in the circle. A. Bely is declared a genius. In him there is genius, but nastily so, such that all the hapless, who do not see genius in the verses of A. Bely, are declared glassy people, bereft of the right to love the native land, bereft even of the right to belong to the living and to know, what is life and what is death. To all, who do not see in the collection of verses[3] of A. Bely a revelation, of the "white arrow" from worlds not here, to almost all of Russia are hurled the words: "Ye be not only glass, but ye, likewise, be neither my contemporary. Neither to me, nor to Andrei Bely, nor us all the living, be with ye in any sort of dealing. Mine is the native land, mine is my human heart, my present hour, my life, my death, our life, our death... But for you, certainly, it has never entered the head, what is life, what is death. Then all the better for you". But if it becomes a matter of choice between A. Krainy and A. Bely, on the one hand, and all of God's world (on the other hand), then one must make bold to prefer God's

[3] The undoubtable qualities of the verses of A. Bely I shall not here touch upon, and indeed is not here the question.

world. What then really is the matter, why all the fuss? What has happened is that A. Bely has gotten to have citizen feelings, which earlier he never suspected he had. The event, perhaps, is important in the life of A. Bely, but not especially important in the life of Russia. There happen to be people, for whom societal feelings awaken quite late, for whom the societal consciousness developes not altogether normally. Certainly it is better late, than never. But such a change ought to be made without the special fuss, and with greater modesty. Andrei Bely and Anton Krainy have discovered for themself an America already long since discovered, but for Russia and for the world, in this they have discovered nothing. It would be hard to consider such a discovery in the verses of A. Bely so promoted by A. Krainy: "Over my native land hath arisen death". Everyone already long since knows and feels, that "death hath arisen". But here A. Bely quite late has come to sense, what earlier he did not sense, and A. Krainy, having learned about this discovery from A. Bely, demands, that we should all acknowledge, that only through A. Bely is it possible to learn about the sufferings of our native land. I did not sense a "searing burn" from the line of A. Bely and therefore I all into the category of persons, who do not know, what is suchlike the "native land", what is suchlike "death", what is suchlike "arisen". And indeed there is hardly anyone who has sensed the "searing scald". No, the religious consciousness has still not won out over the decadent experiences of A. Krainy. He has only introduced into the customary aspects of the decadent circle a novelty -- societal radicalism, but nothing is changed by this. For Anton Krainy the chief thing is still lacking -- a Christian attitude towards people and towards the native land, and there is no acknowledgement of the human worthiness for the enormous mid-mass of mankind, beyond the theme of "inhabitants", yet of which is comprised the nation.

REGARDING A CERTAIN REMARKABLE BOOK [1]

(Otto Weininger: Sex and Character)

The book of O. Weininger, "Sex and Character", has come out in a fine translation and in a fine edition.[2] This book has already brought attention to itself, and it is deserving of attention. It would not be so fine a thing, however, were Weininger to come into a faddish vogue, if there were to obtain the wide circulation of certain of his ideas, which can prove fresh and interesting, ideas, having justification in the passionate subjectivity of his rich individuality, but harmful and trite for mass consumption. And thus one might wish, that Weininger be properly appreciated, while thus one might also wish, that Weiningerism not become a stylish fad. In the youthful book of Weininger there is a sweep of genius, and from this sombre book wafts an air of freshness. This is a very stimulating and inspiring book.

Weininger -- is a son of the German spiritual culture, and in him is felt the spirit of Kant, of Schopenhauer, Schelling, R. Wagner, the spirit of German idealism and romanticism. But in him there is a profound difference from contemporary German culture and philosophy. The book of Weininger, the book of a 22 year old youth, -- is perhaps the most vivid manifestation of contemporary German culture; after Nietzsche there was nothing already in this fleeting culture so remarkable. In this book, the spirit of German idealism and

[1] Published initially in journal "Voprosy philosophii i psikhologii" ["Questions of Philosophy and Psychology"], May-June 1909.

[2] Regretably, another book of Weininger, "The Final Word", full of intuitions of genius, and in which he presents a genuine mysticism, was very badly translated.

romanticism attain to a religious torment. One merely small matter separates Weininger from the religious acceptance of Christianity, and it is this, that he cannot transgress this quirk, cannot undo it. Weininger arrives not at a religious world, but he is pervaded by a reverent, almost religious love for truth and right and he inspires others with a love for perfection. In this, he is akin to such writers as Fichte, Carlyle, L. Tolstoy; he comes across graciously even in those instances, when he expresses evidently false ideas. What enchants in the book of Weininger is not his theoretical ideas, too often exaggerated and inaccurate, but rather an elusive breath of air throughout all this book.

In the book swells the breath of an eternal idealism, a profound and passionate hostility towards positivism, towards the cult of numeric quantities and the transitory, but with a love for qualities and eternity. The most successful aspect would be the specific views of Weininger on womankind, on the bisexuality of the human being, etc. In these views there is much of interest, but I should want to turn attention to altogether different sides of the book. In his teachings about genius, Weininger is most of all ascendant over the spirit of our times, most of all by his own genius. In romanticism there was an eternal side, and this is also developed by Weininger, which leads the spirit of romanticism through the cleansing fire of philosophic criticism. There is the sense likewise of an affinity of Weininger with Carlyle, with his cult of heroes. Our era is in need of the rebirth of the very idea of genius. Almost no one already during our times still connects his dreams about a rebirth of mankind in connection with genius, all tend to connect the dream about a new life with the power of numeric quantities, with mechanical forces. "Universal apperception, all-general judgement, complete extra-temporality" -- here is what Weininger sees as the essence of genius. "It is proper then to call a man a genius, when he lives in a conscious connection with the worldly whole. Genius is but also the Divine within man". "The genius -- this is that man, who attains to the consciousness of his own particular *I*". But in accord with the profound thought of Weininger, "the utmost individualism is the utmost universalism". In genius also is revealed in full the idea of man. He declares to us in eternal moments, that such a man: " is an object, the subject of which serves all the world". *Genius,* in accord with the original teaching of Weininger, is present not only in those people, whom we are accustomed to call geniuses. "Genius is an idea, towards which one approaches closer while another remains afar from it, an idea, to which one approaches quickly, while another approaches it, perhaps, only towards the end of his life". Weininger is an avid adherent of the Platonic teaching about ideas, and towards everything he adopts the Platonic method; for him both the masculine, and the feminine, and genius -- are ideas, with which the empirical activity corresponds to a greater or lesser degree. The idea of genius -- is a basic idea for Weininger; in it he sees salvation, in it -- universality, the fullness of being, and also together with this the self -consciousness of the "I", the affirmation of the person. Genius is the consciousness of values, a positive relationship to things, and moreover with this, genius is a liberation from the power of time -- extra-temporality. Genius for Weininger is distinct from talent, since a basic sign of genius is an universal proclivity, which with talent there cannot be. Genius can obtain with people of simple gifts, and even in people untalented in other moments of life: in the moments of great suffering or ecstasy there can appear genius, the flash of light, the universal acceptance of things. Remarkable likewise is the teaching of Weininger about memory, with which he connects the consciousness of the I, the consciousness of value, genius and extra-temporality. "The ideal of genius would be manifest by suchlike a being, for whom as much as he may have "perception", just as much as has "apperception"". With memory is connected also the need for immortality. Memory is a victory over time, it is the affirmation of one's I against the force of time. In the chapter about logic and ethics Weininger connects ethical and logical norms with memory. He uniquely interprets the normative criticism and makes broad inferences from this teaching.

But most of all it must be mentioned, that Weininger is a remarkable psychologist, a person of clear insights into emotional elements. He quite uniquely comprehends the tasks of psychology, and his merits involving psychology are still to be recognised. Weininger relates with a caustic and sharp-witted spurning of the "soulless psychology"; he wants to return to psychology its lost soul; in this he differs not only from the positivists, but also from the greater part of the Neo-Kantians. Weininger dreams about a new science -- characterology or theoretical biography, which should replace the old, the soulless and abstract psychology. With him there is the idea of a new concrete psychology, which would study what not at all concerned the old psychology, e.g. the psychological problems of "murder, friendship, solitude". Weininger would tend also to study the psychologically concrete problems of -- masculinity, femininity, genius, giftedness, maternalism, eroticism, etc. Many of the psychological observations and generalisations of Weininger are striking in the power of their intuition, without which it is impossible to be a genuine psychologist. Psychology will only then emerge out upon a new and fruitful path, when it is not limited to the investigation of sensations and the elementary and most general emotional phenomena of cognition, of will and feelings, but makes rather the object of its investigation such complex and concrete phenomena, as e.g. idolatry, suffering, childishness, pride, anguish, asceticism, etc. The concrete and complex, the genuinely "psychological" phenomena of modern psychology are not only not being investigated, but they also cannot be investigated given the character of its method. Weininger here does something very exciting, he opens up a new path. Prior to Weininger no one had undertaken such a psychological investigation of masculinity (M and femininity (F. What is striking with Weininger in this area is a mixture of intuitions almost of genius, of profound insights into the character of "woman" together with very inaccurate, unjust and but basic generalities. In the attitude of Weininger towards F there is something tortuous and enigmatic. The passion, with which Weininger denies a depth of soul in F, denies every relationship of F to logic, to ethics, to genius, to consciousness of the "I", to truth and right, -- conceals within him something unhealthy, some sort of experiential fear. True, Weininger speaks not about woman, but about the F, as a Platonic Idea, which can be found also with men, just as the M principle can also be found with women. But the constructs of Weininger are logically arbitrary and unsustainable, since he ascribes to the M everything positively of value and makes man the bearer of the M, and to the F he ascribes everything negative, bereft of value, and makes woman the bearer of the F. The arbitrary, subjective and unjust aspects of the basic outlook of Weininger has not hindered him from saying a bitter truth about women. His teaching about the genida, as a characteristic trait in the makeup of woman. True also is this, that it is a male only that is explaining the feminine genida. Very profound likewise is the teaching about the opposition between sexuality and the erotic. Weininger connects with the erotic the sense of opposition between the person and the race and the sense of redemption and salvation. The F is but the projection into the external world of the sin of the M, and love is a thirst for redemption from the sin. The male never loves the female, and the female is unworthy of love, -- he but moistens in woman the "soul", moistens his own idea of perfection, his own value. Such an idea is purely erotic. The sexual attitude towards woman is however a source of sin and slavery. Weininger arrives also at the preaching of an extreme asceticism, in which he sees a liberation from the F, i.e. from sin and evil. In him is sensed a breath of the Platonic Eros, but poisoned by modernity. In Weininger there is a sense of terror and fright in facing the secret of sex.

In Weininger there is likewise an intense, a passionate sense of the person, the sense of the "I", and a no less passionate, indignant hostility towards the racial aspect. Everything impersonal, elemental, bestial, familial is hateful to him. In this Weininger stands at the very summit of consciousness, and his book with genius reflects on that crisis of the familial element, which is in so impaired a state for modern mankind. The self-consciousness of the person, the consciousness of the higher nature of man rises up against the slavery of the impersonal racial-familial element. Weininger therefore hates the F, since that he sees in this element a principle, hostile to the person, hostile to reason and conscience, binding one to the race, to racial reproduction, to the elemental such as is hostile to immortality. The sense of person and the thirst for immortality lead Weininger to a denial of the maternal. He dethrones maternalism from its pedestal, since he sees a profound opposition between the creativity of new generations and the creativity of spiritual values. For him maternalism is a subconscious, animal-like instinct and therefore not exaltive for women. Here Weininger is close to Plato and to eroticism, as begetting beauty. Vl. Solov'ev likewise followed the path of Plato, but he knew a Christian egress. Weininger wages an incessant struggle against the elemental and the unconscious in the name of reason and of consciousness. In this, he goes against the spirit of the times, the spirit of a decadent consciousness, immersed in the unconscious elements and opposed to all norms. He struggles likewise against the decadent ethics, with its denial of the absolute character of morality, against the modern lack of principle and amoralism. Weininger by his criticism provides a service for a spiritual rebirth, the orienting of man towards eternal values and towards immortality.

Weininger stands upon the groundings of a Kantian philosophy; but he does not emerge as the usual type of Neo-Kantian, -- which is to say a positivist: he understands what is the most important thing in Kant -- his teaching about the duality of human nature, his moral philosophy. Weininger has deep respect for philosophy, in this he is a typical German. He is not only a idealist, but also a spiritualist, he combines the criticism of Kant with the spiritualistic monadology of Leibnitz. But the spiritualism of Weininger is dualistic, he abandons the dichotomy of spirit and flesh, and he is hostile to flesh. If Weininger were to have come to the Christian consciousness through modern philosophy, he would then have surmounted this dualism, and his spiritualism would become monistic, not denying the flesh, but spiritising rather the flesh. In Weininger is evident the deadliness and impotence of an irreligious romantic idealism.

Amidst all the psychological shrewdness of Weininger, amidst his deep understanding of evil in womankind, there is still no true understanding of "the essence of womankind and its meaning in the universe". Weininger puts all his hopes upon an ultimate victory of the masculine over the feminine, which should be a victory of spirit over the flesh, of the world eternal over the world corruptible. And Christianity does see in womankind an evil principle, it teaches, that the female nature is particularly susceptible to evil, but Christianity also teaches, that the female nature in turn is also susceptible to the greatest good, becoming fruitful by the Spirit of God and having given birth in the flesh to the Son of God. Only the faith in Christ could save Weininger from his gloomy views on womankind. He would see, that besides prostitutes and mothers there are also the myrh-bearing women.[3] The teaching of Weininger about the erotic includes within it a partial truth, but he does not arrive at the ides of an erotic union of the make and female in eternal being. The positive meaning of being -- is in the heavenly Eros, just as this is revealed to the religious consciousness at its summits. The Eros of Weininger however is illusory, in it there is not attained real being. The cult of the Madonna for him -- is a delusion, and the dream of love -- an illusion. Man remains alone by himself, and not possible for him towards another and others. Weininger calls for an heroic effort of self-salvation, of liberation by one's own powers from the flesh, from this world, from womankind. But the help is nowhere to be awaited, there obtains no grace. In this idea of self-salvation there is both pride and doubt. Weininger did away with himself, and in the book there are presentiments of this terrible end. He loved Christ and Christianity, but Christ for him was only but a religious genius, only the great founder of a religion. He sees in Judaism that selfsame evil

---

[3] [trans. note: by Christian scriptural tradition, the Risen Christ appeared first to Mary Magdalene and the other MyrhBearing Women, and only afterwards did He appear to the Apostles. Likewise in this vein is the truism, that in general there would be found but few men in church, were it not for the women getting them there].

power, which also is in womankind, and he sees the exploit of Christ in the victory over Judaism.[4] And he awaits a new religious genius, who again will conquer the "Judaism", infecting all our culture. "Against the new Judaism will burst forth to light a new Christianity. Mankind thirsts for the founder of a new religion, and the battle will come nigh to a decisive end, just as in the first years of our era. Mankind anew will have to choose between Judaism and Christianity, between business and culture, between the feminine and the masculine, between the race and the person, between non-value and value, between earth and an higher life, -- between Nothingness and God". If Weininger had sensed, that Christ were not so much the founder of a religion as is rather the religion, he would less gloomily have faced his own fate in the world. But he did sense, that the world is moving towards a new religious life, and that the times ensue for a decisive struggle. Weininger -- is one of the few people of the modern culture, who loudly witnesses to the religious searchings and torments in anticipation of a religious rebirth.

---

[4] The hostility of Weininger towards "Judaism" has nothing in common with the vulgar anti-Semitism, it is deeper and more terrible. From the perspective of Weininger, modern anti-Semitism is itself pervaded by a spirit of "Judaism". In his views upon Judaism, Weininger follows R. Wagner. The question about the opposition of the Aryan and the Semitic culture again becomes strained.

PHILOSOPHIC TRUTH (ISTINA) AND INTELLIGENTSIA JUST-TRUTH (PRAVDA) [1]

In an era of the crisis of the intelligentsia and an awareness of its mistakes, in an era of the re-evaluation of the old ideologies, it has become necessary to put a stop to our attitude towards philosophy. The traditional attitude of the Russian intelligentsia towards philosophy is more complex, than it would seem at first glance, and an analysis of this attitude might reveal fundamental spiritual features peculiar to our intelligentsia world. I speak about the intelligentsia in the traditionally Russian sense of this word, about our narrow-circles intelligentsia, artificially isolated from national life in general. This is an uniquely peculiar world, living up to the present a closed-in life under twofold a pressure, a pressure involving a red-tape situation external -- of the reactionary powers, and a red-tape situation inward -- of an inertness of thought and a conservativeness of feelings; and not without reason do they term it "Intelligentsianism", in distinction from intelligentsia in the broad, national in general, historical in general meaning of this word. Those Russian philosophers, which the Russian intelligentsia has no wish to know, which it refers to as an other and enemy world, likewise indeed belong to the intelligentsia, though foreign to the "Intelligentsianism". What indeed has been the traditional attitude of our specifics-minded, narrow-circle intelligentsia towards philosophy, an attitude, having remained unchanged, despite rapid a shifting of philosophic modes? Conservatism and stagnation in the core emotional composite for us have been combined with a penchant for novelties, for the latest European fads, which never get assimilated deeply. This is the same thing also as regards philosophy.

---

[1] Published in collection of articles in "Vekhi", 1909.

What becomes apparent first of all, is that the attitude towards philosophy has been shallow of culture just the same, as it also has towards other spiritual values: the self-sufficing significance of philosophy is denied, and philosophy gets subsumed to utilitarian aims. The exclusive and despotic dominance of utilitarian-moral criteria, just like the exclusive and stifling dominance of people-love and proletarian-love, bowing before "the people", its betterment and interests, the spiritual smothering by political a despotism, -- all this has led to the result, that the level of philosophic culture has shewn itself for us to be very low, and that philosophic knowledge and philosophic developement have very little spread into the midst of our intelligentsia. A broad philosophic culture can be met with only among individual persons, who themself have already become isolated from the "Intelligentsianism" world. But for us there has been not only little of the philosophic disciplines of knowledge -- this is a correctable shortcoming, -- among us has prevailed suchlike an emotional disposition and suchlike evaluations of everything, that genuine philosophy has had to remain hidden and incomprehensible, and philosophic creativity has had to be presented as a matter of quite another a world and mysterious. Perchance, some will have read philosophic books, outwardly they will have understood what they have perused, but inwardly just the same they will not have become conjoined with the world of philosophic creativity, nor also with the world of beauty. This is to be explained not by defects of intellect, but rather by a direction of will, which has fashioned the traditional, the stubborn intelligentsia medium, having assimilated into its flesh and blood the populist world-outlook and utilitarian approach, even at present not fading away. For a long time among us it has been considered almost immoral to devote oneself to philosophic creativity, -- in this sort of occupation they saw treason towards the people and the people's affairs. A man, too immersed in philosophic problems, would become suspect of indifference to the interests of the peasants and workers. Towards philosophic creativity the intelligentsia related ascetically, they demanded abstention in the name of their god -- the people, in the name of preserving strength for the struggle against the devil -- absolutism. This populist-utilitarian-ascetic attitude towards philosophy has remained even among those intelligentsia currents which, apparently, have surmounted populism and disdained the elementary utilitarianism, since this attitude is rooted in the sphere of the subconscious. The psychological primal core of such an attitude towards philosophy, and indeed in general towards a construction of spiritual values can be expressed thus: *the interests of distribution and levelling within the consciousness and feelings for the Russian intelligentsia have always have dominated over the interests of production and creativity*. This is alike true both regarding the sphere material, and regarding the sphere spiritual: towards philosophic creativity the Russian intelligentsia has related just the same, as it has towards economic productivity. The intelligentsia have always readily accepted the ideology, in which the central focus has concerned the problem of distribution and equality, while the whole of creativity was hemmed off, and here its assuredness had no limits. Towards an ideology however, which at its core posits creativity and values, it has related with suspicion, with an earlier formed deliberate decision to reject and disdain. And suchlike an attitude ruined the philosophic talent of N. K. Mikhailovsky, just as also it did the great artistic talent of Gleb Uspensky. Many tended to abstain from philosophic and artistic creativity, since they reckoned this a matter immoral from the point of view of the interests of distribution and equality, and they saw in this a betrayal of the people's welfare. In the 70's there was even a time, when the reading of books and the increase of knowledge was reckoned as not particularly valuable an occupation and when morally the thirst for enlightenment was frowned upon. That time of a populist dark-obscurantism has passed away already long ago, but the bacillus has remained in the blood. In the recent revolutionary days there has again been repeated a persecution against knowledge, against creativity, against the lofty life of spirit. And indeed up to the present day there remains in the blood of the intelligentsia the selfsame fermentation. All the selfsame moral censures tend to dominate there, albeit with new words adopted at the surface. Up into the present day our intelligentsia youth cannot admit of a self-sufficing significance for science, for philosophy, for enlightenment, for universities, and up into the present matters still get subordinated to the interests of politics, parties, currents and narrow-circles. The defenders of an unconditional and independent knowledge, of knowledge as a principle, hoisted higher than the societal evil of the day, are all still suspect as being reactionary. And to this lack of appreciation for the sacredness of knowledge has always been enabled by the activity of the ministry of popular enlightenment. Political absolutism here also has so distorted the soul of the foremost intelligentsia, that a new spirit can only with difficulty break its way through into the consciousness of the youth.[2]

But it cannot be said, that philosophic themes and problems have been foreign to the Russian intelligentsia. It can even be said, that our intelligentsia always have been interested in questions of philosophic an order, though also not in their philosophic setting: it managed to bestow philosophic a character even to very practical societal interests, the concrete and the particular it transformed into the abstract and the general, questions on the agrarian or of the workers represented to it questions of saving the world, and sociological teachings became tinted for it in almost theological an hue. This feature has been reflected in our journalism, which studied the meaning of life and was not so much concrete and practical, as instead abstract and philosophic even in the investigation of problems economic. Westernism and Slavophilism -- were not only journalistic, but also philosophic currents. Belinsky, one of the fathers of the Russian intelligentsia, knew philosophy but poorly and he did not employ a philosophic methodology of thinking, but all his life the accursed questions haunted him, questions of worldwide and philosophic an order. Themes on philosophic questions occupied the

[2] *Note to 2nd Edition*: The accuracy of my characterisation of the intelligentsia psychology is brilliantly corroborated by the character of the polemics, flaring up concerning "Vekhi". Only did I not expect, that the incapacity to criticise *in essence* the spiritual-reform work in "Vekhi" would prove so widespread.

heroes of Tolstoy and Dostoevsky. In the 60's philosophy was hemmed away and in decline, and scorned by [Pamphil Danilovich] Yurkevich who, in any case, was a genuine philosopher in comparison with Chernyshevsky. But the character of the then enthusiasm for materialism, a very elemental and shallow form of philosophising, all the same reflected an interest towards questions of an order philosophic and worldwide. The Russian intelligentsia wanted to live by and define its attitude towards the very practical and prosaic sides of societal life upon the basis of a materialistic catechism and a materialistic metaphysics. In the 70's the intelligentsia was keen on positivism, and its governing mind -- N. K. Mikhailovsky was a philosopher both as regards interests of thought and range of thought, though without genuine schools and without genuine disciplines of knowledge. P. L. Lavrov, a man of great knowledge and breadth of thought, though also bereft of creative talent, was resorted to by the intelligentsia for a philosophic basis to its revolutionary social strivings. And Lavrov provided a philosophic sanction to the strivings of the youth, usually beginning his fundamentals from afar, with an educating of the muddled masses. The intelligentsia always had their own narrow-circle intelligentsia philosophers and their own trends in philosophy, sundered off from the worldwide philosophic traditions. This home-grown and almost sectarian philosophy satisfied a deep need in our intelligentsia youth to have a "world-concept", answering to all the basic questions of life and combining theory with societal practice. The need for wholistic a societal-philosophic world-concept, was a basic need of our intelligentsia in the years of its youth, and directing its mind became only those, who from general theory had derived a sanction for its societal liberation strivings, its democratic instincts, its demands for justice in whatsoever the matter. In this regard the classic "philosophers" of the intelligentsia were Chernyshevsky and Pisarev in the 60's, Lavrov and Mikhailovsky in the 70's. For philosophic creativity, for the spiritual culture of the nation, these writers provided almost nothing, but they answered the needs of the intelligentsia youth for a world-concept and they provided a basis to the theoretical vital strivings of the intelligentsia; up to the present time still they tend to remain teachers for the intelligentsia and with fondness they are read in the period of early youth. During the years of the 90's with the arising of Marxism there was quite a raining of the mental interests of the intelligentsia, the youth began to Europeanise, began to read scientific books, the exclusively emotional populist type began to change under the influence of an intellectualistic trend. The need for a philosophic grounding to its social strivings began to be satisfied by dialectical materialism, and then Neo-Kantianism, which did not receive widespread a penetration owing to its philosophic complexity. The "philosopher" of the era then became Bel'tov-Plekhanov, who snatched away Mikhailovsky out of the hearts of the youth. Then on the scene appeared Avenarius and Mach, who were proclaimed as philosophic saviours of the proletariat, and Messrs. Bogdanov and Lunacharsky were rendered "philosophers" of the Social-Democrat intelligentsia. On another side there arose currents idealistic and mystical, but this was already an altogether different trend within Russian culture. The Marxist victories over Populism did not lead to any profound crisis in the nature of the Russian intelligentsia, it remained old-believer and populist and in the European trappings of Marxism. It negated itself in its Social-Democrat theory, but this theory itself was for us merely an ideology of the intelligentsia narrow-circles. And the attitude towards philosophy remained as it was previously, if one does not take into account that current of criticism within Marxism, which then passed over into Idealism, but a widespread popularity amongst the intelligentsia it did not have.

The interest among the broad circles of the intelligentsia towards philosophy consisted in the need for a philosophic sanctioning to its societal constructs and strivings, which from a philosophic fashioning of thought would prove unshakable and not subject to re-evaluation, to remain firm, like a dogma. The intelligentsia has no interest in a question, its truth or falsehood, for example, of theory of knowledge by Mach, and what interests it only is this -- is this theory beneficial or not to the idea of socialism, and does it serve the welfare and interests of the proletariat; its interest is not in this, whether that metaphysics be possible and whether metaphysical truths exist, but only this merely, whether or not metaphysics be harmful to the interests of the people, whether it divert away from the struggle against autocracy and from service to the proletariat. The intelligentsia is prepared to accept on faith every philosophy under this condition, that it should provide a sanctioning to its social ideals, and without criticism repudiate every, indeed very profound and truthful philosophy, if such be suspect of being unfavourable or simply critical towards the traditional intelligentsia constructs and ideals. The hostility towards the idealistic and religio-mystical currents, the ignoring of the original aspects and the totality of the creative contributions of Russian philosophy is based upon this "catholic" psychology. The societal utilitarianism in the values of everything, the bowing to "the people", -- then to the peasantry, then to the proletariat -- all this remains a moral dogma for the greater part of the intelligentsia. It even began to read Kant only because, that critical Marxism held promise with Kant to provide a grounding to the socialistic ideal. Then too was accepted even the quite difficult to digest Avenarius, whereby the most abstract, the "most pure" philosophy of Avenarius without his knowing and without his fault suddenly was presented as the philosophy of the Social-Democrat "Bol'sheviks".

In this peculiar attitude towards philosophy is expressed, certainly, all our shallowness of culture, the primitive lack of differentiation, a weak awareness of the unconditional value of truth and of mistakes of moral judgement. The whole of Russian history indicates a weakness of independent mentally speculative interests. But this bespeaks also features that are positive and of value -- the thirst for an wholistic world-concept, in which theory gets aligned with life, the thirst for faith. Not without basis does the intelligentsia relate negatively and with suspicion towards abstract academism, towards a cleaving apart of a living truth, and in its demand for wholistic a relationship to the world and to life there can be viewed a feature of subconscious religiosity. Yet it is also necessary to sharply make the distinction of the "right hand" from the "left hand" within the traditional psychology of the intelligentsia. It is impossible to idealise this feebleness of theoretical philosophic interests, this low level of philosophic culture, the absence of serious philosophic disciplines of knowledge and an incapacity for serious philosophic thinking. It is impossible also to idealise this almost maniac-like inclination to evaluate philosophic teachings and philosophic truths with criteria that are political and utilitarian, amidst this inability to investigate the appearance of philosophic and cultural creativity in its essence, from an absolute perspective of its value. At the present hour, the history of the intelligentsia is in need not of self-applause, but rather of self-criticism. We can transition on towards a new consciousness only through repentance and self-examination. During the reactionary years of the 80's they were wont with self-boasting to speak about our conservative, truly Russian virtues, and Vl. Solov'ev did an important thing, challenging this part of society, summoning it to self-criticism and repentance, laying bare all our ills. Then began the times, when they happened to speak about our radical, likewise truly Russian virtues. During these times it was necessary to summon a different part of society to self-criticism, to repentance and an exposing of ills. It is not possible to be perfect, for if one be situated in a rapture over one's own great attributes, then from this rapture fades also the genuinely great merits.

In light of its historical condition, there occurred with the Russian intelligentsia a sort of misfortune: *the love for a levelling sense of justice, for the societal good, for the people's welfare, ran parallel a path apart from the love for truth, almost that it extinguished the love for truth.* And philosophy is a school for the love of truth, foremost of all for truth. The intelligentsia has been unable to relate uncovetously to philosophy, since that it had a mercenary attitude towards truth itself, it demanded from truth, that it should become a weapon of societal turnabout, for the people's benefit, for the happiness of people. It succumbed to the temptation of the Grand Inquisitor, which demanded the repudiation of truth in the name of the happiness of people. the basic moral judgement of the intelligentsia is comprised in the formula: the heck with truth, if by its perishing the people will live better, if people will be happier; down with truth, if it stands in the way of the sacred cry of "Down with Autocracy". It would seem, that a falsely directed love for man kills the love of God, since the love for truth, as also for beauty, as also for every absolute value, is an expression of love for the Divinity. The love for man has been false, since it has not been based upon a genuine appreciation for man, as begotten of and equal as regards the One Father; it has been ,on the one hand, a commiseration and pity for the man from "the people", and on the other hand, it has gotten transformed into a worship of man and worship of the people. An authentic love for people is however a love not against truth and God, but the rather in truth and in God, not a matter of pity, denying the dignity of man, but rather an acknowledgement of the birthright image of God in each man. For us, in the name of a false love for man and love for the people, there has been wrought as regards philosophic searchings and currents, resultant methods akin to being held under suspicious observation and investigation. Hence, in the sphere of philosophy no one basically tended to enter, the populists forbade entry out of a false love for the peasantry, the Marxists -- out of a false love for the proletariat. But the similar attitude towards the peasantry and the proletariat involved an insufficient appreciation for the absolute significance of man, since this absolute significance is grounded upon the Divine, and not upon the human, upon truth, and not upon special interests. Avenarius seemed better than Kant or Hegel not because, that they had espied truth in Avenarius, but because, they fancied, that Avenarius would prove the more conducive to socialism. This also means, that special interests are set higher than truth, the human higher than the Divine. To refute philosophic theories on the basis that they are not favourable for populism or the Social-Democrats, means to be contemptuous of truth. A philosophy, under suspicion of being "reactionary" (and what only do we not see termed "reactionary"!), gets listened to by no one, since the philosophy itself per se and truth are regarded as of little interest. The narrow-circle musings of Mr. Bogdanov will always be shown preference over the remarkable and original Russian philosopher L. M. Lopatin. The philosophy of Lopatin demands serious mental effort, and from it do not flow any sort of programme slogans, while towards the philosophy of Bogdanov it is possible to relate exclusively on emotion, and it can all be packed off into a five kopeck brochure. Among the Russian intelligentsia the rationalism of consciousness is combined both with an exclusive emotionality and with a weakness of self-appreciated mental life.

Both as it is regarding philosophy, so also towards the other spheres of life, wherein there has predominated for us a demagogic attitude; the disputes over philosophic trends in the intelligentsia circles bear a demagogic character and are accompanied by an untrustworthy glancing sideways with the aim to learn, what pleased whom and what instincts it answered to. This demagoguery demoralises the soul of our intelligentsia and creates a stifling atmosphere. There developes a moral cravenness, and it quenches the love for truth and boldness of thought. Lodged within the soul of the Russian intelligentsia is a thirst for justice upon earth, a thirst sacred in its foundation, which gets distorted. The moral pathos degenerates into monomania. The "class" explanations of various ideologies and philosophic teachings get transformed by the Marxists into some sort of sickly obsessive *idee fixe*. And this monomania has infected the greater part of our "leftists". This partitioning of philosophy into "proletarian" and "bourgeois", into "leftist" and "rightist", the affirmation of two forms of truth, the useful and the harmful, -- all this is a sign of mental, moral and overall cultural decadence. This path leads to a dissolution of an all-obligatory universal consciousness, with which is connected the worthiness of mankind and the growth of its culture.

Russian history has created the intelligentsia with emotional an inclination, which has run contrary to objectivism and universalism, hindering a genuine love for objective, universal truth and values. The Russian intelligentsia has related with mistrust towards objective ideas, towards universal norms, since it presupposed, that suchlike ideas obstruct the struggle against autocracy and service to "the people", the welfare of which has been set higher than universal truth and good. This is a fatal trait of the Russian intelligentsia wrought by its sad history, a trait, for which our historical authorities have to answer, having crippled Russian life and in fateful a manner having shoved the intelligentsia exclusively into a struggle against political and economic oppression, and has all led to this, that in the consciousness of the Russian intelligentsia the European philosophic teachings have become assimilated in distorted a form, adapted to serve specific intelligentsia interests, while the most remarkable features of the philosophic thought get altogether ignored. Distorted and adapted to our home-grown conditions is indeed what has happened with scientific positivism, with economic materialism, with empiro-criticism, and with Neo-Kantianism, and Nietzscheanism.

Scientific positivism has been assimilated by the Russian intelligentsia altogether wrongly, altogether unscientifically and it has played altogether different a role, than it has in Western Europe. Towards "science" and the "scientific" our intelligentsia has related with reverence and even with idolatry, but by science it understood a particular materialistic dogma, and by the scientific a particular faith, and always a dogma and faith, exposing the evil of the autocracy, and the falsehood of the bourgeois world, a faith, of salvation for the people or the proletariat. Scientific positivism, as with everything Western, has been assimilated in a very extreme form and has been transformed not only into a primitive metaphysics, but also an especial religion, a substitute to all former religions. science itself and the scientific spirit have not taken root for us, have not been assimilated by the broad masses of the intelligentsia, but rather only by few. The learned among us never enjoyed any special esteem and popularity, and if they were politically indifferent, then their science itself was regarded as not genuine. The intelligentsia youth began their learning of science through Pisarev, through Mikhailovsky, through Bel'tov, through their own home-grown narrow-circle "studies" and "thinkers". About genuine studies, however, many have never even heard. The spirit of scientific positivism itself per se is neither progressive nor reactionary, it is simply concerned with a researching of truths. We however as regards the scientific spirit have always understood it in context of political progressivism and social radicalism. The spirit of scientific positivism itself per se does not exclude any sort of metaphysics, nor any sort of religious faith, but likewise it also does not assert any sort of metaphysics nor any sort of faith.[3] We however by scientific positivism have always tended to understand it in context of a radical denial of every metaphysics and every religious faith, or more precisely put, scientific positivism became for us identical with materialistic metaphysics and socialistic faith, while not one mystic, not one believer can deny *scientific* positivism and science. Between mystical religion itself and positivist science itself there cannot exist any sort of antagonism, since their spheres of competency are completely different. The religious and metaphysical consciousness actually does deny the unique soleness of science and superiourity of scientific knowledge within spiritual life, but science itself has only to gain from a limiting of its domain. The objective and scientific elements of positivism have been poorly assimilated among us, but all the more passionate have been those elements of positivism, which have transformed it into a faith, an ultimate understanding of the world. The attractive aspect for the Russian intelligentsia was not the objectivity of positivism, but rather its subjectivity, its making a god out of mankind. In the decade of the 70's positivism was transformed by Lavrov and Mikhailovsky into a "scientific sociology", which became the home-grown, the narrow-circle philosophy of the Russian intelligentsia. Vl. Solov'ev quite cutely said, that the Russian intelligentsia always thinks according to the strange syllogism: man is descended from the apes, consequently, we ought to love one another. And scientific positivism has been assimilated by the Russian intelligentsia exclusively in the sense of

---

[3] I have in view not *philosophic* positivism, but rather *scientific* positivism. The West created the scientific spirit, which there also was transformed into a weapon of the struggle against religion and metaphysics. But Slavic extremeness is foreign to the West. The West created *science* religiously and metaphysics neutrally.

this syllogism. Scientific positivism has been merely a weapon for the affirmation of the realm of a social seeking of justice and for a final extirpation of those metaphysical and religious ideas, upon which, according to the dogmatic presupposition of the intelligentsia, rests the realm of evil. [Boris Nikolaevich] Chicherin was far more learned a man and in a scientific-objective sense quite greater a positivist, than was Mikhailovsky, yet it did not hinder him from being a metaphysical idealist and even a believing Christian. But the science of Chicherin was emotionally remote and adverse to the Russian intelligentsia, whereas the science of Mikhailovsky was near and dear. It is necessary, finally, to admit, that the "bourgeois" science is namely also the authentic, the objective science, whereas the "subjective" science of our populists and the "class" science of our Marxists has far more in common with a peculiar form of faith, than it does with science. the veracity of the "spoken from on the highest authority" is confirmed by all the history of our intelligentsia ideologies: the materialism of the decade of the 60's, the subjective sociology of the 70's, and by the economic materialism upon Russian soil.

Economic materialism likewise has been inaccurately assimilated and subjected to the selfsame distortions, as with scientific positivism in general. Economic materialism is a teaching primarily objective, it posits at the centre of the social life of society the objective principle of productivity, and not the subjective principle of distribution. This teaching sees the essence of human history to be in a creative process of a victory over nature, in an economic constructiveness and organisation of productive powers. The whole social structure with the forms of distributive justice inherent to it, all the subjective outlooks of social groups, are but subordinate to this objective productivity principle. And it mustneeds be said, that in the objective-scientific side of Marxism there was an healthy grain of truth, which was asserted and developed by the most cultured and learned of our Marxists -- P. B. Struve. In general however, among us the economic materialism and Marxism were misunderstood, were assimilated "subjectively", and adapted to the traditional psychology of the intelligentsia. Economic materialism lost its objective character upon Russian soil, the production-constructive momentum was shunted off to secondary a plane, and on the primary plane appeared the *subjective-class* side of Social-Democratism. Marxism among us underwent a populist transformation, and economic materialism was rendered into a new form of "subjective sociology". Russian Marxists came to have an exceptional love for equality and an exclusive faith in the nearness of a final socialistic outcome and the possibility of attaining this outcome in Russia even a bit earlier, than in the West. The objective momentum of the truth ultimately sank down into a subjective momentum, into a "class" perspective and class psychology. In Russia the philosophy of economic materialism was transformed exclusively into a "class subjectivism", even into a class proletarian mystique. In light of suchlike a philosophy, awareness could not be oriented towards the objective conditions of developement in Russia, and of necessity this awareness got swallowed up by that for an attainment of an abstract maximum for the proletariat, a maximum from the point of view of the intelligentsia narrow-circle mentality, not wanting to know of any sort of objective truths. The conditions of Russian life made impossible the flourishing of an objective societal philosophy and science. Philosophy and science came to be understood in intelligentsia-subjective a manner.

Neo-Kantianism was subjected to lesser a distortion among us, since it enjoyed lesser a popularity and circulation. But all the same there was a period, when we wanted too exclusively to employ Neo-Kantianism for a critical reforming of Marxism and as a new grounding for socialism. Even the objective and scientific Struve in his first book made the transgression of too great a sociological interpretation of [Alois] Riehl's theory of cognition, he gave the gnosseology of Riehl an interpretation conducive to economic materialism. And at one time we considered [Georg] Simmel almost a Marxist, although with Marxism he has little in common. Then the Neo-Kantian and Neo-Fichtean spirit became for us the weapon for a liberation from Marxism and positivism and a means for the expression of impending idealistic outlooks. But creative Neo-Kantian traditions in Russian philosophy however there was not, the genuine Russian philosophy went by other paths, about which will be discussed further on. Justice demands one to admit, however, that the interest towards Kant, towards Fichte, towards German Idealism has raised our philosophic-cultural level and has served as a bridge to higher forms of philosophic awareness.

Empiro-criticism for us was subjected to incomparably greater a distortion. This extremely abstract and refined form of positivism, having emerged from the traditions of German trends of criticism, was perceived as almost a new philosophy of the proletariat, with which Messrs. Bogdanov, Lunacharsky, and also others considered possible to convert into something home-grown, something their very own. The gnosseology of Avenarius is so general, so formal and abstract, that it does not affect the deciding of any sort of metaphysical questions. Avenarius resorted even to a letter symbolism, in order not to get connected to any sort of ontological positions. Avenarius is terribly afraid of having any remnants of materialism, spiritualism etc. Biological materialism is inadmissible for him the same, as is every form of ontologism. The seeming biologism in the system of Avenarius is unlikely to lead to error; this is a purely formal and so overall general biologism, that any whatever "mystic" could accept it. One of the most cerebral of the empiro-criticists -- [Hans] Cornelius, admitted even of the possibility to count in a god amongst the prior-existing. Our Marxist intelligentsia has however assimilated and interpreted the empiro-criticism of Avenarius exclusively in a spirit of biological materialism, since this seemed profitable by way of a justification for a materialistic perception of history. Empiro-criticism became not only a philosophy of the Social-Democrats, but even of the Social-Democrat "Bolsheviks". Poor Avenarius also did not suspect, that in the dispute of the Russian intelligentsia between the "Bolsheviks" and the "Mensheviks" there would be dragged into the struggle his innocent name, having since well departed the living. The "Critique of Pure Experience" suddenly was rendered quite almost the "symbolic book" of the revolutionary Social-Democratic faith confession. In the broad circles of the Marxist intelligentsia they hardly read Avenarius, since to read him was not easy, and many, certainly, sincerely came to think, that Avenarius was a verymost mental "Bolshevik". In actuality however, Avenarius had just as little a relationship to the Social-Democrats, as does whatever other the German philosopher, and his philosophy with no less a success might be employed, for example, by the liberal bourgeoise and even find justification in the teaching of Avenarius concerning the "maximum preservation of life" with its "rightist" inclination. Chiefly however it mustneeds be said, that if Avenarius were so simple a matter, as Messrs. Bogdanov, Lunacharsky et al suggest, if his philosophy were a biological materialism with the head's brain at the centre, then he would have had no need to devise his various systems S, freed of any premises, nor would he be admitted a powerful mind, with an iron-logic, as happens even today with his antagonists.[4] True, the empiro-critical Marxists no longer still term themself materialists, ceding materialism to such backward "Mensheviks" as Plekhanov et al, but empiro-criticism itself assumes with them a materialistic and metaphysical hue. Bogdanov diligently preaches a primitive metaphysical aspect of his own, mentioning the names of Avenarius, Mach and other authorities, and Mr. Lunacharsky has even fashioned out a new religion of the proletariat, based upon Avenarius. European philosophers tend, in the majority of instances, to be abstract and quite detached from life, and they do not suspect the sort of role they play in our narrow-circle intelligentsia disputes and squabbles, and they would be very astonished, if it were told them, how their ponderous thoughts are rendered into light-weight brochures.

But among us an altogether indeed sad twist has befallen Nietzsche. This solitary hater of every sort of democracy has been subjected by us to a very shameful democratisation. Nietzsche has

[4] Avenarius did not succeed in getting free of "premises", his gnosseological perspective is very piecemeal, with wisps of "materialism", and "spiritualism", and whatever, but it is not simple.

been hacked into pieces, made use of by all, each for his own domestic aims. Suddenly it seemed, that Nietzsche, who thus also died thinking, that he was needful to no one and would remain the solitary upon the lofty heights, -- suddenly it seemed that Nietzsche was very much needful for shedding light on and reviving Marxism. On the one side, we had an entire herd of Nietzschean-individualists milling about, and on another side, Lunacharsky prepared a vinaigrette salad from Marx, Avenarius and Nietzsche, which for many hit the spot, and seemed savory. Alas for Nietzsche and alas for Russian thought! What dishes do they not serve to the hungry Russian intelligentsia; and all partake of it, all eat of it, in the hope, that it will win out over the evil of autocracy and will liberate the people. I fear, that even the most metaphysical and most mystical of teachings among us will likewise be adapted for domestic use. And the evil of Russian life, the evil of despotism and slavery will not be conquered by this, since it is not to be conquered by the distorted adoption of various extreme teachings. And Avenarius, and Nietzsche, and indeed Marx himself will very little help us in the struggle against our age-old evil, distorting our nature and rendering us so unreceptive to objective truth. The interests of theoretical thought for us have been humbled, but the very practical struggle against evil always has assumed the character of a confession of abstract theoretical teachings. For us, true has been termed that philosophy, which aided in the struggle against autocracy in the name of socialism, and an essential side of the struggle itself has been a recognition of the obligatory confession of suchlike "true" a philosophy.

The same psychological peculiarities of the Russian intelligentsia have led to this, that it looked at original Russian philosophy the same way, as it did the philosophic content of Russian great literature. A thinker, of suchlike a calibre as Chaadaev, has gone altogether unnoticed and has not been understood even by those, who make mention of him. It would seem, and there has been every basis for this, that Vl. Solov'ev should be acknowledged our national philosopher, and around him be created a national philosophic tradition. It is indeed impossible to create these traditions around Cohen, Rickert or whatever German, foreign as such to the Russian soul. The philosophy of whatever the European land would be proud to have a Solov'ev. But the Russian intelligentsia has not read nor known of Solov'ev, has not accepted him as their own. The philosophy of Solov'ev is profound and original, but it does not have socialism at its basis, it is foreign both to populism, and to Marxism, and cannot be readily rendered into a weapon of struggle against autocracy, and therefore does not provide the intelligentsia a suitable "world-view", and thus he seemed foreign, more remote, than the "Marxist" Avenarius, the "populist" Aug. Comte, and other foreigners. The greatest Russian metaphysician was, certainly, Dostoevsky, but his metaphysics was something the broad strata of the Russian intelligentsia would nowise bear to shoulder, and he was suspected of every sort of "reactionism", and indeed he actually provided reasons for this. With grief it mustneeds be said, that the metaphysical spirit of the Russian great writers has not been discerned as something akin to itself by the Russian intelligentsia, as something genuinely positive. And it remains to be seen, as to which is the more national, these writers or the intelligentsia world in its own prevailing mindset. The intelligentsia also did not admit L. Tolstoy to be in its own authentic image, but was reconciled with him over his populism and at one point was subject to the spiritual influence of Tolstoyanism. In Tolstoyanism there was all the selfsame hostility towards higher culture, towards creativity, an assertion of the sinfulness of this luxury.

Particularly pitiful seems to me to be the obstinate refusal of the Russian intelligentsia to familiarise itself with the rudiments of Russian philosophy. And Russian philosophy consists not only of such a brilliant figure, as Vl. Solov'ev. The conceptions of a new philosophy, surmounting European rationalism on the basis of an higher consciousness, can be found already in Khomyakov. Along the side stands the significantly substantial figure of Chicherin, from whom one could learn much. Then too there is also Kozlov [Alexei Alexandrovich, 1831-1901], Pr. S. Trubetskoy, Lopatin, N. Lossky, and finally, the little known V. Nesmelov -- a very profound figure, a product of the spiritual academies and on that basis cut off from and remote to the intelligentsia heart. In Russia philosophy there is, certainly, many a variation, but there is also something in common, something unique, the forming of some sort of new philosophic tradition, distinct from the prevailing traditions of contemporary European philosophy. Russian philosophy at its core involves a tendency to continue on with the great philosophic traditions of the past, the Greek and the German, in it still live the spirit of Plato and the spirit of classical German Idealism. But German Idealism has halted into a stage of extreme abstraction and extreme rationalism, culminating in Hegel. The Russian philosophers, beginning with Khomyakov, gave sharp a critique to the abstract idealism and rationalism of Hegel and passed on not to empiricism, nor towards neo-criticism, but the rather towards a *concrete idealism*, to an ontological realism, to a mystical fulfilling of reason as engendered by European philosophy, but which had lost its vital being. And in this it is impossible not to see the creative fundaments of a new path for philosophy. Russian philosophy conceals within it a religious interest and reconciles knowledge and faith. Russian philosophy up to the present has not provided a "world-view" such as would only be of interest to the Russian intelligentsia, in the narrow-circle sense. Towards socialism this philosophy has no direct relationship, although Pr. Trubetskoy also terms his teaching about the sobornost'-communality of consciousness as a *metaphysical socialism*; concerning politics this philosophy, in a quite literal sense of the word, is not interested, although in the finest of its representatives also is concealed a religious thirst for the Kingdom of God on earth. But in Russian philosophy there are features, akin for it to those of the Russian intelligentsia, -- the thirst for an integral world-understanding, an organic confluence of truth and good, of knowledge and of faith. Hostility towards abstract rationalism can be found even among the academic mindsets of Russian philosophers. And I think, that a concrete idealism, connected with a realistic attitude towards being, can become the foundation of our national philosophy of creativity and can create a national philosophic tradition,[5] of which we are so in need. The quickly shifting abstract fads among European teachings ought to be opposed by a tradition, a tradition which ought however to be both universal, and national, -- then only will it be fruitful for culture. In the philosophy of Vl. Solov'ev and the Russian philosophers akin to him in spirit, there lives universal a tradition, in common with Europe and in common with mankind, but certain tendencies of this philosophy can create a tradition that is national. this would lead not to the ignoring and not to the distorting of all the remarkable figures of European thought, the ignorings and distortions by our cosmopolitan-minded intelligentsia, but rather to a more profound and critical penetration into the essence of these figures. what we need is not the narrow-circle opinionising, but rather a serious philosophic culture, universal and together with this, national also. Truly indeed, Vl. Solov'ev and Pr. S. Trubetskoy -- are finer Europeans, than Messrs. Bogdanov and Lunacharsky; they are bearers of a worldwide philosophic spirit and, together with this, national philosophers also, since they set the foundations for a philosophy of concrete idealism. Historically formed prejudices have led the Russian intelligentsia to a frame of mind, amidst which it was unable to perceive within Russian philosophy a basis for its own distortion of pravda-truth, of righteously just-truth. Our intelligentsia indeed has esteemed *freedom* and yet espoused a philosophy, in which there is no place for freedom; it has esteemed the *person* and confessed a philosophy, in which there is no place for person; it has esteemed *progress* and confessed a philosophy, in which there is no place for the meaning of progress; it has esteemed the *sobornost'-communality of mankind* and confessed a philosophy, in which there is no place for the sobornost'-communality of mankind; it has esteemed *justice* and all sorts of lofty

---

[5] Truth cannot be national; truth is always universal, but the various nationalities can be called to a revealing of individual aspects of truth. Traits of the Russian national spirit suggest, that we are called to create in the field of religious philosophy.

things and yet confessed a philosophy, in which there is no place for justice and no place for any sort of lofty things. This has been an almost continuous aberration of consciousness, wrought by all our entire history. The intelligentsia, in its best parts, fanatically has been ready for self-sacrifice and no less fanatically it has confessed materialism, negating every self-sacrifice; the atheistic philosophy, which always has attracted the revolutionary intelligentsia, could not provide sanction for any sort of sanctity, yet amidst which the intelligentsia itself bestowed on this philosophy a sacred character and it esteemed its materialism and its atheism fanatically, with almost Catholic a fervour. Creative philosophic thought would remove this aberration of consciousness and provide it a way out from its dead-end. Who knows, what sort of philosophy will become the fad of tomorrow for us, perhaps, a pragmatic philosophy of James and Bergson, which will be made use of the same as with Avenarius and others, or perhaps, some whatever new novelty? But with this we shall not have advanced a single step forward in our philosophic developement.

The traditional hostility of the Russian intelligentsia towards the work of philosophic thought is expressed also in the character of the latest Russian mysticism. "Novyi Put'" ["The New Pathway"], a journal of religious searchings and mystical mindsets, has most of all suffered by the absence of a clear philosophic consciousness, and has reacted towards philosophy almost with contempt.[6] The most remarkable of our mystics -- Rozanov, Merezhkovsky, Vyach. Ivanov, -- though also they provide rich material for new settings of philosophic themes, yet still manifest an anti-philosophic spirit, an anarchistic denial of philosophic reason. Vl. Solov'ev, combining in his own person a mysticism together with philosophy, noted, that a low regard for the principle of reason is characteristic of Russians. I should also add, that a non-love towards objective reason can be

[6] The exception consists of N. M. Minsky, who propagandises a meonic philosophy. But Minsky -- is a rationalist right down to the marrow of his very bones.

found alike both in our "rightist" camp, and in our "leftist" camp. Amidst all this, Russian mysticism, in its essence very valuable, is in need of philosophic objectivisation and normalisation in the interests of Russian culture. I would tend to say, that the Dionysian principle of mysticism needs to be combined with the Apollonian principle of philosophy. Love for the philosophic investigation of truth needs to be inculcated both by the Russian mystics, and by intelligentsia-atheists. Philosophy is one of the paths of the *objectivisation* of mysticism; the utmost and indeed full form of such an objectivisation can only be through positive religion. The Russian intelligentsia has regarded Russian mysticism with suspicion and hostility, but of late there has begun a turnabout, and there is a danger, that in this turnabout there will be alike shown hostility towards objective reason, the same as also the inclination of the mystics to compromise themself to be of utility to traditional societal aims.

The intelligentsia consciousness demands radical reform, and the cleansing fire of philosophy is called to play not small a role in this important deed. All the historical and psychological givens tend to indicate, that the Russian intelligentsia can transition on to a new consciousness only upon the basis of the synthesis of knowledge and faith, a synthesis, satisfying the positively valuable need in the intelligentsia for an organic co-uniting of theory and practice, of "pravda-truth" [pravda as istina/truth] and "pravda-justice" [pravda as spravedlivost'/justice]. But at present we are spiritually in need of an acknowledgement of the value of truth in itself, of humility in the face of truth and a readiness for renunciation in its name.[7] Such an approach would introduce a refreshing flow into our cultural creativity. Philosophy indeed is an organ of the self-consciousness of the human spirit, and an organ not individual, but supra-individual and communal. But this supra-individualness and sobornost'-communality of the philosophic consciousness is to be realised only

[7] Humility in the face of truth has great moral significance, but it ought not to lead to a cult of moribund, abstract truth.

upon the basis of a tradition universal and national. The reinforcing of suchlike a tradition ought to enable a cultural rebirth for Russia. This long desired and joyous rebirth, the awakening of slumbering spirits demands not only a political liberation, but also a liberation from the oppressive grip of politics, that emancipation of thought, which up to the present has been difficult to meet with in our political liberation figures.[8] The Russian intelligentsia has been such, as Russian history has rendered it, in its psychological mannerism is reflected the sins of our sick history, of our historical powers and our eternal reaction. the now senile autocracy has distorted the soul of the intelligentsia, enslaved it not only outwardly, but also inwardly, since it has negatively defined all the evaluations of the intelligentsia soul. But it is unworthy of free beings in everything always to blame external forces while in their own guilt seek to justify themself. The intelligentsia itself also is to blame: the atheistic aspect of its consciousness is the fault of its will, it itself chose the path of the worship of mankind, and by this it has distorted its own soul, and has deadened in itself the instinct for truth. Only an awareness of the guilt of our mentally-graspable will can lead us to a new life. We shall free ourself from external oppression only then, when we shall have freed ourself from inward slavery, i.e. when we place upon ourself answerable responsibility and cease with everything to blame forces external. Thereupon will be born the new soul of the intelligentsia.

---

[8] Note to 2nd edition: Political liberation is possible only in connection with a spiritual and cultural renewal at its core.

BLACK ANARCHY[1]

The interests of the political struggle and of the political parties interfere with an evaluating of "The Union of the Russian People" from a moral point of view, to perceive in it a phenomenon, characteristic of the condition of Russian culture. It is impossible to deal with the "truly Russian" people such as one might with a reactionary-political party, to view them as exclusively political opponents. The "Union of the Russian People" does not have a relationship to politics in the strict sense of the word. This "union" is but a disorderly rabble of savage elements, of barbarity, of pagan darkness and moral wantonness, pent up for ages within the Russian people. This -- is the debauchery of the primitive Russian anarchistic dissoluteness of instincts, not knowing any sort of norm, this -- is a final flare-up of that moral idiotism, which was fed by the power of too chronic a despotism. In the "Union of Russian People" is a sense of the Eastern savagery and darkness, and at times it shows *the muzzle of the beast* and lays bare the atavistic experiences of cannibalistic instincts. The "truly Russian" people in its masses stands on the other side of good and evil, of truth and lie, their thoughts, feelings and actions are situated outside the control of conscience and reason. herein there is not immorality and stupidity, here there is something even more primitive, something antecedent to the very arising of moral and rational evaluation. I speak not about the Russian people, naive and direct in its devotion to the good old days, profound and good even in its "reactionism", genuinely religious, but about those misfits, which dub themself with the name of the "Russian people". One can be a political conservative, a proponent of state absolutism, a guardian of historical traditions and legacies, and together with this a man of high culture and lofty moral

[1] Published in "Slovo", 17 April, 1909.

consciousness. Our Slavophils were conservatives. Conservatism has a right to existence in each society, and for us the rise of a socio-intellectual conservatism is even desirable in the interests of the organic developement of the nation. But it is impossible to term the "truly Russian" people as conservatives, they -- are destroyers and anarchists in the most savage and most literal sense of the word. The "truly Russian" people are only possible amidst an anarchistic condition of society. It is likewise impossible to term them monarchists and nationalists. The idea of monarchy as a positive basis of national life is only as foreign the same, as is every and any idea; monarchy for them is but a tool, which they want wholly to subjoin to their instincts and their whims. They are far moreso than anarchists, than monarchists. Sufficiently in witness to this are the innumerable attempts of the "soiuzniks" ["unionists"] to usurp power for themself, to shout with the impudence, with which they ascribe to themself the power to do as they please, along with the bragging of Mr. Markov II concerning this. Likewise foreign to them is the idea of nation in its creative significance, their nationalism is but a wild instinct, an unmitigated wont for avarice and paganly dark self-praise.

Those same dissolute herd instincts, which once found expression in the revolt of Stenka Razin and Pugachevism, at present find expression in the Jewish pogrommes and in all the acts of pogromme and scandals of the "soiuzniks". This -- is an anarchy of slaves, having stirred up a chaos of savagery, of unbridled force, with the intent of transforming it into a weapon of struggle against the revolution.

There exists the opinion, that the Black Hundreds (not hundreds alas) is a religious reaction, the reaction of the old beliefs of the people against the new spirit. This is, granted, actually a religious reaction, yet not a reaction of Christian religion, but rather of a dark and primitive pagan religion, of pagan superstition and idolatry. In our black reaction has rise up also a pagan mode of Christians, binding them to time and the temporal in the world, instead of the eternal truth and right of Christianity. With the soiuzniks, pagans as regard the wont of their hearts, there is no reverence towards the sacred, nor humility towards on high, there is not even a respect for churches, which they regard possible to defile with societal scandals and political fanaticism. There have been instances, when the "truly Russian" people forcibly have burst into church, perpetrated violence against the priest, and transformed the temple of God into a tool of savage democracy. The Church, just like the monarchy, just like nationality, is necessary for them only as a tool for their savage whims. These people are full of superstition, but bereft of reverence before the holy. Christianity cannot defend the death sentence, violence against conscience and the darkness, all this can only be defended by the pagan mode of the dark "christians". The "Union of the Russian People" is also a pagan-mannered union; there should be set in opposition to it a Christian union, which would inspire a creatively-constructive character of healthy religious reaction against non-belief. Christians can be adherents of whatever political form as pleases them, monarchy, republic or even *something else, since all political forms* possess a relative and temporal significance, but Christians cannot be defenders of beastliness, cruelty, violence, darkness. I think, that an absolutist, in being an implacable opponent of the death penalty, and an opponent of every violation against conscience etc, is from a Christian point of view more tolerable, than a constitutionalist being a proponent of the death penalty and cruelty.

The Slavophils were proponents of an ideal absolute monarchy, but they intended, that the absolute monarchy should serve towards good and freedom, that it should be humane and Christian, that it should enlighten its people and protect the weak from the strong. The "Union of Russian People" holds dear first of all not the absolutism, but rather that it can execute and commit violence, can rot any enlightenment and deaden the conscience, can be an obedient tool of its instincts and whims. Absolute monarchy can be enlightened and humane only as long as it is wanted and loved; when it ceases to be wanted, it becomes an intolerable despotism. An absolutism, proceeding through the control of consciousness of all the people, ought to be transformed into constitutionalism. The basic contradiction in the construction of an ideal state absolutism is in this, that it wants to be properly loved, wherein it cannot be forcibly imposed, and together with this it imposes itself, commits violence, when it is not loved. The same contradiction is there also in the construct of socialism.

The "Union of Russian People" as regards its cultural and moral aspect stands still lower than that ruling power, which does much evil, but all the same acknowledges a certain minimum of cultural norms. The denial of *obligatory* norms binding for all mankind comprises the chief feature of the "truly Russian" people. The denial of *an universal consciousness* by the "truly Russian" people lays bare their pre-christian and pagan nature. Christianity is an universal truth and an all-human truth and it therefore cannot be reconciled with a wantonness of instincts, with capriciousness and greed, be it personal, group or national. The "truly Russian" nationalism is quite real a paganism, a paganism standing at a level of developement, prior to the formation of an all-human consciousness. With the "truly Russian" people there becomes impossible community upon the basis of all-human norms of conscience and reason. The same can be said about certain representatives of the camp directly opposite, madly obsessed with the class point of view. But these latter have at least the advantage of not blasphemously calling themself Christian. Over and over it must be emphasised, that this is a matter not within politics and not within a preference for this or some other political form, this matter involves something far deeper: *in the absence of the elements of an universal consciousness, binding upon every human being, it is a matter involving a moral, cultural and religious savagery.* The "truly Russian" people are in need of an elemental moral enlightenment, of an acceptance of the universal norm of life into their own flesh and blood.

Among the Russian clergy, particularly the churchly upper hierarchy, there at present predominate members of the "Union of Russian People". At a missionary session in Kiev, at this session of the superstitious Russian paganism, all our pre-Christian savagery found expression. According to the teachings of the Christian Church, belonging to the clergy hierarchy, even the highest, is no automatic guarantee of Christian qualities. The human side of the Christian Church within history has tended to be particularly polluted by the spirit of evil, in place of the holy there has tended to be such a measure of abomination, such as is not met with in other spheres of life. The defense of the death penalty, for example, is a genuine cannibalism, the demand of bloody sacrificial offerings to the god of vengeance. But the Divine sanctity of the Church is not diminished by the human scale of measure, which in its decay is but a greedy attitude towards the Church.

I can have a close association, just as with kin, so also with a man of quite opposite political views and beliefs, but I cannot have such an association with a man, practically denying the universal norms of good and truth. Political tolerance cannot be extended to the "Union of Russian People", for herein is needful a *moral intolerance*, is needful a merciless moral struggle against our chronic moral turpitude and savagery. By their attitude to the jubilee of L. Tolstoy, the "truly Russian" people have placed themself outside of Russian culture and the national Russian spirit. It is impossible to regard the "Union of Russian People" exclusively as a joke, although for jest and laughing their stupidity and churlishness provide no few opportunities; it is impossible also to relate to this "union" exclusively as one might to a reactionary political party. A moral and religious censure is necessary, because these people use religion for their own dirty purposes. Obstructing the path of the national and religious rebirth of Russia, the path of the creation of a great and free national culture, stands the destructive "Union of Russian People" together with those in secret at the top, who support in Russia the darkness, the fanaticism and anarchy of hooliganism. This obstacle has to be swept out of the way by the creative effort of all the nation, having matured to universal a consciousness of good, but on the condition only that the creative powers of the nation do this in the name of the sanctity of all the people and all mankind. To the "Union of Russian People" there needs to be opposed a patriotic and national enthusiasm. The destructive powers, acting in the name of ideas exclusively negative, in this condition merely tend to sustain the black phantasm. And in the existence of the black phantasm, of the black anarchy, we are all guilty: it seems that the power of reaction is but the objectivisation of our weakness and sins.

II.

Religion. Church.

NIHILISM ON A RELIGIOUS SOIL [1]

K. P. Pobedonostsev is dead. With him there is so much connected, together with him there grew up a whole epoch of Russian history, moreso even than an epoch: in his person and in his deeds was clearly embodied the connection of Orthodoxy with state absolutism. Pobedonostsev -- was a remarkable type: a sincere ideologue of our historical nihilism, of the nihilistic attitude of the official Russian Church and of the state towards life. Pobedonostsev -- was a thinker neither profound nor individual, his ideas were rather superficial, too typical, and he shares them with those historical forces, which he served, and which he ideologically supported. Pobedonostsev evoked towards himself a burning hatred, he was the hope of the dark powers, and the prolonged suchlike years were a nightmare of Russian life. But when one reads him, the hatred weakens: there resound within him such sincere notes, a sincere humility before that above, love for the nation, a romantic attachment to the old way of life. In Russia there were few intelligent and sincere defenders of theocratic autocracy, especially amongst those, who stood in power and directed the state mechanism. Pobedonostsev was amongst the number of those few.

Of what sort was the basic feature of Pobedonostsev, his "character trait that strikes the mind"? *Unbelief in the power of good*, the non-belief of the monstrously divided official Russian Church[2]and the Russian state. The power of Pobedonostsev, the unimaginable authority of this man over Russian life was rooted also

---

[1] Published in "Vek", 6 May 1907.

[2] I speak here all the time here not about the Universal Church, not about Orthodoxy as the preserver of Divine sanctity, but about our national Church in its historical and empirical, its human side.

in this, that he was a reflection from above of the historical Russian nihilism. A nihilistic attitude towards man and the world on the soil of the religious attitude towards God -- here is the pathos of Pobedonostsev, in common with the Russian state-governance, set within an historical Orthodoxy. Pobedonostsev was a religious man, he prayed to his God, he saved his soul, but towards life, towards mankind, towards the world process he had an unreligious, an atheistic attitude, he did not see anything of the Divine in life, nor any sort of reflection of Divinity in man; only a terrible, a gaping abyss of emptiness was revealed for him in the world, the world was not for him the creation by God, he never had a sense of the Divineness of the world soul. This spectral, this ghastly old man lived under the hypnotic power of evil, he believed infinitely in the might of evil, he believed in evil, but in the Good he did not believe. The Good he considered impotent, pitiable in its lack of might. He -- was among the number of those hypnotised by the fall into sin, shutting off the genesis, cut off from the mystery of God's creation. The devil rules the world, defines the course of universal life, penetrates into human nature right down to its roots; the good, the Divine do not possess any objective power, upon the good it is impossible to build life, with the power of good it is impossible to tie together any sort of historical perspectives. Just like Marx, Pobedonostsev looks upon human society as upon a mechanism of forces. The fatal process of the fall and decay of mankind, the increasing powers of evil can be halted only by force, only however by evil, only by the despotic state authority, which the Church sends forth into the world to freeze the growth of life, to constrain the liberation of life. Pobedonostsev bore within himself a grudge against the world life and against mankind, he was suspicious and mistrustful to the point of psychosis. But this nihilism of Pobedonostsev, this atheistic attitude of his towards the world is not something by chance individual, connected with personal events in his life, this is a worldwide fact, a fact, lodged within the religious consciousness of historical Orthodoxy.

Historical Orthodoxy has not manifest within itself the religious truth about man and the world, in it religiously is only an attitude towards death, not towards life. Orthodox Christianity is a teaching about individual salvation in Heaven, about the departure from the world, which is all infected by evil. In the ascetic consciousness there is no teaching about the meaning of universal world history, about the triumph of religious truth upon the earth. Orthodoxy does not believe in the Kingdom of God upon earth, only in Heaven does it expect it, and the earth it leaves to the devil. One only good deed can and ought to be done upon the earth -- to hold back the course of evil, to halt it, to curb it by force, to freeze it down. And in Orthodoxy there is the teaching about the religious significance of the state, which the Church empowers, not to build the Kingdom of God upon the earth, but rather to restrain the kingdom of the devil, by force to stop the world from the ultimate catastrophe. The uniting of Orthodoxy with state absolutism came about on the soil of a non-belief in the Divineness of the earth, in the earthly future of mankind; Orthodoxy gave away the earth into the hands of the state because of its own non-belief in man and mankind, because of its nihilistic attitude towards the world. Orthodoxy does not believe in the religious ordering of human life upon the earth, and it compensates for its own hopeless pessimism by a call for the forceful ordering of it by state authority.[3]

State absolutism is the teaching of Orthodoxy about this, how to arrange the earth, how to hold back the victorious course of evil in the world. Russian absolutism they call theocratic, but this is not very precise; the blessing of absolutism by Orthodoxy is the result of the non-belief of the Orthodox Church in the possibility of theocracy upon the earth, nor the Kingdom of God, nor the Truth of God upon the earth. Since God's Truth is not for the earth, but for Heaven, then upon the earth let it be to the state might by force to hold back

---

[3] Here my basically accurate thought is not altogether accurate and is too exaggeratedly expressed. The image alone of St. Seraphim of Sarov introduces the corrective to my formulation.

mankind from evil, -- this is the gist of the Orthodox teaching about absolute monarchy.

Non-belief in the objective power of good upon the earth, non-belief in the meaning of world history, in the non-mediated might of God Himself within the earthly community, -- this non-belief is also the basis of state positivism, the apotheosis of state authority. Catholicism likewise did not believe in the Divineness of mankind, in the might Divine within earthly human history, and it created a teaching about the arrangement of the earth under the assist of Papism. Papocaesarism and Caesaropapism, the Pope, the Vicar of Christ, and the Byzantine emperor, the Vicar of Christ, -- alike they grew out of an unreligious, atheistic attitude towards earthly mankind, which cleaves to non-belief in God-manhood and in the God-manness of historical fates, in a non-belief in this, that Christ Himself wilt reign upon the earth (Chiliasm).

These -- are the two pseudotheocratic currents in world history, alike opposed to true theocracy, hostile to faith in the reign of God Himself upon the earth. In the coming true theocracy Christ will tend not to have a vicar-substitute, He Himself will rule the world, His truth will reign sovereign; Godless mankind, recognising as worthwhile only forceful restraint, will become a free God-manhood.

The nihilistic side of official Christianity was clearly bespoken in Pobedonostsev. Both in theory and in practise, he was perhaps a most typical representative of the idea of pseudo-theocratic absolutism, of an Orthodox Christian non-belief in the possibility of good upon the earth. In Pobedonostsev there is, as it were, a finishing-off of the historico-fatal process in Christianity, of the extinguishing of faith in the Providence of God, in God's guidance of the destinies of mankind. The suspicion and mistrust of Pobedonostsev regarding the world and man is not something merely personal, he has it here in common with the whole historical Orthodox life-sense, in common the seeing only of evil in everything. For Pobedonostsev, as also for the official teaching of the Orthodox Church, everything in a fatal manner comes to ruin, to the triumph of evil; for Pobedonostsev, as in general also for Orthodoxy and official

Christianity, eschatology is something foreign, there are no great historical tasks, there remains no place for historical perspectives, there is no meaning in the process of history, there is no awaited religious triumph in the end time, the victory of Christ upon the earth. Pobedonostsev has an hatred for life, he does not see the Divine in the world, he does not sense the image of God in man, and terrible to say, he learned this from Orthodoxy, it was from the official Christianity that he garnered his nihilism. This is something to ponder. I do not think, that with Pobedonostsev there was a vivid feel for Christ, he was infinitely remote from Christ, in his heart he did not know Christ; but the feel of Christianity, a closeness to the Church, a sincere attachment to its spirit was tremendous in him. Pobedonostsev -- was of a tragic type, for this was one of those, in which Christianity has killed Christ, one for whom the Church has shut off God. Christ rendered God infinitely close to man, He filiated mankind into being sons of the Heavenly Father; the spirit of Pobedonostsev makes God infinitely remote for man, it recasts the son into a slave. An emissary from the state to watch out for the Church, for long years guiding the Russian state in the name of the Church, a bureaucrat in Church and a theocrat in state matters, a man of might, dreaming about Heaven and along the way having gained utmost power upon the earth, -- he was a living corpse. In his veins flowed not blood, but some other deadly fluid, and he did not believe that in other people there did flow blood, human blood he did not value. The body of Pobedonostsev was terrifying in its morbidity, its being like parchment, and one could barely believe that it might resurrect, since resurrection was foreign to this man.

Pobedonostsev -- was the enemy of everything taken to wing, of everything taken to flight, of everything fully alive, instead he shoves man down to the hated earth. He is a worshipper of simplicity, he fears complexity, he preaches humble satisfaction through small deeds. Pobedonostsev is for order first of all and always and in everything, he fears the irrational and the problematic, he is in his manner a positivist and utilitarian, he believes only in impersonal institutions. Servility and groveling are characteristic of the official

Christianity, they are sanctioned by our local Church, while at the same time condemning boldness and bravery, the impulses afar and ascent higher.

Why does Pobedonostsev, a sceptic in everything, so believe in the state, in its goodly nature? Only the state power seemed to Pobedonostsev fine and good, the sole bright spot on the earth, and here his scepticism halts short. This is understandable. Pobedonostsev saw the whole task on earth to consist only in this, to halt, to interrupt, to freeze down everything (in the expression of the reactionary genius K. Leont'ev), and of creative tasks there are none. Everything decays and decomposes on earth, but the state at its best and by its might is not subject to this process, it halts the decline and decay. For everything else -- non-belief, for the state -- faith. This faith in the benefit of state might, saving the world from evil, the fanatics for the state have accepted this irrationally, in vivid contradiction to the light of reason and conscience. We know only too well, that the state also is subject to decline and decay, and that power often renders itself evil and godless.

Pobedonostsev and the Church, in its historical finiteness, and in its blessing of absolutism as though they did not want truth and joy upon the earth, and instead they see the good in this, -- that the evil, contrary to Christianity, they wish as though to torment man with, so as to his soul. All this, however, is that theory and practice of the Grand Inquisitor, not believing in mankind, saving it mistrustfully and by force. The atheistic spirit of the Inquisitor moves within Pobedonostsev, and he, just like that terrible old man, he repudiates freedom of conscience, he fights temptation for the small things, he defends a religious utilitarianism. Not only is Christ clouded over by the Church, but the Church itself is imperceptibly transformed for Pobedonostsev into a means for state control; by a strange, but appropriate irony of fate, the bureaucrat and statesman within the Church is rendered in Pobedonostsev all the stronger a theocrat and heavenly dreamer in the state. I repeat, and I do not doubt, that Pobedonostsev was a religious man personally, that his spirit was nourished by the cult and the sacraments of the Orthodox Church, but for the world and for mankind there was nothing religious in him, only a desolation, filled with the spectre of state might. Pobedonostsev was far remote from the Slavophils, since unlike them he did not possess the wide historical perspectives, he shared not their earthly religious utopia, and foreign to him was any sense of a mission. Pobedonostsev is more Orthodox than the Slavophils, he understands better, that regarding questions about the earth, about mankind, about the world -- in Orthodoxy there is the desert place, and that from this Orthodoxy one does not derive a just community, an holy corporeality. The ideal of Orthodox sanctity -- is in the withdrawal from the world, monasticism, the hermit-anchorite, but since the delimited ideal of sanctity as given is attainable but by few, there then remains the compromise with the world, the expression of its sinfulness and depravity -- the state, limited in nothing, coercive, as though demonstrating the impossibility of a religious sociality.

For Pobedonostsev there is no God-manhood, just as for him there is no historical Orthodoxy, for him there is only the inhuman God and the godless man, and for him Christ did not unite man with God. In God there is nothing of the human, in man -- there is nothing of the Divine, of the Divine-human body, containing all the fullness of life, it is not and will not be upon the earth -- all these negations are very characteristic for the historical Church, for the old religious consciousness. The truth of humanism is discovered in the secular culture, outside of religion and as it were contrary to Christianity, but ultimately this is the truth of Christ, the truth of the God-Man. The Kingdom of God upon earth is dreamy nonsense for people on the outside of a religious consciousness, and only a new religious revelation can bring to light both the truth of the dream, and its ruinous falsehood. To transform the revealed truth about the God-Man into the as yet unrevealed truth about a God-Mankind -- here is the universal religious task, before which stands the contemporary world at the door aknocking.

That, for which Pobedonostsev lived, what he loved, what he supported in idea, now has come undone, the whole system has collapsed, and not a stone upon a stone remains. And to some it would seem, that the quite totally outdated Orthodox Church is dying and decaying, that Orthodox Christianity has ceased to be a power in this world, since it was against this world. The monstrous hysterics of priestmonk Iliodor and others, certainly, is a symptom of decay, and in it there is nothing organic. But the gates of Hell will not prevail against the Church in its holiness. The death of Pobedonostsev is significant only in that it coincides with the death of nihilism on religious soil, with the death of the spirit of death. This nihilism has not vanished completely. There remain the "Iliodors", and periodically there will arrange pogroms of culture, but the strong, the predominative sacramental nihilism defining the course of history this will no longer be, and already is not.

The new religious consciousness rises up against the nihilistic attitude towards the world and mankind. If a religious rebirth be possible, only then on this soil will there be the revealing of the religious meaning of secular culture and earthly liberation, the revealing of the truth about mankind. For the new religious consciousness the declaration of the will of God is together with this a declaration of the rights of man, a revealing of the Divine within mankind. We believe in the objective, the cosmic might of the truth of God, in the possibility according to God to guide the earthly destiny of mankind. This will be the victory of the true theocracy, whether over a false democratism, -- the apotheosis of the quantitative collectivity of human wills, or so also over the false theocraticism, -- all that apotheosis of the human will within Caesaropapism or Papocaesarism. Christ cannot have human vicarage in the person of the tsar or high-priest. He -- is Himself the Tsar and High-Priest, and He will reign in the world. "Thy Kingdom come, Thy Will be done on earth, as it is in Heaven".

THE QUESTION CONCERNING THE RELATIONSHIP OF CHRISTIANITY TO THE SOCIETAL MOVEMENT [1]

In the No. 18 issue of "Vek" I read through the D. V. Philosophov article, "The Church and Revolution", and then the reply of V. Sventsitsky, "Concerning the New Religious Consciousness", and these articles so roused me, that I decided to enter the fray, the fulsome dispute, inherent to out religious ferment. There have been raised questions both great and vexing, barely finding explanation, and with religious experiences all still not credible. Neither Philosophov nor Sventsitsky have proven satisfactory for me, though I evidently am more of like mind with the former, than with the latter. The frame of mind within both articles seems to me non-religious, moreso revolutionary than religious, moreso human than of God. I speak only about the articles here, not the people.

What is *Orthodoxy*? This is the basic question, about which the discussion only involves, but between them neither Philosophov, who assaults Orthodoxy, nor Sventsitsky, in defending Orthodoxy, attempt even to explain, -- *what* for them is Orthodoxy. Under "Orthodoxy" might be understood the Universal Church, but there might be understood also the historical local Church, there might be understood the fullness of religious truth, but it might be -- also only a portion of revealed truth, there might be termed "Orthodox" all that is genuine and right in the Christian religion, but there might also be termed thus the historical deviations and falsehood. I would like, finally, for someone to say clearly and authoritatively, what actually is the Orthodox Church, all across the board, whether an object of veneration or an object for condemnation. What sort of inalienable marks are there that substantially belong to Orthodoxy, and what can

[1] Published in "Vek", 24 June 1907.

be subjoined or taken off from it without alteration of its essence? How long with impunity can Orthodoxy be called either that, whatever pleases thee, or that, whatever that displeases? Looking here at Catholicism, there is a sense of solidity and clarity of features, not permitting of doubt. The "Brotherhood of Zealots for Churchly Renewal" and the more radical "Christian Union" reckon it possible to remove from the historical body of the Orthodox Church whole series of signs, to cast away a whole series of attributes on the basis, that these do not involve the essence of Orthodoxy, not about the mystical body of the Church, but rather about historical accretions, about human searchings and deviations. Some prove to be moderates on the cleansing of Orthodoxy, while others are more radical, but both the moderates and the radicals alike continue to term themself "Orthodox". The MostHoly Synod is not an inward mark of the Orthodox Church, but rather an impaired outgrowth, autocracy does not have any sort of inward connection with Orthodoxy, the historical organisation of the Church does not derive from Orthodox mysticism, and with Orthodoxy can be united progressiveness, a love for the sciences and the arts, and one can be a Cadet [i.e. Constitutional-Democrat party], a worker or populist sort of socialist, regarding monasticism a mistake etc etc. Contemporary reformers and renewalists find it possible to remove from Orthodoxy all the aspects unacceptable to them and leave only that, what pleases them, and equally alike to subjoin and enrich Orthodoxy with the comforts won by progress.

Sventsitsky goes so far, that there remains in Orthodoxy only the sacraments alone, everything else he refuses. But I would ask Sventsitsky, the most revolutionary minded reformer: is there for him an Orthodox fullness of religious truth, a fullness of Revelation, does it include for him in Orthodoxy everything Divine, revealed to mankind, everything, that God in His providential plan had to reveal to mankind for its return to His bosom, for the salvation of the world? Sventsitsky regards only the sacraments as genuinely of God in the Orthodox Church, everything else he regards as human, an accretion, false, even diabolical and of the Anti-Christ. And I would ask Sventsitsky further: what sort of source does he draw upon as a criterion of judgement over the Orthodox Church, over the whole of Christianity within history, for a [Last-Judgement sort of] separating within it of the right from the left? The sacraments alone, taken abstractly from the whole plenitude of religious truth and religious existence, still cannot per se provide this criterion. In the sacraments of the Orthodox Church tend to partake those also who are reactionaries, and the indifferent, and those confessing a liberal "semi-truth". I am afraid, I am very afraid, that Sventsitsky has taken his criterion for passing judgement upon Orthodoxy, for the casting out from it and the subjoining to it, not from a religious source, but from a source mundane and secular, from the truths of revolution, and not from religion, from the truths of the Social-Revolutionaries and the Social-Democrats, from the revelations of human progress, and not from God. I do not intend by this to cast a shadow of suspicion upon the religiosity of Sventsitsky, God spare me, I point only to the difficulty of the question, to the unclearness of the setting of this question with Sventsitsky, on the impossibility for him to hold on to Orthodoxy. Sventsitsky, just like Philosophov, inevitably flounders on the question: ought it to be expected, that God will still reveal something to mankind for the completion of the world process of salvation, for the realisation of the promises and prophecies of the Kingdom of God, does there continue the cosmic religious process of the influence of God upon mankind, or is the religious process of revelation already completed and therein remain only its human assimilation, with the spreading and supplementation of truth ultimately already revealed? Least of all should I want to pass myself off as a man, to whom there has been revealed that which is unknown to others, but I believe, that the settings of this question are apparent to me, and not only to me, but to all those who go in search for "the new religious consciousness".

I put to Philosophov the same question concerning Orthodoxy. Just what is Orthodoxy for Philosophov? Falsehood, a misunderstanding or an incomplete truth? Does Philosophov acknowledge any sort of sanctity in the Orthodox Church? If

Orthodoxy in all its senses is a lie, a deviation, a misunderstanding, if there be no sanctity, then the religious history of the world is bereft of all meaning, there is broken asunder every religious thread, there is lost faith in the Providence of God. Then there is nothing for us to continue on with in the world, we -- are then but beggars, not having received any sort of inheritance, just like the proletariat, just like the irreligious revolutionary apostates. If with Sventsitsky it is unclear what metaphysically is insufficient for Orthodoxy, then with Philosophov it is unclear, what still metaphysically there is in Orthodoxy. It is evident to all, that Philosophov looks upon autocracy as a terrible evil, as something diabolical, whereas he looks upon revolution as something good, as something divine. According to his scheme of things, Orthodoxy gives blessing to absolutism, is inseparably connected with it, and it condemns revolution, and is altogether disjunctive with it. But for me there is a misunderstanding here: if within Orthodoxy there is though but some portion of truth, though but a spark of the Divine, though but some bit of sanctity, then how can this truth, this Divine, this sanctity be connected with such a diabolical evil, as absolute power, how can it justify and sanctify the state -- the kingdom of this world? With Philosophov it remains in general unclear, why the world-denying, ascetic metaphysics of Orthodoxy organically and mystically should include in itself such a fierce and insane world-order, so esteem the world, that it should organise and defend an autocratic state, that it should want such a "kingdom"? It would indeed seem, that an ascetic metaphysics, in its practice clearly expressed in hermitism and monasticism, at present in decline, but formerly glorious, always anarchistic in relation to the world and its kingdoms, -- it would seem that it bears no sort of passions, connected with the earth. But here suddenly is brought up the priestmonk Iliodor [Trufanov], the "Union of the Russian People", etc etc. All this breathes forth with earthly, with worldly passions, everything is ludicrously attached to a "kingdom", altogether nowise ascetic. But indeed the Eastern Christian mysticism, which is most authentic and universal in Orthodoxy, has bequeathed something altogether different:

passionlessness in regard to the world, the theosis-deification of man by way of an inward acceptance within himself of Christ and a definitive withdrawal from the world and its prince, amidst union with God and bliss within God, and not in the worldly state. Or is all this tied up with a fatal misunderstanding and blind chance? But indeed in world history, full of religious meaning, there cannot have played such a role of misunderstanding and blind chance.

It seems to me, that Philosophov has provided an unclear and dangerous formula, as regards its consequences, for that which is correct within the basis of his thoughts. Orthodoxy has grown up psychologically and historically together with an absolute state, whereby the Orthodox sense of social community -- is reactionary, and this -- is an empirical fact, demanding an investigation. I assent, that Orthodoxy is not connected with absolutism mystically, that this very idea of a connection, put forward by reactionaries and revolutionaries alike, is absolutely absurd, since from the Orthodox metaphysics it is inwardly and organically impossible to specifically derive tsardom, or any other sort of state for that matter. That which in Orthodoxy is authentically Divine, holy, and is so indeed, has then no sort of connection with absolutism, nor with reaction just as not with revolution, nor in general with any sort of societal community, nor with anything temporal. The metaphysics of Orthodoxy does not contain per se *any sort* of a binding teaching concerning societal community, it is impossible, absolutely impossible to deduce from it any sort of state (mystically impossible namely, but historically everything is possible, in it there is not revealed as yet the full truth concerning mankind and its earthly fate, in it there is still not a positive religious anthropology. And thus so it ought to be in an ascetical religious metaphysics, foreordained to orient man towards the heavens, turning him away from the world full of its sinfulness, to teach man to conquer the order of nature, in which reigns the law of corruption and decay. Orthodoxy has preserved the Divine truth in the person of its saints and ascetics, but it cannot direct the historical fate of mankind towards a sacred societal order, towards God-manhood, it has still not known the call for this.

The historical church, not having realised in itself the teaching about a righteous society, has fatefully adapted itself to a pagan society, having united itself with the traditions of a pagan realm. Every state power and every state form is of a non-Orthodox Christian origin, all are purely pagan and pre-Christian in origin. A coercive state authority acts thus, as though Christ had never appeared in the world, its foundations are lodged in that God-apostacy, which led to the primieval chaos; against this chaos the pagans were helpless, mankind struggled with the bloody task to organise itself into a state. The absolute state, whether Russian or any other, is a pagan idea and possesses a pagan and pre-Christian origin, an unlimited and despotic power afraid of nothing -- this is a legacy of the primieval savagery and chaos. In vain and without success in the formulation of his scheme does Philosophov attempt to give all this a tone of religious justification. Historical Orthodoxy came to be united with a pagan state, with a non-Christian and anti-Christian imperialism only because, that in its metaphysics it contained no sort of definitive societal ideal, no sort of historical perspectives, no sorts of expected truth upon earth. This is a connection purely negative, and not positive; Caesaropapism is an human temptation, the temptation of a mankind, not yet having accepted Christ within itself and therefore seeking for external props, and not the especial metaphysics of Orthodoxy. Sventsitsky is correct, when he says, that herein act "powers, contrary to Christ". Papocaesarism and Caesaropapism -- are two great temptations within Christian history, two forms of concession to the prince of this world, the hypnotic effort from the lustre of his realm. Orthodoxy is an uncompleted truth, and it is completed with falsehood, as long as there ensues not the day of God's completion; in it there is not a religious anthropology, and hence there has remained an empty spot, seized upon by the prince of this world. The Orthodox princes of the Church and the laity can just as much as they like religiously justify absolutism, but this will still be a purely human opinion and human justification, whereas Orthodoxy itself is unable religiously to give justification whether it be to absolute power, or to revolution, or to whatever towards the earth might be oriented as a positive societal construct. There was not discussion on this at the OEcumenical Councils.

Catholicism with its Papocaesarism, with its materially tangible authority -- was far greater an historical pitfall, far more terrible a temptation. At the same time while Eastern Christian mysticism preserved the genuinely Divine, -- though also still it did not include in itself a full sense of the human, Catholicism lost a connection with the Divine, in it tended to predominate the human aspect, reflecting a false anthropology, a false theocratic social community, the temptation of the prince of this world, having assumed religious a guise. Papocaesarism is characteristic to the metaphysics of Catholicism, insofar as it is false, whereas the incomplete truth of Orthodoxy cannot however sanctify any sort of evil, whether it be of Papocaesarism, or of Caesaropapism.

The frame of reference in the articles of Philosophov and Sventsitsky does not seem religious to me, since they make quite abusive use of arguments, borrowed from considerations of revolution and progress. One might tend to think, that revolution and progressiveness are dearer to them than is religion, that the human as it were should supplant the Divine. The religious man ought not to assault Orthodoxy or defend Orthodoxy per motives non-religious, and "worldly", almost utilitarianly so. It is impossible to posit the sanctity of Orthodoxy as dependent upon whether it justifies either autocracy or revolution. It is important to decide the question, whether the truth of Orthodoxy be also the fullness of truth, whereas in contrast autocracy, reaction, progressiveness, revolution, everything political and everything human and earthly should possess but a subordinate significance, a relative and conditional value, all which should be humbled before the holy and Divine. In Sventsitsky there is too much the sense of the psychology of the Social-Revolutionaries or the Social-Democrats, of the unique emotional composite of the Russian radical intelligentsia; in his tone is sensed moreso the revolutionary fanaticism and demonism in the spirit of Ibsen's "Brand", than there is of Christian love and religious humility.

In Philosophov there is too noticeable an intent to subordinate religion to the societal question, to religiously justify revolution, to revalue religion in regard to the criteria of secular culture. Both are tempted by revolution as a fact, both desire, that religion should serve in the grandiose historical fracturing. But religion cannot serve whether it be revolution, or reaction, or progress, or the despotic state; both revolution, and the state power ought to be humbled before the sanctity of religion. God preserve us from a politicising religiosity and from a religious politicism; the terrible experience of Catholicism ought to teach us much. We should sooner want to be neo-Orthodox, than neo-Catholics, to dedicate our will to God, than falsely assert the human will.

The revolutionary struggle against absolutism is to a remarkable degree outmoded, has become an anachronism, since after the halfways played-out revolution we have entered into a period of quite pitiful a constitutional monarchy; earlier was the proper time to think about the religious lie of absolutism. But the most important thing of all to realise is this, that the struggle between revolution and absolute power, between progress and reaction is the clash of two self-asserting human wills; both sides act in their own name, rather than God, they want everything for themself, to enrich themself. At the basis of the Russian absolute state rests a God-apostacy, human self-assertion, and the selfsame self-assertion lies at the basis of the Russian revolution. Christians (all, be they "old" or "new" alike) can the same as little be Social-Revolutionaries or Social-Democrats, as they can members of the "Union of Russian People" or Oktobrists, since they cannot justify terror and class hatred, cannot by force exert social truth. Religious radicalism is altogether just what political radicalism is, and it would be well for Sventsitsky and Philosophov to be mindful of this. political excitement quite often becomes gripping and demonically obsessive and it has little in common with inspiration. Just like the reactionary, so also the revolutionary passions in fatal a manner pass over into demonism, into a mad capricious self-assertion, into human self-conceit. Revolutionism is as it were an extortion of absolute benefit by purely human and outward means, and it stands in a servile dependence upon violent reaction. "Cadetism" [Constitutional-Democrat party], despite its aspect of being spiritually bourgeois, in the sphere of mundane politics appears still the lesser evil. In "Cadetism" there is not such a self-conceit and self-assertion, there is not the beastliness of greedy will, this is moreso neutral and humanitarian a means; many of the Cadets understand, that the inner maturing is more important, more substantial, more radical than external turnabouts, though they lack for the actual creative ideas.

A religious movement, connected with the name of Christ, cannot simply stand either on the side of reaction, nor on the side of revolution, nor can it justify either the mono-cratic nor the people-cratic. The revolutionary consciousness can see true revolution only in the uniting of the human will with the will of God and ought to say *its own say*, not reactionary and not revolutionary, its own theocratic say. Religion is called to transform the struggle of self-asserting human wills into a struggle against every self-assertion and self-deification of the human will. "Thy will be done", not mine, not a limited human will, nor the will of one man of a social class or position, or even of the whole people, but Thy Divine and absolutely righteous will. This is the path in Christ, its beginning is already revealed to the world, but its end however is not yet clearly visible. And certainly priestmonk Iliodor [Trufanov], or archpriest [Ioann] Vostorgov are tempted the same by the prince of this world, and godlessly self-assertive the same, having a sick self-conceit the same, as do either the "Bolsheviks" or "maximalists". Iliodor clearly betrays Christ for the "world", heaven -- for the earth, his passions are not Orthodox-Christian, but rather worldly-pagan, in him stirs the chaos of the primieval savagery. What sort of Orthodox monk is Iliodor indeed! He is not a monk and he is not Orthodox, he is too immersed in the politics of the world order, in his obsession and demonic frenzy he is akin to the extreme revolutionaries. All the reactionary pogrommists, all the members of the "Union of Russian People" are as much in need of the immersion in Baptism, as are also the revolutionary maximalists. Social and political revolutionism is therefore already non-religious, since it denies the difficult and the long inner effort of victory over sin, with the willful refusal of self-assertion, and since there is in it too much self-conceit and self-smugness.

I am against the appearance of a new pseudo-theocracy, involving just as much the same human lust for power, as also the Catholic, a new self-assertion of the human will, though it be in Christian a guise. It mustneeds be remembered, that the essence of the religious life, connected with Christ, -- is in the voluntary renunciation of one's own will, of human volitional greed, of every will to power. "Thy will be done" -- in this and only in this is the essence of a theocratic societal order. With prayer is begun every religious life, and the prayerfulness, the inner uniting with God ought to be carried over also into societal life, onto the path of history. For the mystical act of self-renunciation, the voluntary forsaking of human self-assertion, from its own, and only from its own limited will is needed a tremendous power of will, non-volitional -- this is an higher form of volition, this passionlessness -- is an highest passion. Herein is ultimate freedom, the proper assertion of person (in God, in Whom is lodged the idea of my person, and not in the natural world, within the demonic chaos), is the authentic triumph of the rights of man. Theocracy can only be an ultimate devoting of oneself to the will of God, but I fear that with Philosophov and Sventsitsky theocracy would prove to be a new autocracy, a demonism of the will, an apotheosis of the human "we". There is too much the same feeling within it of that selfsame human will, which is there in the revolutionaries and the statists. Only after a religious act of self-denial, involving a mysteried conjoining with the will of God, a mystical victory (initially individual) over egoism and ambition, over the illusory self-affirmation, -- would there open up for us a religious anthropology, the truth about the Divine humanity -- God-manhood. It would become clear, that the human conceited opinion of self and self-deification serve to the destruction of *man*, since the authentic and absolute Man is only Christ -- the God-Man, and the authentic and absolute mankind can only be in God-manhood, in which is alive the Spirit-Comforter sent by Him. But according to the prophecies, a theocracy, in the worldly view, would be only an oasis, it cannot become an overall form of human life, since within time itself the prince of this world is victorious. The atheistic and anti-Christian governments will thus tend to persecute believers.

Philosophov and Sventsitsky ought to acknowledge, that for genuine revolutionaries and progressives, religion -- whether it be that Christianity old or new, Orthodox or of some third testament of the Holy Spirit, will always remain reactionary, since the hopes of the religiously Christian and the hopes of the revolutionary progressive are directly opposite. The revolutionary progressive hopes rest upon human self-assertion and self-deification, upon the expectation that with its self-deification mankind, having spurned God, will lead this world to an absolute perfection. This is an anti-Christian eschatology. In progress there is another side, there is a genuine truth, but hereupon religion ought to stand upon its own feet, to draw forth the criteria from its own unfathomably deep source, and not conform itself to the idol of progressiveness.

Revolutionary eras can assume a superficial approach to religion and by this they tend to distort the religious movement. A process transpires of adapting religion to the ends of the world process. in such epochs the social liberation movement sometimes assumes a religious form, and the religious movement enters in as a component part of the social movement. The same thing is happening also for us in Russia. and it seems to me, that equally alike, -- just as with the more moderate and to a significant degree the "Brotherhood of Zealots for Church Reform, so also the more radical "Christian Union of Struggle", cannot per se be called a religious movement, although the participants may be quite religious. This is one of the forms of the liberation movement and has its significance in the general course of the societal developement of Russia. Whether a priest be a Cadet, a populist socialist or an SR {Social-Revolutionary], it matters not. Philosophov is correct, when he proposes to concentrate on a religious metaphysics. I should say, that there mustneeds be found an inner and religious source, which would provide the religious movement the right to express *its own* say. It is impossible to find this source in a mechanical subjoining to revolution. They tend to forget, that the essence of religion -- is in a sacramental communion with God; the official Christianity has long since already forgotten about this, and we also tend to forget, caught up as we are in external events and facts.[2] The truly new, the religiously new, "history-surmounting" Christianity mustneeds anticipate an organic connection with the old sanctity, with that what already has been attained by religious experience, i.e. within the Church. The New Testament did not abolish the Old Testament, did not declare it false. So also the revolution of a Third Testament, towards which metaphysically the world is moving, can only be as a final fulfillment of the Testament of Christ. But those, who assert an incomplete truth in its exclusiveness, like the Old Testament sort keepers of law, impede the fulfillment of God's promises, they run contrary the prophecies.[3] Orthodoxy, an absolute Orthodoxy perfected on earth, has still not arrived. Its perfection will not be a Lutheran Reformation, but incomparably greater.

---

[2] Religious renewal can be accomplished only by inwardly-religious a pathway, and not externally-societal.

[3] Vl. Solov'ev says: "In the developement of religion the falsehood and error consist not in the supporting of whatever may have been from a particular stage of developement, but in the exclusive affirmation of one aspect of them and in the denial of all the others on account of and in the name of this one aspect. In other words, *the falsehood and error are manifest in the futile attempt to hold back and halt the religious process*" (italics mine). This is something students of Solov'ev should not hesitate to keep in mind.

THE DISPUTE OVER CHURCH AND STATE IN RUSSIA [1]

> *Woe unto the shepherds of Israel, who do feed themselves! Ought not the shepherds to feed the flock!...*
>
> *Here I am against the shepherds, and I shalt exact Mine sheep at their hands and give them no more to feed the sheep, and I shalt snatch Mine sheep from their jaws, and they will not feed upon them...*
>
> *For thus saith the Lord God: I shalt herewith search out Mine sheep and look upon them...*
>
> *I shalt feed My sheep and grant them rest...*
>
> Book of Prophet Ezekiel (34: 2-15)

There is many a corrupt lie in our life, but there is no greater lie, it would seem, than that, upon which is posited the relationship of church and state. There is no other area, in which insincerity, the conditional and extraneous considerations have to such a degree been elevated into a principle. A Christian state there never has been and never will be, but the state passes itself off as Christian, and Christianity is rendered an aspect of the state. Let them point out, where it is foretold, that the ruling power on earth should belong to the Christian faith, that the world should become subject to Christian rule? There exist prophecies, that the prince of this world will be victorious upon earth, and that believers, standing up on the side of the Lamb, will be persecuted. The victory of the prince of this world, true, will be religiously an illusion, but empirically all the more and more felt and noticed. There are no sort of religious justifications for

---

[1] Published in the anthology collection, "Questions of religion", 1908, written in 1907.

a forceful upholding of faith, for the coercing aspect would sooner serve to the confirming of non-belief.

All the experiences of the Christian community within history have been up to the present a compromise with paganism, in the West having assumed the form of Papocaesarism, and in the East -- of Caesaropapism. Thus in the West was created the pseudo-Christian society with the rule of the pope at the head, of the pope as the vicar of Christ upon earth, and in the Byzantine East a no less pseudo-Christian society with the rule of the tsar at the head, the tsar as vicar of Christ. But both in papism and tsarism, under the guise of Christianity, there alike has lived the pagan principle of power, pagan imperialism. The compromise of Christianity and paganism has had a providential mission within history. But Christianity has been transformed from persecuted into persecutor, Christians have ceased to be martyrs and have become martyrers. The lie and falsifications are bound up with the basis of the religious authority of papism and theocratic imperialism. We have but to call to mind the forgery, known under the name of the "Grant of Constantine". The Christian and theocratic state is however a lie, because Christian theocracy should be a kingdom of grace, but the state however is a kingdom of law, a pagan kingdom. Blessed Augustine provided the groundwork for medieval theology in a mixing up of law with grace. Mankind in the process of its self-awareness sensed the lie of the Christian state, the religious falsehood of an autocratic papacy and a theocratic autocracy, it noticed the switched substitute, which has been a great temptation within Christian history, and was one of the temptations by the devil, spurned by Christ in the wilderness. The Reformation, and later also the progressive falling away from Christianity and from religion in general, was the result of the pitfalls involved in the attempt to create a Christian state, to organise a religious ruling authority over the earth. This was a false, a counterfeit religious anthropology, and mankind, as it were temporarily left to its own devices, answered this lie and forgery with a secular and non-religious humanism. Humanism came to prevail over the inhuman and false theocracy, both the papist and the imperialist. In place of the human self-assertion and love for power, veiled over as Divine power and in the guise of religious authority, humanism began openly and honourably to affirm man and a purely human ruling power. And herein certainly the truth was on the side of humanism, but it was a relative and incomplete truth, for at present it has already transformed itself into a lie, into a new deception.

Unbelief has all more and more progressed, but the false connection of church with the state has as it were remained untouched, it has all more and more poisoned the wellspring of religious life. Society has been rendered atheistic, and an enormous portion of it does not even know, Who Christ was; in the soul of the people there has dimmed the sense of religious sanctity, and the conditional and coercive lie of the official state religion continues to corrupt human souls. Religion has become utilitarian a tool of the kingdom of this world. Then only is force applicable in matters of faith, when faith itself no longer exists, when religion is impotent, when the heart has deadened. Every forceful upholding of church and faith by the state power is the result of unbelief in the power of Christ. The faith of Christ will revive only then, when it is persecuted and it persecute not. Suspicious are those pages of Christian history, when Christianity attempted to become a compulsive earthly power, allured by the temptations of the devil. On the side of the persecuting and coercive has never been the Holy Spirit, but rather the spirit of the "Grand Inquisitor". In the constant confusing of the Holy Spirit with the spirit of the Inquisitor, of free effort with compulsion -- is a source of horror within religious history. Christ brought into the world freedom, and not coercion, and the New Testament of man with God was a testament of love. The redemption of the world was a renewal of human nature, with a mystical act of returning to man the freedom, lost in the fall into sin. Christ freed the world from the slavery of the devil's chains, He affirmed in the world the cosmic possibility of salvation for mankind, and has become the path of salvation. Christ did not appear in the image of tsar and sovereign, He was abased and crucified, and empirically as it were defeated by the evil of this world. And within Christian history there was not apparent the miraculous might of Christ, His testament of love endured blow after blow, failure after failure. Where is the power and the glory of the Gospel kingdom? In what is the meaning of this powerless Kingdom of Christ upon the earth, why do the miracles not reveal to mankind, that Christ -- is the sole Tsar and Sovereign? Why did the Son of God appear to the world in the image of the Crucified One, lacerated by the worldly power? The "Grand Inquisitor" understood the religious meaning of the apparent powerlessness of Christ in the world, when he said: "Thou dost rely upon the free love of man, so that he should freely follow after Thee, entranced and captivated by Thee". The Inquisitor was an enemy of freedom and therefore he could not but be an enemy of Christ. The historical church, having spurned freedom of conscience, being saved by force, by Caesar passing himself off as God, and to God -- the things that are of Caesar; and a church, having become official and part of the state, is infected by the spirit of the Inquisitor, therein committing blasphemy against the Holy Spirit. The reigning might of Christ over the world will appear only in a theocracy, in a kingdom not of this world within this world (a thousand years kingdom), in a miraculous revoking of the order of nature, of the kingdoms of the prince of this world. The Coming Christ will come in power and in glory, but those only will enter into His Kingdom, who freely have loved the Crucified One, those who have looked upon the lacerated and humiliated -- God, and have believed without miraculous force.

The persecution by the government of priests, thirsting for religious renewal, the disdain of society towards religious searchings -- is not this a symptom of an incipient religious renewal? Has there not already happened before our eyes the separation of God from Caesar?

The historical drama of the Christian Church consists in this, that the Church was not of earth, it did not include within itself a religious truth concerning the earthly community and the earthly fate of mankind, but in its empirical relations to the earth it became too earthly, it fell under the power of the prince of this world. In Catholicism, the world-denial of the Church was transformed into a world-enslavement, the Church ascetically denied everything worldly, in order to restore everything worldly, but subordinated already to its own power, subordinated, and not transfigured. The power of the Catholic Church tended not to be a Divine and supra-worldly power, but nonetheless human and worldly. Catholicism worked out a pseudo-religious teaching concerning man and mankind, and papism sought to organise mankind upon the earth. In Orthodoxy there tended to be an attitude of indifference towards the earth, and the disbelief in a possibility of truth on earth led to a pseudo-religious blessing of pagan-Tatar-Byzantine absolutism. The ascetic Orthodoxy began, why however so, to guard the pagan state, it supported the earthly instincts of self-preservation. In these antinomies of the Church, in these antitheses of an ascetic world-denial and the world-affirmation of the state there was a profound inner meaning. Then only would the Christian Church not be subject to the master of this world and not be historically compelled to accept the pagan laws of life, to not enter into compromise with the pagan deification of the state, if it had its own religious ideal of society, if there were included in it already the power to guide as Christian the fate of history. But the Christian societal ideal has still not been given, the Christian meaning of the history of human culture has still not been revealed. The way out from the crisis can only be in the uniting of Christianity together with a righteous humanism in the surmounting of inhuman gods and godless mankind, in the revealing of an authentic and fully religious anthropology, with the teaching about mankind as God-manhood, about man as in the image and likeness of God, absolutely realised in the God-Man [Christ]. The human element, in itself per se, affirmed naturally and abstracted from absolute being, -- is illusory, it leads to the semblance of being, to actual non-being. Only a mystically real reuniting of the human with the Divine leads to salvation and resurrection. This reuniting is accomplished individually in the God-Man, the New Adam, and it ought to be accomplished collectively in God-manhood, in the new society of God.

In Russia for us during the era of revolution, the falsehood of the old union of church and state has reached proportions unendurable for the conscience. Our revolution -- is worldly, it is non-religious and in much even anti-religious, but it has shaken to the very foundations the old lie of the "Christian state" and exposes the lawless connection of the Christian Church with the pagan state, it discloses the whole incompatibility of the law of Christ, which is not of this world, with the law of coercive force, which is of this world. Subjected to the liberative impetus of the revolution, the Church ought to posit the question concerning a Christian society, for even the world liberation movement tends to posit the question about a free church. Church and state would meet face to face, and then the masks would be torn off, and both sides would have to openly declare, by what sort of law they live, what they love more: Christ or the prince of this world, God or the godless elements of the world. The ruling power formerly veiled itself under a religious sanction, though not only did it not fulfill its religious vocation, but went directly against the Testaments of God; the ruling power hypocritically held forth with the view, that it upholds the faith, that it guards the Church, though the Church least of all has need of such an upholding, since it has been said, that "the gates of hell will not prevail against it". Our society is atheistic, it long ago fell away from the faith in Christ, but it is obliged to prevaricate, to pass itself off as Orthodox. Christianity has not been accepted by the world in genuine a manner, this acceptance too often has become superficially in word only and therefore already there cannot be an authentic Christian power in the world. The government itself has nothing in common with Christ, it confesses religion as a state condition and utility. The churchly hierarchy itself has clearly apostacised from Christ, since the hierarchical principle, the principle of an human love for power is put higher than God and His law. The bishops in their spirit are nowise distinct from governors and the directors of departments. The realm long since already has ceased being subject to the spiritual authority of the clergy and being guided by the religious inspiration of prophecy. The priesthood has been subordinated to the realm, and prophecy has completely dried up. In the official Church creative life has ceased, it does not as it were seek to fulfill its promise. The Synod, titled MostHoly, justifies everything, that makes for power in its name, and it condemns everything, that for its power is useless; as such, it cannot possess any sort of spiritual authority, it evokes only disdain for it. We are mindful of the shameful page in the history of our local Church, or more correctly, the activity of the churchly hierarchy: the 9th of January and the Synodal missive. The speaking of the hierarchs of the Russian Church in defense of the death penalty will remain forever shameful.

Long since already there has been talk about the Church Sobor-Council, and there is hope, that the Sobor will revitalise the deadened religious life, that it will renew the Church. But the Sobor is a fiction in the interests of the princes of the Church, the faithful servants of the state. The state power and the churchly hierarchy alike act in the name of the human love for power, of self-interest. And it is not matters concerning Christ that interest the "christian" hierarchy, but rather matters of state and churchly rule of power, matters of the earthly kingdom, in which long already they do reign and which they have no wish to forsake. The religious consciousness of the progressive portion of the clergy and Orthodox laity, participating in the liberation movement, is such however, that it lacks the power to overcome the vexing inertia of the hierarchical principle, to spiritually alter matters of rule. For a religious victory over the principle of the official hierarchical authority, over the principle of human self-interest and self-deifying, there is needed not so much a religious reformation, as rather a religious revolution. Only the revealing of a genuine religious anthropology, of the religious teaching concerning man and mankind, will lead to a victory over a spiritual and state power which has betrayed its appointed destiny, over the lie of a "Christian" state. Then the liberation movement will cease to seem to the popular mind an apostacy from faith, and the realm will cease to be called Christian. Terrible as it is to say: "Christianity" in our time has been rendered into a conventional lie, shut off from the love of Christ, and in the name of Christ it has become necessary to surmount the official "Christianity", to conquer the human lie, the historical encrustation in the name of Divine truth. The pagan lifestyle and the human kingdom have been passed off by history as a Christian lifestyle, as the Kingdom of God, and all the revolutions of the world justly have doubted the veracity of the religious sanction for society, they caught sight of the fraud.[2] The Christian, the authentically Christian societal order, the Kingdom of God, theocracy, has not yet been seen by the world. Not the Western papism nor the Eastern Caesarism -- for this is the Kingdom of God; this Kingdom will be free, in this Kingdom it will be the power of God that rules the world, and not that of man. Mankind ought to free itself from the dubious and fraudulent theocracies, in order to prepare the soil for a true and authentic theocracy.

The ultimate separation of church and state ought to be the inevitable and universal result of the differentiating process in modern history. Both the sincere friends of the Church and its sincere enemies acknowledge this separation as something good, since neither sincere faith nor sincere unbelief can stand for the hypocritical and false connection, inherited from the old sins of papocaesarism and caesaropapism, rooted in ideas, long since already bereft of power. The connection of church with state at present has become contrary to nature, both from the churchly religious point of view and from the state point of view, the societally positivist perspective, since it is impossible to serve two gods. The Church as regards its religious essence cannot be transformed into a state, as it was in Catholicism, nor be subordinated to the state, as it was in Eastern Orthodoxy, in Byzantium and Russia; the Church itself can only become a realm, a kingdom not of this world yet in this world,

---

[2] The principle itself of the ruling power was religiously justified in the words of the Apostle Paul. The ruling power has its own mission, for as long as the world resides in evil, and thus it averts anarchistic disintegration, and struggles against chaos. But the Apostle Paul did not thereby construct a "Christian state", he but rather gave justification for the pagan ruling power as not in vain.

when within it will be a fullness of the revelation concerning the earthly fate of mankind. This will be a replacement of the state by the Church. The Church religiously will supplant the state, will surmount the necessity of a state for those, which dwell in it.[3] Christ in the Universal Church cannot have a vicar, whether in an human pope, or in an human tsar,[4] in it Christ Himself, is HighPriest and Tsar, and within God-manhood will dwell the Holy Spirit.[5]

At present, the completed and ultimate separation of church from state in France is a fact of prime importance not only social, but also religious; with this separation is connected the hope of a new religious consciousness.[6] Let there take shape an openly atheistic, anti-Christian state, let the master of this world openly, sincerely, respectfully be what he is, let his "kingdom" show itself and appear for what it is, and cease passing itself off as a Christian kingdom, cease hiding itself behind the skirts of religious authority. In the ancient East and in Rome both pagan and Rome Catholic, in Byzantium and in Russia the kingdom, the state always was and always is pagan, both in its origin and in its spirit, un-Christian in its

---

[3] But this will not abolish the necessity of the state for those, which have not accepted within themself the law of Christ. Forceful rule is necessary for the world. Governance -- is something mystical.

[4] This was acknowledged by Khomyakov, who defended religious freedom more strongly than anyone.

[5] I do not think to deny the historical only, but even the religious inevitability of the existence of the churchly hierarchy. Mankind can come to the universal priesthood only through the hierarchical priesthood. But even in a religiously justified hierarchy there is a pitfall on the side of regarding as Divine the human will of the hierarchs, substituting as a vicar of Christ.

[6] This does not hinder us from admitting, that in its actual methods of the separation there was much that was ugly and shameful.

tasks. Imperialism however in all its historical forms is contrary to the spirit of Christ, in it is one of the temptations, spurned by Christ.

The worldwide historical separation of church from state can become as it were a prelude of the coming, the final separation in the world of those, that will stand on the side of the Lamb, apart from those His enemies, the final division of good and evil. The Coming Christ, in accord with prophecies, will find in the world the Church, the Bride of Christ, having prepared itself for meeting its Bridegroom, and also the kingdom of the prince of this world, a godless society, a mankind regarding itself a god. The defenders of a state church and a Christian state cannot justify themself by the meaning of the prophecies, nor can they connect their idea with a religious meaning of history. These people gaze exclusively backward, they do not see anything ahead. In Russia the hypocritical connection of the state with the Church is sustained by a moribund imperialism in the name of self-preservation. Among the people lives a faith, that the kingdom upon earth ought to be of God, in it is still alive the hope, that the truth of Christ has power in the world, that this truth can be safe-guarded and realised. This chiliastic expectation as regards the incompleteness of the religious consciousness of Orthodoxy is bound up with an absolute power, representing the truth of Christ upon earth, in connection with a dream, and not with actuality.[7] The religious element of the people's soul, dark still in its awareness, is exploited by the worldly powers to their own benefit, and the churchly hierarchy in its human self-interest and love for power gives blessing to this exploitation. To remove from Russian absolutism its religious sanction -- means to undo its final prop in the consciousness of the people, means to expose not only the historical sins of the ruling powers, but also the historical sins of the churchly hierarchy, the human, its quite human lie. A static Orthodoxy, taken within its historical limitedness, has not the ability to pronounce this

---

[7] The chiliastic expectation amidst the darkness of religious awareness likewise readily passes over among the people into a revolutionary opposite enthusiasm.

judgement upon the ruling powers, cannot separate itself from the state, and is too ingrown with the human kingdom, to lead the world to the Kingdom of God. But the official Orthodoxy got a jolt, and now a religious crisis is occurring in the depths of life, and the passage over to a new religious consciousness is inevitable. The revolution has produced a complete turnabout in the relations of church and state, but all the revolutionaries and secular liberators do not even suspect the depth of the Church problem, of all the importance of this problem for the fate of Russia. Do even the Church reformers, the priest-renewers and laity, returning to the faith of their fathers, suspect this? In Russia, the separation of the Church from the state cannot be that of a transforming of religion into a partial matter, this separation can be connected only with a religious rebirth, not a decline of faith. In the churchly revolution will spring forth a sprouting of theocracy.

I fear, that not only the liberator atheists, but also the liberator Christians, will account it not significant an occurrence. It would be absurd to presuppose, that in the societal sphere there has to occur a turnabout, while in the religious sphere everything can remain the same old way. On the basis of this reinvigoration of the old religiosity by a new and irreligious societal awareness, it would create a tragic aspect of impotence for our progressive clergy, a sense of hopelessness for our renewal movement, a spiritual incapacity and faintness of heart. It is indeed quite apparent for the spiritually perspicacious, that a societal-churchly turnabout, the liberation of the Church from the age-old and false connections with the pagan worldly state and from the grip of the human pseudo-hierarchism, resulting in the censure by the Church against the evil will of the ruling powers can be accomplished only by way of a religious turnabout, one not only societal. The best part of our clergy however are so powerless in the struggle with the state powers, with the Synod and the princes of the Church, since it has nothing religiously to oppose the old powers, since it stands with them on one and the same religious ground. Against Messrs. Vostorgov and Iliodor the progressive priests fight with secular a weapon -- humanism, liberalism, democratism etc., but a sufficiently powerful religious weapon they have not, since the black hundredists are just as Orthodox, as are the white hundredists of the Russian clergy. Only a new religious consciousness can provide a way out from the condition of incapacity and hopelessness, can conquer the unbearable dualism, since to the reactionary religious consciousness would be opposed a liberating religious consciousness, a vital religious fire. And only then will the religious consciousness be new, creative, liberative, when it includes within itself a religiously autonomous, and not worldly, ideal of society, i.e. the City of God. The new religious movement stands upon the path of the perception and construction of a theocracy, an authentic Kingdom of God upon earth, not the kingdom of a pope or some other man, but the Kingdom of Christ. The Church at this step of religious consciousness, which is called "Orthodox", cannot as yet reign in the world; it has been subordinated to the kingdoms of this world, since it has not had its own say about earthly truth. Here is why with the persecution of the priests, with the falsehood of the Synod, with the lie of a Christian state power it needs to be looked into from far deeper a point of view, than usually it is. There is posited a problem incomparably more profound, than that of a mere change in the organisation of the Church, a mere societal renovation. The clash of the finest priests versus the Synod is only a symptom of the beginning rupture of church and state, the clash of those thirsting for a renewal of religious life versus the hierarchy of the Church -- is a symptom of the collapse of a false hierarchic authority. But the ultimate liberation of the Church from the state and from human an hierarchy, such as passes itself off as Divine, can be brought to completion only by entrance into the Universal Church, supra-historical, not "Orthodox" and not "Catholic", or more accurately, genuinely Orthodox. In this religio-societal process will be perhaps many a step, where herein might be worked out a tactic of struggle, but the setting of the tasks ought to be radical. Upon the complex path of religious developement will perhaps be many a sobor-council, of greater or lesser significance, but only a new and authentic

Universal Sobor [OEcumenical Council], inspired by the Holy Spirit, will appease the thirst of those seeking the City of God, will remove the torment of religious revolutionaries, will halt the wrangling of the old and the new religious consciousness, will reconcile the historical faith-confessions in the plenitude of the supra-historical faith-confession, will work out the dogmatics concerning God-manhood as regards the earth. Religious life has been free and tragic, since there has not been on earth an absolute authority, there has not been a material point, in which there should be collectively incarnated the Spirit of Christ. The suffering experience of mankind will lead, certainly, to this incarnation, and the Church will become, certainly, Universal and mighty, and there will have transpired a miracle for faith.

It would be mistaken to think, that in Russia there can be a Reformation, similar to that of the Lutheran. The religious thirst already cannot be satisfied by Protestantism, and indeed Protestantism is foreign to the soul of the Russian people. In Protestantism there was a moment of great truth, of the religious affirmation of person and freedom of conscience, but in its ultimate developement Protestantism, which was a reaction against the falsehood in Catholicism, lead instead to rationalism, to the replacement of Christian mysticism by humanistic a morality, to the decay of the very idea of the Church. The role of Protestantism within history is fully played out, and in our era all the less can there be any expectation of the discovery of the Universal Church from the warmed-over ideas of the Lutheran Reformation. With us, there is perhaps a not-large Protestant-reformation sort of current, it already has begun in the rationalistic sects among the people, in a portion of the intelligentsia, those exposed to the influence of Kant and L. Tolstoy, and it can attract those of a rationalist mindset, and some sober progressive priests, but never will this current take hold universally with the people. The religious turnabout, which needs to carry a searching mankind out onto the path of the Universal Church, and which is ensuing in Russia, can only be mystical, and not rationalistic. This -- is a turnabout on cosmic a scale, within it is disclosed truth concerning mankind as the centre of the Divine Cosmos, and in it is opened up the mystery of creation. Dostoevsky was for us a prophet of this turnabout. All the rivulets stream together into a mighty religious torrent, a torrent universal, but it is a bad thing, when the rivulet passes itself off as already the wide ocean, and in this is the danger of sectarianism. We wish most of all for a Russian religious ferment, very diverse in its appearances, of *universal a consciousness*, a fullness of the religious consciousness, since only in this full, universal consciousness will there ultimately be decided the question concerning the relationship of the Church to the state, a most tormenting question of human existence. The false connection of church and state, instead of uniting heaven and earth, ultimately has made a rift between them, and to transcend their ultimate rift with this old connection is possible only in the name of theocracy.

CHRIST AND THE WORLD [1]

(Reply to V. V. Rozanov)

V. Rozanov is one of the greatest Russian prose writers, a genuine magician with the word. V. V. Rozanov frightens Christians, both the old, and the new. They are embarrassed to have to ward off his blows, they consider him a very dangerous opponent of Christ, as though Christ could have dangerous opponents, as though the deed of Christ could be struck undeflectable blows. And Rozanov is an enemy not of Christianity only, not of "historical" Christianity, but first of all of Christ Himself. Christianity is not so repulsive for him, the whole of Christianity was a compromise with the "world", within Christianity has become pervasive a principle of household management, within the elements of Christianity has coalesced a familial way of life, and Christianity has created the strangely-felt way of life of the white clergy, for Christianity has decided to eat its "jam-preserves", to be fruitful with children, and it accepted within itself almost the whole "world". Christ for Rozanov was worse than Christianity: Christ was pitiless towards the world, Christ was frightening with His world-denial. The whole of Christianity however has been humanly complaisant, condescending towards the weak, and Christianity within history did not pose so sharply the dilemma: "Christ" or "the world"; it adopted some from Christ and some from the world. And Rozanov is not so altogether hostile to the Christian way of life. To much of this way of life he is attached, his unctuous love for family grew out of this lifestyle. Rozanov is an enemy of

---

[1] A formal Paper, read at the 12 December 1907 session of the St. Peterburg "Religio-Philosophic Society". Published thereafter in "Russkaya mysl'" January 1908. (*Translator note*: text includes Berdyaev's 1944 revisions).

Christ, and only the absence of genuine bravery compels him to mask this hostility and lead into error good people, who continue to think, that Rozanov demands merely the readjustment of Christianity, that his aims are reformational, that he is prepared to accept Christianity, but with reservations, with theatrics and jam-jelly, with the pleasures of the world. The times are so gone to ruin, that Rozanov appears as a reformer of Christianity, when in fact he is a terrible and implacable foe of the faith of Christ, more terrible indeed than was Nietzsche. A brilliant and charming literary talent, with boldness and a perceived concreteness in the positing of questions, a strong mystical sense -- all this is impressive in Rozanov, and he almost hypnotises amidst the reading of his articles. But he is not so terrible a devil, as they point him out to be. A philosophic and religiously bright consciousness without especial effect might find a tangle in the very setting forth of Rozanov's theme, and this tangle is not by chance, not from some pervasive mental weakness of Rozanov, but rather a fatal tangle, ultimately in intent dispatched for ends such as Rozanov's.

The theme of Rozanov, and to a remarkable degree also of "Novyi Put'" ("The New Pathway"), and both the former and the current "Religio-Philosophic Gatherings"[2] -- was of Christ and the world, the relationship between Christ and the world. Rozanov with extraordinary talent and brilliance developed in his article, "Ob Iisuse Sladchaishem i o gor'kikh plodakh mira" ("On Jesus MostSweet and the Bitter Fruits of the World"), and it is this article chiefly that I shall address in the present reply. From God there is the child-Christ and the child-world. Rozanov sees an irreconcilable hostility between these two children of God. For whomever Jesus is the sweeter, for that one the world is rendered bitter. In Christ the world is embittered. Those, who have come to love Jesus, have lost their taste for the world, all the fruits of the world have become bitter out of the

---

[2] *Berdyaev's 1944 revision note*: The Peterburg Religio-Philosophic Gatherings of 1903-1904 were meetings of Russian writers, religious seekers, together with hierarchs of the Church.

sweetness of Jesus. All this was written with an amazing vividness, glaringly, boldly and at first impression dangerously. One mustneeds choose between Jesus and the world, between the two children of God. It is impossible to unite Jesus with the world, it is impossible to love them both at the same time, it is impossible to sense both the sweetness of Jesus and the sweetness of the world. The family, science, art, the joy of earthly life -- all these are bitter or tasteless for the one who has tasted of the heavenly sweetness of Jesus. In the marvelous expression of Rozanov, Christ -- is an one of a kind flower, and this means all the flowers of the world set in comparison with Him. In the "Imitation of Christ" is praised this sweetness of Jesus and the bitterness of all the fruits of the world. And in the "Confessions" of Blessed Augustine it is filled with a fondness for Christ and a dislike for the world. Rozanov himself does not like to dot the i, he is given to equivocation, and he never makes the decisive deductions, leaving it to the conjecture of the reader. But the dilemma is suchlike: if Christ is Divine, then the world is demonic, or if the world is divine, then Jesus is demonic. Rozanov is attached to the world with all his being, he loves in the world everything worldly, he feels the divineness of the world and the sweetness of its fruits. Jesus MostSweet became for him demonic, and the face of Christ -- darkened.

Rozanov's settings of the question produce a very strong impression, whereas all the expressions of the apologetes of Christianity are but insipid and weak. Rozanov speaks concretely and at first glance clearly, he provides a feeling for the question in all its acuteness, he stuns and hypnotises. He is crude, when he drags a monk into the "theater", but the monk actually is presented as hapless. The chatter of the official defenders of the Church is not convincing, and the impression remains with everyone, that Rozanov has proven, has graphically demonstrated the absolute opposition between Christ and the world, the absolute incongruity of the sweetness of Christ with the sweetness of the world. Christ for Rozanov is the spirit of non-being, the spirit of the diminishing of everything in the world, and Christianity -- is a religion of death, an apology for the sweetness of death. The religion of birth and life ought to declare irreconcilable war against Jesus MostSweet, as a poisoner of life, a spirit of non-being, the founder of the religion of death. Christ has hypnotised mankind, has inspired a dislike for being, a love for non-being. His religion has acknowledged as but solely beautiful -- dying and death, sorrow and suffering. Rozanov writes quite talentedly, he speaks very vividly, he says much that is accurate, but his very point of departure -- is false, and his very settings of the question -- are illusory and confused. *Rozanov -- is an ingenious philistine*, and his question ultimately is a philistine, bourgeois, everyday ordinary question, but formulated with brilliant talent. Rozanov also tends to strike hold with this, in that he bespeaks something close to the philistine heart, that the question about the sweet and the bitter fruits of the world grabs hold the attention with the bourgeois of this world, it throws into confusion the official Christianity, further still transported into philistinism. Rozanov's family, jelly-jam, theatres, pleasures and joy of the felicitous life are acceptable and close to every philistine realm, which sees in this also the essence of this "world" and it is "this world" which would as it were be saved from the hypnosis of Jesus MostSweet. For Rozanov, being is what is, and the "world" is the sweetness of the lived life. This is very deep, in this -- is power.

Rozanov suggests, that every philistine-fellow knows, that the "world" is suchlike, he sense it as the bearer of the joys of being, with the family, the sweets, the adornments of life, etc. The philistine-fellow knows, but the philosopher does not know. The question about the *world* is very unclear and undefined, and in this passing off of the unclear and undefined in place of the clear and defined, the passing off of the sought for in place of the found -- lies all the slyness of Rozanov and the empowerment of all his whole secrct. What is the suchlike world, and about what sort of world is it being spoken? What sort of content does Rozanov invest in the word "world", and is this world the aggregate of empirical appearances or of the positive fullness of being? Is the world everything of the given, a medley of the authentic with the illusionary, the good with the evil, or only the authentic, the good? If the question about the world be taken as applying to the aggregate of everything empirically given, in which the sweetness of jelly-jam occupies the same spot as would also the sweetness of the greatest of artistic works, then this question for us is almost not worth the interest. The eternal in the world and the perishable in the world cannot be taken in the same regard, and the very settings of the question about the world without any differentiation of values is impermissible. Such a world is a "world" in parentheses. Our factually given and investigated world is a medley of being and non-being, of actuality with the illusory, of eternity with the perishable. What sort of world is Rozanov fond of, what is it from the world he would affirm, in what sort would live? I am afraid, that Rozanov demands from religion a factual mishmash of the genuine and valuable, all mixed up with the false and worthless. But the religious is not a question about the world, rather it is the question about the authentic, the real world, about the fullness of being, about the values of the world, about the extra-temporal, the imperishable content of the world. Simply to affirm "this world" -- means to affirm the law of decay, of servile inevitability, of necessity and sickness, deformity and falsification. The world lies in evil, but the positive fullness of being is a supreme value and good, and the valued and joyful in the world is an actual being. Rozanov can only succeed in standing afront the evil of this world, to deny this evil he cannot, to confront the results of this evil is beyond his powers. From whence is death, at the same time hateful to Rozanov and to all of us, from whence hath death come into the world and wherefore been taken hold by it? Does Rozanov consent to acknowledge death as an essential part of this world, which he so loves and which he defends against Christ? Not from Christ hath death come into the world: Christ came to save from death, and not to bear death to the world.

Christ came to separate the genuine and the valuable in the world from the false and the worthless, the Divine from the diabolic. Christ -- is the Saviour of the genuine world, that which is authentic and of the fullness of being, the Divine cosmos, wounded by sin, and not the inauthentic world, not the chaos, not the kingdom of the prince of this world, not the non-being. Christ hath judged the perishable, the illusory and chaotic world: the Kingdom of Christ is not of this world, and Christ taught not to love this world, nor that which is of this world. But worldly factuality is neither of this world, nor of that world, but a medley, an admixture of that other world with this, the wounded and sickened creation, both being and non-being, both the valuable and the worthless. Christ had to have come, since that the old world, the sinful world fallen away from God, had rotted, rust undercut all the foundations of the world, and anguish encompassed the world. The old immanent feeling for life, so captivating for Rozanov in paganism and Judaism, was conjoined together with a transcendent feeling. A tragic experience thus transpired always at the threshold of every religious turnabout. The old world, left on its own, could not save from the perishing, within this world it had not the power to save from the power of the all-encompassing death. Self-deification is ruination, the theosis or making-Divine by the Son of God is salvation. Rozanov desires an immanent salvation through the world and he repudiates the transcendent salvation as non-being and death, he sense the divine within creation, but he is deaf and blind to the tragedy, bound up in the rift betwixt the creation and the Creator.

Rozanov's feeling for the world can be termed an *immanent pantheism*, in it is lodged a powerful primal-feeling of the divinity of worldly life, a non-mediated immediate joy of life, but very weak in it is the sense of the *transcendent*, quite foreign to him is a transcendent anguish and expectation of a transcendent exodus. Rozanovism is a peculiar mystical naturalism, the deifying of the natural mysteries of life. In the XX Century, during the sunset years of human history, Rozanov is living out the naturalistic phase of religious revelation, he thirsts for a world-wide historical childhood and naiveté, and he fails to notice the senility and decrepitude of this restoration of the first days of mankind. Rozanov's naturalistic pantheism is the senile lapsing into childhood with mankind. Only in deep old age can be remembered the days of childhood and youth, the relishing of past delights. And Rozanov, the mystic Rozanov, in whom there are ingenious insights, deifies the good and the joys of this life, he worships familial felicity, looking forward with a childlike enthusiasm to the sweetness of jelly-jam, and then imperceptibly taking a tumble over into an apology for his everyday ordinary aspect and philistinism. He identifies the world with the felicitous life of the natural familial sort. He wants as though ultimately to deify the life of the natural familial sort. But we have seen already, that this "world" so dear to Rozanov is all still subject to the law of decay, and Rozanov lacks the ability to repose such, as in death did Abraham, Isaac and Jacob, blessing their posterity, in him there is not such a strength of the impersonal, fine indeed only for that world epoch; even he does not consent to live but in his posterity, and he is deeply caught up in the final phases of the worldwide religious revelation, and his blood is infected with Jesus MostSweet. A restoration never transpires as it was intended to be restored.

And as fine as the religion of Babylon was in its time (but for its time it was a poor one, since then already there were higher forms of religion), after Christ and the whole experience of modern history the restoration of the Babylonian religion is folly or child's play. Historical science has sufficiently dissuaded us of the existence of a Golden Age, and the religious consciousness can see in the sweet remembrance of a Golden Age not some sort of earthly epoch in the past history of mankind, but rather a sense of its own extra-temporal and extra-worldly closeness to God, transgressed by sin. We have lost paradise, but this paradise was not Babylon, nor Judaism, nor paganism, nor overall any earthly past of mankind, as Rozanov is inclined to think, but rather the heavenly origin of mankind. Yet as we see, Rozanov is oriented not only backwards, he looks forward also and he conjoins with this the expectations of an earthly paradise in the future. Unexpectedly for him, he is prepared to give a mystical hue to the array of the Babylonian turret-tower, and he would justify the deification of the old natural world upon the social arrangements of the future. He imperceptibly approaches the pathos of positivism and greenly naive radicalism, and with rapid strides he gets almost to Pisarevism, but he remains an artist, not having been wrought an artisan.

Rozanov is a man *immersed in being*, in him there is an intense sense of a man immersed in life and with a very weak sense of person. Personal self-consciousness for Rozanov is almost entirely lacking, just as it tends to be lacking in modern man. Rozanov also therefore lacks the awareness of the tragedy of death, the tragedy of personal fate, the terror at the individual perishing. Rozanov has something in common with L. Tolstoy, in the feel for life, in them there is mutual aspect, in that they sense worldly life akin to the Old Testament manner. Just like Tolstoy, Rozanov facing the world unwraps "the child's diaper with its green and yellow" and with this diaper he wants to conquer death and personal tragedy. The "Kreutzer Sonata" was only a revenge side of this diaper. Both L. Tolstoy and Rozanov arrive at a reinforcing of the everydayness, at a philistinism inconsistent with their religious searchings. Rozanov decides thus the problem of death: there were two men, and between them were born eight children, two die, but in the eight there is a triumph and life is increased. Salvation then from death -- is in the shattering of each being into a multiplicity of pieces, in a bad infinity, and consolation for the person -- lies in the disintegration of the person. Rozanov opposes to death not eternal life, not resurrection, but rather birth, the arising of new and other lives, and so on without end, without exit. But this method of salvation from the tragedy of death is possible only for a being, which senses the reality of the race and does not sense the reality of the person. This consolation tends to delimit human reproduction on a par with cattle breeding.

In the Old Testament and aboriginally-pagan racial mindset, the person was obscured, hardly awake from the sleep, into which its sin had cast it. The whole of world history was a gradual awakening of the person, and in our much troubled and much complicated epoch the person has awakened with a shriek of terror and helplessness, torn away from its racial aspect and only now able to attach itself to something new. Rozanov pulls the person backwards towards the racial element and he wants to convince the world, that to return is possible, that it is necessary but to renounce Christ, to forget Christ, that Christ is the culprit behind the hypertrophy by the personal by means of sensing, that if Christ were not, there would not be the tragedy of death, it would not be felt so sickeningly and the terror of death and destruction come but from a glance at the diaper, soiled in green and yellow. The world for Rozanov is the race and a living for the race, whereas the person is somewhere on that other side of the world, with Christ. The feeling of the person and a consciousness of its tragic fate -- is transcendent, it goes beyond the borders of that which Rozanov terms the "world", and therefore so tragic and tormentive is its fate in this world.

But everything that has been of value, genuine within the history of the world, was *transcendent*, it was a thirst to go beyond the boundaries of this world, to break out from the restraining circle of immanence, it was an exit to another world, and the penetrating of another world into our world. The transcendent becomes immanent to the world -- here is in what lies the meaning of world culture. The whole of human creativity has been a troubling over the transcendent, over another world, and never has creativity been a reinforcing of the joys of the natural racial lifestyle, it was never an expression of the sufficiency of this life. Creativity has always been an expression of insufficiency, a mirroring of the torment of dissatisfaction with this life. It is not only art, philosophy, culture and all the creativity of culture which per se indicate the transcendent distress of mankind, but also love, sexual love, so very close and dear for Rozanov, standing at the centre of everything, -- this too has been a thirst for a transcendent egress, an unsettling desire to break free from the bounds of this world. Sexual love is already more, than this "world", it is already a dissatisfaction with this "world". And Rozanov himself acknowledges the transcendent character of sex.

To justify love, art, philosophy, all the creative impulses -- means also to reveal their transcendent character, to see in them the potential for an egress from this world. Family is still this world, it has delimited horizons, but love is already another world, it is an expanding of the horizons to infinity. Positivism is of this world, forever with delimited horizons, but metaphysics is of another world, it is remoteness. The immanent pantheism, towards which Rozanov gravitates, is likewise a poetised sort of pantheism, a peculiar perspective of a mystical positivism. The societal order of the human realm is of this world, and all this is a delimited horizon, but the vision of the unification of people within a Kingdom of God on earth is already of another world, the surmounting of every restriction. People love to talk about Greek culture and the affirmation of the world within it in contrast to a world negation within Christianity. But the greatest things in Greek culture -- were an egress from this world, a consciousness of the immediately obtaining world, it was already a path towards Christianity. The whole Medieval culture, rich with creativity, and full of beauty, was built upon a transcendent feeling. In this culture there was also love, with the cult of the Fair Lady, and art, and philosophy, and chivalry, and public festivity. Was all this, in light of Rozanov, an affirmation or a negation of the world? I include all these examples to effectively show all the shakiness of the settings about the "world". That "world", which Rozanov so frets about, does not at all exist.

To religiously justify history, culture, the flesh of the world -- does not mean to justify family, the racial lifestyle and "jelly-jam". It means rather to justify the transcendent thirst as regards an other world, *embodied* within world culture, to affirm in this world a thirst for an universal exodus forth from the natural order of nature, of evil and decay.[3] I am emboldened even to think, that between the world and the family, in the name of which first of all Rozanov rose up in

---

[3] It suffices but to read through Justin the Philosopher, Ireneius of Lyons, and other apologetes and teachers of the Church, in order to perceive, how inaccurate is that viewpoint, which sees within Christianity an hostility to the flesh of this world. Christianity in particular has defended the flesh of the world and the earth from the spiritising negation by Platonism, Gnosticism, etc.

revolt against Christ, there exists a deeply irremedial opposition. The family itself makes pretense to be the world and to live according to its own law, the family detaches man off from the world, not infrequently it deadens man for the world and for everything, that is created in the world. Between the world and the family there exists quite greater an antagonism, than between the world and Christ. It has already been sufficiently demonstrated and shown, that nothing so gives hindrance to an universal sense of world life and the worldly ends of history, as the fortress of the racial family. And not only between the family and the world does there exist an opposition, the opposition exists also between the family and love, in the family love all too often becomes buried away.

Every reinforced and delimited way of life is opposed to creativity, to the age-old antagonism with the universal and the worldwide. But Rozanov wants us to put the familial lifestyle before the universal, before the great world of God. The hostility of the racial lifestyle and the racial family to universal creative impulses does not require any especial proofs, the fact is all but evident. Here is why Rozanov's "world" presents itself to me as a fiction, which seems clearly discernable for the common everyday consciousness. This "world" is an hodgepodge of being with non-being, and the religiously important thing is not the question about the "world", but rather the question about worldwide historical creativity in this "world", that of *being*. And the immanent religion of this world is but an apotheosis of philistinism, one aspect of which Rozanov comes nigh to. This "world", taken in itself, is but only worthy of the fire, but in its history there is affirmed an other, a genuine world, in it there is a Divine-human connection, in it there are creative impulses towards the Divine cosmos, in it there is the universal path towards a new heaven and a new earth, in it there is deliverance from evil, and with these matters is connected the religious question about the affirmation of the world.

All more and more a degenerated monasticism denies not the world, -- this world via the smuggler's pathway penetrates into the monastic lifestyle, there is much of the jelly-jam in the monasteries and little of the Gospel "mourning with ashes", -- monasticism denies creativity, the penetration into this world of an other world, it denies the history of the deliverance from evil of this world. Monasticism has gotten mired down in this "world", it has sundered its connection with the ascetic Christian mysticism; furthermore, the official Christianity has already become transformed into the lifestyle, of which there is much that is dear to Rozanov's heart. But monasticism continues to deny the values of the world, it contemns creative impulses, it is hostile to deliverance from the powers of this world, it esteems the evil of the world and the justification of its existence. Monks, bishops, the princes of the Church, the historical masters over religion -- these usually are people of quite worldly a lifestyle, the established rulers of this world. We cannot believe, that these people are not of this world, and their seeming denial of the world is but one of the ruses of this "world". And we tend to rise up against the hierarchs of the Church, against the official Christianity, not in the name of the world, but in the name of an other world, in the name of creativity and freedom, in the name of the thirst to break forth from the bounds of this world, rather than to reinforce them. The worldwide historical significance of ascetic Christian mysticism -- is in a challenge to the whole natural order, a struggle against natural necessity, in the theosis-deification of human nature in union with Christ, in the victory over death. This asceticism of the Christian saints was not unintelligible or evil, it had a positive mission, it had cosmic consequences in the deed of the salvation of the world. But where now are the saints? Is it possible still in our time to speak about the existence of an ascetic mysticism? For us, the act of surmounting in Christian asceticism is not a denial of its great mission, it is not an acceptance of this world. The new religious consciousness affirms not this chaotic and servile world, but rather the cosmos, the sacred flesh of the world. The flesh of the world, that which ought to be sanctified, liberated and saved -- is transcendent, as much transcendent as also is spirit. This flesh is not material matter of this world, this flesh is manifest as a result of the victory over the burden and fetters of the material world. Chiliastic hopes towards the completion of history by a Kingdom of God upon earth, a sense-perceptible realm of Christ, is not the expectation of a kingdom of this world: chiliasm is not a kingdom of this world, but rather in this world. And with chiliasm is connected the world-historical resurrection of the flesh, a religious affirmation of the flesh of the world. What sort of flesh however is it that Rozanov loves, what sort of religion of the flesh does he preach?

The question about the origin and essence of evil for Rozanov is unresolved, and it is not even posited. Pantheism is always one-sided, it does not sense the tragedy of the world, enclosed in it is only part of the truth. If the world is so fine and divine, if in it itself there is an immanent justification, if there is unnecessary any sort of a transcendent egress from world history, then it is incomprehensible, from whence hath appeared the evil of this world and the terror of the here and now life. For Rozanov, evil is some sort of an unintelligible, an accident, a fatal mistake of history, going off on a false path. From whence is it that Christ appeared, from whence is the power, according to Rozanov, of His dark visage? Why does the religion of death have such an hypnotic hold over human hearts? Why does death mow down worldly life? Rozanov is unable to answer even one of these questions. He hides himself away from evil, within the joy of familial life, in the sweetness of being, and with jelly-jam he wants to sweeten the bitter pill of life. Rozanov cries out: I am fed up with tragedy, the sufferings have exhausted me, I want to hear nothing about death, I cannot take already the dark rays, I want the joys of life, I want only to accept the divine world. Overwhelmed by everything, all exhausted, there is nothing thou canst do, evil is actual, and not an hypnotic sleigh of hand. Sex, cries out Rozanov, -- here is salvation, here is the divine, here is the overcoming of death. Rozanov wants to set up sex in opposition to the Word. But sex is poisoned at its source, sex perishes and is subject to decay, sex is something dark, and only the Word can save him.

And if there be seen in Christ a dark principle of non-being, hostile to the divine world, then this is already a very profound failing of pantheism, this is a fracture, which pantheism cannot bear up under. But Rozanov is quite the mystic, he quite latches onto the Person of Christ, in order to explain rationalistically the mysterious might of this Person. Rozanov senses this irrational mystery. But the evil of the world -- is likewise an irrational mystery, and a pure pantheism comes to an halt before this mystery with a sense of helplessness and awkwardness. Rozanov says right out, that the religion of death has come from Christ. But let him also say right out, from whence the death has come, how can it be compatible with an immanently divine world.

The extolled "world" of Rozanov is a cemetery, in it everything is poisoned by a deadly venom. Rozanov wants in the cemetery to grow the flowers of divine life and to console himself with the fertility of the rotting corpses. Rozanov apotheosises the biological fact of birth, but the mystical enigma of life is contained not within the biological birth in time, it is connected with the mystery of death. Rozanov does not want as it were to see the *duality of human nature*, its belonging to *two worlds*, he closes his eyes to the opposition between the eternal impulses of man, between the potentiality of absolute life lodged within himself and the relativity of the here and now life of man, the limitedness of all here and now realisations. But religion does possess this metaphysical and anthropological taproot, within the duality of human nature there is rooted a religious thirst. The religion of Christ denies within this world its sense of limitation and servile bounds, denies it in the name of an absolute unlimitedness and freedom -- herein lies the meaning of the opposition. If Rozanov had a deep sense of person, a feeling for the tragic antinomy of each individual human being, he would then not have posed thus the dilemma: the "world" or Christ. Beforehand would have had to be posed the dilemma: *the world or the person*. In the "Rozanov world", the person perishes together with all its own absolute potentialities. But Christ has appeared: in Christ the person is saved and there is realised all its own absolute potentialities, its filiation-sonship to God, wherein it is called to participation to Divine Life. Christ also is in this world, in which is affirmed the being of the person in the Divine economia. And therefore the dilemma -- "Christ or the world" is stripped of all religious significance, or else comes to assume a meaning other than Rozanov's. True being is the person, and not the race, the true universal union of persons is the Divine-human Sobornost', and not impersonal nature. To affirm the fullness of being in the world -- means to affirm an other, an authentic world, and not the natural order. But Rozanov does not believe in the supra-natural, he brushes off every distinction between a mystical sensation and an empirical sensation (this also is an immanent pantheism), and therefore the religion of Christ presents itself to him as an illusionary comfort, and not a real egress. I propose for Rozanov one question, upon which everything depends. Was Christ resurrected, and what then becomes of this dilemma, -- the world or Christ, -- if Christ was resurrected? Believing in the reality of the Resurrection, would he have suggested, that the religion of Christ is a religion of death? But Rozanov, together with all the rationalists and positivists, is compelled to see in the Resurrection only an hoax, merely a myth, and for him in Christ it is death that conquers, and not life. Herein however the struggle of Rozanov with Christ ceases to be mystically terrible. It would be terrible, if that while believing in the reality of the Resurrection, he nonetheless had the wherewithal to demonstrate, that the religion of Christ is a religion of death. That "real" social reforms are by far more effective for life, than the "illusionary" Resurrection of Christ, -- we have heard this from all the positivists and we are not in the least afraid of this. Rozanov imperceptibly tumbles down the slippery slope towards a vulgar positivism, the adolescent fuzz on the chin forces its way through for him and the strange impression yields in him thc youthful attraction with radical social ideas. The things, that Rozanov now speaks about, are things usually talked about at an incomparably younger age. Soon he will outgrow the honeymoon period of his romance with positivism and socialism -- the consequent results of an irreligious European culture.

A former conservative, a reactionary almost, Rozanov, as a contributor to the *Russkii Vestnik* and the *Moskovskii Vedomosti*, has begun to flirt with revolutionary elements, and imperceptibly he has been reborn a radical. But his political uninformedness, I would say, ignorance almost, precludes Rozanov from getting a grasp on the existing political currents, he remains foreign to politics in the unique sense of the word. To the great chagrin of all those, who read this first-class writer, and hearken to his words, his physiognomy remains twofold, his radicalism seems wanting in seriousness, a caprice of his temperament. I think, that the attraction of Rozanov towards a social radicalism, his love for the "left" has deeper a root. Rozanov feels, that the workings of an immanent pantheism and a naturalistic mysticism can profit from the union of socialism with a degenerated religion, its union with the progressive social approach of this life. Socialism promises to enrich and to organise both the natural world and natural mankind. A pantheism of Rozanov's type could enrich and poetise the prosaic setting of the social order, could perhaps inspire joy for the material life. His immanentist attitude towards this world and the joys of this life and his hostility towards the transcendent set him at one with socialism and even with positivism. But the "left" are such bunglers, that they have no desire to make use of Rozanov, and Rozanov continues to endure no little abuse from them: Rozanov, certainly, always remains the mystic, in him too strong is the direct immediate feeling, and he would never consent to be shuffled off to the kitchen, because of his extreme talent his spunk would always be more powerful than his silly "leftwardness", his dilettante and trite radicalism. There is an authentic and deep radicalism, and the radicalism underlying Rozanov's setting forth of the question of sex and the flesh is quite more genuine, more sincere and remarkable, than his flirting with the "left".[4]

There are merits to Rozanov in his criticism of official Christianity and official churchliness which as such are tremendous, while by his themes he has done a service to the new religious

---

[4] What I wrote initially was more than two years ago. Rozanov has since then quite changed, having returned to his original settings. And subsequent years have seen from him a series of brilliant, religiously penetrating articles.

consciousness. With an unusual radicalism, he has set before the Christian consciousness the question about its attitude towards the life of the world and in particular towards the source of life -- towards sex. He has had a great influence upon Merezhkovsky and "Novyi Put'", and he has all but set the themes of the "Religio-Philosophic Gatherings". He has done much for the betterment of the position of those born out of wedlock. People are quite apprehensive of Rozanov, yet they are quite preoccupied with him, and his influence on the one hand has been beneficial and creative, but on the other -- harmful and quite suffocating. Rozanov has hypnotised everyone with his dilemma of "Christ or the world", while all the same this dilemma that Rozanov posits, does not exist. It is generated by a confusion and obscurity of consciousness. The theme of Rozanov is very vital, very frustrating for official Christianity, for the church coffers, but Christ it does not touch upon, towards Christ it involves perhaps a weakness of consciousness, merely as in an eclipse. When Rozanov says, that Christian marriage does not exist, that the Church in effect sanctions against love, when he posits the question about the sacramental mystery of marriage thus, that if this sacrament genuinely exists, then in the Church there ought to happen the union of the sexes, -- in this he is empowered and radicalised, and has ingeniously made bold with what is important for us. The official Church cannot and has not answered Rozanov anything. But what has this religiously-pervasive question in common with the theosis-deification of this world, immanently assumed, with the attempt to defeat Christ by a lifestyle? The historical Church very much even acknowledges the familial way of life, and in general lives off of it, but the sacramental mystery of love it does not acknowledge, it does not see the transcendence of the mystery of marriage. The official churchly establishment is hostile not to this world nor to the manner of life crystalised within it, it is hostile to the cosmos, to the Divine flesh of the world, and in this is the tragedy of the Church. The Church as it were is hostile to the very idea of the Church as a cosmic organism. But there has been born a new religious consciousness, thirsting for a transfigurative flesh, and not the aboriginal flesh of old. The aboriginal, the pagan, perishable flesh continues by a stealthy path to live on in the Church, but the new resurrective flesh within it there is still not, it is not manifest. Rozanov pronounces his own judgement upon the Church as the representative of this old, pagan perishable flesh, which moreover also occupies too much a place in the Church. Here is why the "Religio-Philosophic Gatherings" did not succeed thus in falling under the sway of Rozanov.

Christ -- is the perfect, the Divine Child of God, the Image of the Cosmos. The ChristChild is the absolute norm for the world-children. In the Name of His Son, the Logos, God hath created the world, through the Son the world is filiated in sonship to God, it returns to the Father. Christ is the Divine Mediator between God and the world: if there were not Christ, then the world would not be the child to God, and the pantheists could not perceive even their own partialised truth -- the divineness of the world. Only the world, having accepted into itself Christ and having entered into Christ, only such a world is wrought into a child of God, and divine. This world is fallen away from God, and therefore it lies in evil, and therefore its divineness is fractured, impaired, and our world -- is but doubtfully divine. But the world retains a connection with God, and this connection in the mystical order of being is the Son of God, the God-Man, of God and of the World, the eternal Intercessor. This connection was incarnated within history in the Person of Christ. Through the God-Man, of God-of-World -- the world becomes divine, is deified. Between Christ and the world there exists only what seems empirically an opposition, issuing forth from the weakness of the human consciousness, but underneathe it lies hidden the mystically-real union. Within the historical bounds of Christianity the conjoining of Christ and the world is insufficiently seen, inasmuch as the cosmic epoch of redemption has not been brought to completion. Only within the Divine dialectic of the Trinity is there ultimately perfected the conjoining of the world with God, only in the Church to come will the flesh of the world resurrect. In the Spirit disappears every opposition betwixt the two children of God, between the world-child and the ChristChild. Christ hath manifest Himself the God-Man, the Holy Spirit manifests God-manhood. In God-manhood transpires the theosis of mankind, the theosis of the worldly flesh. But the new sacred flesh cannot be the old pagan and perishable flesh, that about which Rozanov concerns himself: into the new world indeed will enter all the elements of our world, transfigured however, and nothing destroyed, but all enlightened. We look forwards, and not backwards, we look to the coming Kingdom of God, and not to a lost paradise of the past. We desire to be as though it were religious revolutionaries, and not reactionaries. By a capricious historical irony, religious reaction sometimes is combined with a social revolutionary trait. Rozanov strives not towards the realm of the Spirit, not towards the realm of God One in Trinity, but towards a realm of God the Father: the realm of God the Father cannot still yet be, it is incompatible with the mystical dialectic of the Trinity, ultimately co-uniting the Creator with the creature, and it would nowise differ from the atheism, from which pantheism is separated only by an elusive boundary.

In the world is being born a new religious spirit. This spirit is deeply connected with the very old, with that which was eternal in the old soul, but within it are being revealed new horizons. For the new religious outlook and consciousness, -- having lived through the whole experience of modern history with all the profound doubt and negation, the question about the Church has to be posited otherwise, than it was for the consciousness of old. We seek the Church, into which as it were has entered all the fullness of life, the whole worldly experience, everything of value in the world, everything within history that has been of authentic value. Beyond the walls of the Church nothing ought to remain, except non-being. The Church is a cosmic power, the deified soul of the world, and the Church is also the Divine world, the imperishable connection betwixt God and the world. Entry into the Church is also an entrance into the authentic world, and not a leaving and going out from the world. People of the old religious sensibilities and the old religious outlook go into the Church to save themselves from worldly life, to atone their sins accumulated in the world, but everything by which they live they then leave at the church-yard gate, everything that is most precious for them, most dear in their lives, all the creative impulses, their fond dreams, all the complexity of their experience, the whole path of world history -- all this does not enter with them into the Church, does not venture to go within. This dualism we can no more endure, this dualism has become godless, it deadens the religious life, it is a blasphemy against the Holy Spirit. Within the Church there ought to be everything that is dear for us, everything that is precious for us, everything that is suffered by us in the world, -- our love, our thought and poetry, the whole creativity excluded from the Church for us by the old consciousness, all our great worldly people, all our anticipated hopes and dreams, everything, transcendent in our life and in worldly life. The Church ought to be the plenitude and fullness of life, the richness of being, and not a seminary priestmonk's cowl, which those in power keep their hands upon.

Dostoevsky and Vl. Solov'ev did more than anyone for the new religious impetus, and these were our greatest people, our teachers, but their religious soul was still half the old. Dostoevsky and Vl. Solov'ev were very complex people, having lived deeply through all the experience of modern history, having passed through all the temptation and the doubt, yet in them was accumulated much of the new riches. But into the Church they came as of old, all their riches did not enter in with them into the Church, all their experience did not render this Church more expansive and spacious, within the Church they but negated themself. The religio-philosophic system of Vl. Solov'ev is far broader than his churchly religiosity, in it there is the idea of God-manhood, but in his Church there is still not a divine-human life. Dostoevsky in his "Legend of the Grand Inquisitor" reveals religiously the remote, he senses the unspeakable religious freedom, but he goes into the Church with a mindset closed to all horizons. Wherefore I think, that none of the existing historical churches is the universal Church, none yet contains within itself the fullness of revelation, but the world seeks for the Universal Church, it thirsts to devote its life to it.[5]

Rozanov says, that we are pantheistic with the idea of the Church, but that this pantheistic tendency has nothing in common with its immanent pantheism. The Universal Church, containing all the fullness of being, is the Church of God One in Trinity, the Church of the Holy Trinity; in it ultimately disappears the seeming opposition between the world and Christ. In the light of the new consciousness is born yet another dilemma: the Christianity of the official-chambers, or Christ. The Christianity of the official-chambers is the old world, the old lifestyle; Christ is a new world, contrary to every lifestyle.

---

[5] By this, however, I certainly do not deny, that the path to the utmost fullness of the Universal Church lies through the sanctity of the historical churches, through their sacramental mysteries.

CATHOLIC MODERNISM AND THE CRISIS OF THE CONTEMPORARY CONSCIOUSNESS [1]

I.

When one scrutinises French culture, one is ever the more struck by it in the fragmentation, the disjointedness, the absence of a centre: there are no dominating thoughts nor thoughts, dominating over life, there is no singular and organic consciousness. The external ordering of life, an external national unity, a perfected mechanism of external culture is united with an anarchy of spirit, with a desolation of the popular soul. The French are orderly and content, compared to us. And for us, as Russians, unhappy and sick of soul, for us it is difficult to sense the vital soul of France. And in Paris there tends to be everything, along the various corners of the great city one can find, whatever interests him, whatever his soul desires. But these corners are broken away from the centre of life, one might have lived all one's life in Paris and not yet know anything about them. The inhabitants of Paris usually know only their own block they live on and know almost nothing of what is happening on the next block over. Thus also in the life of a spirit of what is happening on a block, and the people of a block know little about others. The French are very taken up with politics, each Frenchman reckons himself a great political expert and has his own plan for the saving of fatherland, and likewise the world. This -- is in all the city-clocks, this, -- is common to the life of France. There is still something else that is in common -- literature, quite morally vile novels, distributed in an enormous number of copies. Many think, that besides the novels and the

---

[1] Originally published in "Russkaya mysl'", September 1908.

politics, in France there is at present nothing, not anything inspiring in the politics and novels. This view on modern France is too generalised and too remote. From such a perspective one can discern only the general contours and it is impossible to catch sight of important details, the separate corners, in which transpires the crisis of the contemporary consciousness.

At a distance it would seem to me, that in modern France there are no signs of a religious stirring, there is no sort of philosophic thought, that France is almost entirely positivist in outlook, at ease in the triumph of a spiritual philistinism. This is true only in part. In the crannies of French culture one can notice a philosophic and religious ferment, and the beginning somewhere of the crisis of positivism. There is at present in France the talented philosopher Bergson,[2] a struggler against intellectualism, proclaiming a philosophy of action and opening the doors of his philosophy to mysticism and religion. Bergson has become all the more popular and the young hearken to him, he is strange, and at first glance in a completely incomprehensible manner he exerts an influence of two varied and contrary currents in French life: upon the Catholic modernists and upon the syndicalists. The neo-Catholic LeRoy [Le Roy, Le Roi, Edouard, 1870-1954] and the syndicalist Georges Sorel [1847-1922] have come out against Bergson's philosophy of action, against his anti-intellectualism. Yet however one evaluate this philosophy, it is impossible not to see in it a reflection of the crisis of positivism, a protest against the intellectualism, with which the old positivism infected the spiritual atmosphere.[3]

There exist in France both the neo-Catholics, -- modernists, as they are wont to be called, and the neo-Protestants. They publish

---

[2] The chief work of Bergson -- is "L'evolution creatrice", in which he subjects evolutionary theories to a deep-thoughted critique.

[3] Vide the recent book of the acclaimed philosopher Boutroux [Emil, 1845-1921], "Sciense et religion", in which is an entire chapter, "La philosophie de l'action".

journals, they organise conferences, which are frequented, moreover, by a special public. There is a Social Catholic movement, which is grouped around the society "Sillon" and which is very energetic in its striving to unite the orthodox-sort Catholicism with democracy, a republic and social reforms.[4] But the foremost place amongst these currents indisputably belongs to Catholic modernism.[5] Modernism is a movement primarily mental, but it is closely connected with the crisis of Western Catholicism and the crisis of the contemporary European consciousness. And Catholicism and the contemporary consciousness -- are facts of first-rate importance within the developement of world culture. Modernism attracts to itself the attention of wide segments of society and has become the evil of the day thanks to a papal encyclical. A particular stir was created by abbe Alfred Loisy [1857-1940], who not long ago came out with a book entitled, "Simples reflexions sur le decret du Sainte-Office et sur L'encyclique". This book sold out in several days and caused an upheaval in the Catholic world. In this book Loisy and not without some pride says, that those, who now officially are called modernists, several years back were called Loisyites, and he attempts to give answer for the whole of modernism to the holy Roman inquisition and the pope, for their having in a most decisive manner condemned the modernists and all their books.

In Catholic modernism there is many a varied shade, and Loisy justly protests against mixing up all the shades together under a general condemnation. But nevertheless there can be ascertained two basic currents within modernism: the one philosophic, the other exegetical. Social Catholicism with Marc Sangnier [1973-1950] at

---

[4] Vide L. Cousin, "Vie et doctrine du Sillon".

[5] I consider a most remarkable document of the life of a religious soul in France to be in the work of Huysmans [Joris Karl (Charles Marie Georges), 1848-1907], that hero and martyr of decadence, infinitely foreign to the modern triteness. Huysmans is more interesting and deeper than the "modernists".

the head stands off to the side from modernism; modernistic doubts are foreign to this current, and it meets with more indulgent an attitude of the pope, despite its social reform tendencies.[6] On the other side, the social aspirations are foreign to modernism, yet this is nonetheless a current, though in protest against intellectualism, which is primarily intellectual, and its sphere -- is the workings of consciousness. The modernism is an effort at uniting Catholicism with a new spirit, with the modern scientific consciousness, similar to how Sillonism attempts to unite Catholicism with modern democracy. In the words of Loisy, the modernists have therefore become modernists, because they -- are modern people, people of our era, because contemporary culture has entered into their very flesh and blood, because the very fiber of their being has become modern. And the Catholic Church continues to stand with hostile an attitude towards the spirit of the times, to find itself in an eternal opposition to everything modern, to philosophy, to science, to the progress of culture. The official philosophy of the Catholic Church as before remains the philosophy of Thomas Aquinas, and his intellectualistic scholasticism even in the XX Century continues to define the Catholic consciousness. The neo-Catholics, contaminated by the spirit of the times, have come to doubt Thomas Aquinas as a consummate master of religious and philosophic consciousness. Forsaken by the Catholics, the modernists have wanted to taste the sweetness of that freedom of investigation, which already long since was affirmed within Protestantism. But is it possible to remain good Catholics, having entered upon the path of free philosophising and free exegetics? The modernists seem to have two sorts of conscience -- a conscience Catholic and a conscience contemporary, and they are left swaying between two truths -- the truth of the Catholic Church, a truth they cannot disown, and the truth of modern philosophy and modern scientific exegetics, with which they are infected.

---

[6] Pope Leo XIII was an inspirer of Social Catholicism, and the cardinals -- colleagues of the deceased pope, up through the present support the Sillonists at Rome.

Philosophic and exegetical doubts disunite the modernists, they have caught the sickness of the objections of the contemporary consciousness against faith, against miracles and against tradition. Thomas Aquinas provides no sort of saving from these doubts, he but intensifies and strengthens them. There is the need to get free of Thomas, in order to justify the Catholic faith in facing the contemporary consciousness. Together with this, against the modernists boils the old Catholic blood, they are caught up in a fight with all their essence against the Church and the pope, while the authority of the Church is dearer to them than Christ, and the church hierarchy they esteem as a great cultural historical power. In contrast to the Protestants, the modernist Catholics see in the Church the dynamic power of Christianity within history. The Church for them is a religious developing, a living history, and they justifiably want to turn backwards, to the Gospel and the first centuries of Christianity. This attachment of the modernists to the Church, this greater proximity for them to the Church, rather than to Christ, puts them in a tragic and inescapable position for a clash with the pope.

The chief representative of the philosophical current of modernism at present appears to be LeRoy [Le Roy, Le Roi], author of the book, "Dogmes et critique", a student of Bergson, a sharp-witted metaphysician, subjecting the idea of dogma to philosophic analysis.[7] Leroy contends philosophically against Scholasticism, against intellectualism in the investigation of dogmas, while the old rationalistic foundation of the Catholic faith he wants to replace with a new and voluntaristic foundation, and to arrive at a moral dogmatism, a teaching about dogma as a fount of action. The dogmas for LeRoy and the philosophers of modernism possess not a theoretical, but rather practical significance. It is clear, that herein the spirit of Kant wins out over the spirit of Thomas Aquinas. In this the

---

[7] In France in the same direction have been active Blondel [Maurice, 1861-1949] and Laberthonnier [Lucien, 1860-1932], and in England Newman [John Henry Cardinal, 1801-1890], one of the chief inspirers of modernism.

modernists are fully modern, they fully reflect the spirit of the times and the contemporary condition of consciousness.

The chief representative of the exegetical current in modernism appears to be Loisy, the author of serious investigations in Biblical and Gospel history, a Catholic priest, making bold to fight for the freedom of exegetics.[8] Loisy is not at all a philosopher, he is an erudite historian of Christianity. He is a profound thinker, and with all his Catholic blood he differs from Harnack and has written an entire book against Harnack,[9] but he does the same as does Harnack, and like the latter he lacks the ability to philosophically defend his faith. "Das Wesen des Christentums" of Harnack and "L'Evangile et l'eglise" of Loisy -- are two fundamental books, characteristic of Protestant modernism and of Catholic modernism. These are two answers to the doubts, evoked by the modern scientific spirit, the spirit of historical investigation, knowing no mercy, -- the response of a neo-Protestant, who loves Christ, and of a neo-Catholic, who loves the church. And neither of them believes in the God-Manhood of Christ, the one from a German Protestant sincerity and uprightness, the other from a French Catholic cleverness and sense for ambiguity. In absolute religious truth, in religious realism have alike experienced doubt both LeRoy with his voluntaristic philosophy, and Loisy with his erudite exegetics. The truth of contemporary philosophy and contemporary historical science has seemed stronger than the old religious truth, has seemed as though not dependent upon it neither in time, nor in science, nor in philosophy. Why however are LeRoy, Loisy and all these modernists so frightened of the spirit of the times, so passive in the face of the contemporary consciousness, so powerless to defend their faith against the pressure of scientific and philosophic doubts? Because

---

[8] Vide "Les Evangiles synoptiques", "Le quatrieme Evangile", "Histoire critique du texte et des versions de Ancien Testament" and other works.

[9] Vide "L'Evangile et l'eglise".

their blood is too infected by the historical sins of Catholicism, they have been poisoned by the age-old hostility of the Catholic Church towards progress, towards science and philosophy. Those, for whom Thomas Aquinas has been the final word on human culture, the supreme word on science and philosophy, are objectively defenseless against the spirit of modernity, when they happen to doubt the absolute and final significance of Thomas. For those, who have imbibed into their own flesh and blood the idea of the absolute authority of the pope and with this idea have bound up belonging to the Church of Christ as dear to their heart, -- for these the freedom of the modern spirit holds especial temptation. modernity, the freedom of science and philosophy have opened up for the modernists that same seductiveness, which the forbidden beauty of a woman had for the medieval monk. Both Thomas Aquinas and Pope Pius X stand in the way of this wondrous beauty and they do not permit it, they threaten excommunication and eternal perdition. But is this woman so beautiful, is the forbidden modernity so attractive?

In modernity, in the consciousness of modern man, long since already freed from both Thomas and from the pope, and indeed from all religion, there is occurring a crisis, the reverse of that which transpires with Loisy, LeRoy and others like them: modernity thirsts for faith, thirsts anew to discover the lost sanctity, to go along varied paths towards religious rebirth. The modernist Catholics are overdue in their attempts to unite Catholicism with the spirit of the times, the spirit of the times will soon move on and forsake those positions, upon which they intend to solidify their renovated faith. The modern Catholics want to reform and renew Catholicism with that modernity, which historically itself is a product of the sins of Catholicism and which from its new sins can be set free only by a new and fuller faith. It wants to replace the old Catholic intellectualism with a modern voluntarism and by this to breathe life into the decrepit Catholicism. But the contemporary voluntarism has become hopelessly blind, people come to it out of despair, having lost all faith and all awareness of the meaning of life.

In essence, LeRoy has come to doubt on dogma, the modern consciousness hinders him to believe in dogma in the old way, he has sensed philosophic impediments, and the old Catholic philosophy cannot defend him against the spirit of the times. It is evident to everyone, that LeRoy has sincerely wanted to remain a good Catholic, fervently to be attached to the faith, but he is too "modern", his old religiosity is combined with a new irreligious consciousness, and this consciousness is terrified of the miraculous. In the contemporary consciousness of cultured European peoples lives the prejudice, that the impossibility of miracle has been proven and shown. LeRoy has had doubts first of all in the existence of absolute truth and in the existence of the organ for its apperception. In following the modernising philosophy LeRoy spurns any great and absolute reason, he renounces any legacy of the Logos, as revealed in the history of the human consciousness. The modern voluntarist Bergson is closer to him, than are the great philosophic traditions of the past, he has lost hold the thread, which stretches through the whole of world culture from Plato to Schelling. LeRoy is very sharp-minded a philosopher, but foreign to him are the testaments of a free knowledge of God. Together with this, LeRoy is impelled to break with religious realism, he fatally goes over to a religious symbolism. A man of the contemporary philosophic spirit, a follower of Bergson, though too a faithful son of the Catholic Church, he cannot realistically investigate the dogmas, he cannot affirm the higher reason within the dogmas. For LeRoy the dogma is not so much a fact of the mystical order, for real and apperceptive by faith, a real and objective fact dwelling outside man, as rather a subjective condition of man himself, his moral activity. The dogma is needed for activity, for the practical in the religious life. Pensee-action -- is here the basic word. The moral dogmatism of LeRoy is reminiscent of the practical reason of old Kant, though also LeRoy cannot be termed a Kantian in the precise sense of this word. Bergson and LeRoy, certainly, are bound up with the spirit of the Kantian practical reason, the Kantian voluntarism, but they are distinct from the German neo-Kantians, within their mindset is a national French particularity. All this current of the philosophy of action is akin to the spirit of the brilliant American philosopher and psychologist, James.[10]

Kant left man facing a terrible abyss, having cut off the path to the apperception of transcendent realities. Absolute truth as a reality, according to Kant, is unattainable for man, religious realism has reached its end-point, and for hapless and helpless man there is left only the right of exerting the will, volitional activity, the moral activity to create for oneself a religious activity. The objectively lost faith needs subjectively to be recreated. The Christian dogmas, which earlier were perceived as a real and objective activity, for the modern consciousness -- are a lost paradise. But the need for religion has remained, it is needful to life, for morality, and there remains only the possibility to affirm the dogmatic actions, the dogmatic moral postulates. LeRoy is to much the Catholic, to formulate the condition of his consciousness such as I tend to formulate it, but the core of the crisis, which occurs with people like LeRoy, it seems to me however, can be expressed thus. Faith in the God-Manhood of Christ and in the Resurrection of Christ is needful to religious life, for moral activity, for contemplative practice. Indeed so. But is Christ really, mystically really the God-Man, was Christ resurrected, and the sins of the world redeemed and the world saved by the fact of the appearance of Christ, a fact, in its objectivity towering over not only all our human condition, but also over all this world? LeRoy as a good Catholic believes, that Christ -- is the Son of God and has risen in the Resurrection, but as a philosopher, as a "modernist", he is perplexed and unconvinced. The eternal reason and the temporal reason have become dissonant.

Loisy, representative of the other current of modernism, in his reply to Harnack sets the Church higher than Christ. And this is quite characteristic for his Catholic blood. Christ is perceived only through the Church, Christ has passed over into the Church and as it were has

---

[10] Vide William James, ""L'experience religieuse".

become dissolved into it. It is impossible to feel Christ Himself, and a return to Christ would be a reactionary renovation. There remains only one path -- the furthermost developement of the Church itself. But Loisy is gripped by exegetical doubts, and Biblical criticism tempts him. History, i.e. scientific history, imperceptibly assumes for him the character of a supreme criterion. He thus often states, that he might be suspected of a twofold accounting, that as it were there exists for him two truths -- the one historical and scientific, the other religious and theological. In his latest book Loisy defends himself against this suspicion and straight-out says: "That, which is historically false, I account false everywhere".[11] After this revealing acknowledgement, which clearly indicates, that exegetical doubts have gained the upper hand over his faith, he consoles himself and us with this, that "the legend or myth can denote its own religious truth, it can express a moral feeling". Bereft of objective truth, Loisy wants then to recreate it subjectively, as something morally necessary for life, for the practical.

What sort of meaning do the exegetical doubts of Loisy possess? I understand still the philosophic doubts, but the doubts of historical investigation itself per se do not possess any principal significance for faith. It is possible philosophically to assert, that towards every religion, thus also towards Christianity, can only be one attitude -- the historical, that every religion is but an object of historical research. Then one would therein consciously and philosophically deny, that there is in man any organ for the apperception of the religious within history, except for scientifico-historical research. Harnack, a very remarkable, a very erudite specialist in Christian exegetics, has gotten himself hopelessly entangled in this regard. He has set himself the task, amidst the help of historical research and to which he ascribes the significance of a supreme criterion of truth, the task to determine "the essence of Christianity", which earlier he had defended religiously. There

[11] Vide "Simples reflexions", p. 62.

obtains a vicious circle: "the essence of Christianity" is the religion of Harnack, acquired by him through an unmediated and direct religious sensing, but the historical investigation, unaware of its religio-philosophic limitations, holds forth with the view, that it is defining the "essence", which for scientific investigation is always elusive.[12] The position of Loisy is worse still. Harnack -- is a Protestant rationalist, he consciously confesses Christianity as a moral teaching; Loisy -- is a Catholic (though also a modernist), he has grown up attached to the Church such that no sort of exegetical doubts can tear him away from it, yet together with this he wants to transform the scientifico-historical research into a supreme criterion of truth. What however then happens with *religious apperception*, with a sensing of Christ as Saviour, a primal sensing, not dependent upon any sort of science, nor upon any sort of history! Harnack in his capacity of rationalist denies a real religious apperception, for him there remains only a moral religious feeling. Loisy as it were admits a religious apperception in regards to the Church but denies it in regards to Christ. Christ is surrendered into the hands of exegetical investigation.[13] That which remains untouchable in Christ for historical investigation, then passes over instead into the Catholic Church, the dynamic power of human progress, which becomes higher than Christ, which outgrows Christ and perhaps also outgrows itself, as the modernists would have it. A more hopeless, shaky and ambiguous position, than this, upon which Loisy and others like him stand, is difficult to imagine. He does not believe in absolute

---

[12] For me it is gnosseologically indisputable, that the religiosity of the object demands the religiosity of the subject. In this position is a limitation to every scientific investigation of religion. The mysteries of religion obtain only for a religious receptivity, and demand devotion.

[13] The image of the Son of God manifest in history is apperceived through the sacred tradition of the Church, but the Church itself -- is a mysteried universal society of the living and the dead -- apperceived only mystically.

religious truth, and in standing for the Church, he wants to resist the pervasive grip of relativism, the historical relativity of everything, subjected to scientific investigation. The reply of Loisy to the pope and the Holy Inquisition produces a distressing impression. There is the feeling, that the man has gradually lost his faith, but is afraid to admit this himself. It is incomprehensible, why he stands up for the Church, why he strives for a justification. Loisy has become vexed, and his tone is such, that it ill becomes those paltry people to judge about his erudite investigations. And moreover for an erudite man, an investigator of Christian history, there should be no need to squander time on explanations with the pope and the Catholic Church.

II.

The Russian religious searchings of every sort are very different from what we see in the Catholic modernism. The texture of our religious thought is altogether different. Christ is closer for our direct religious sense, than is the more external churchliness, our religious thought asserts an absolute truth, we aspire towards religious realism, and not a mere symbolism; for us the search for the City yet to come, -- the Kingdom of God on earth, is bolder, than it is in the West. Within Orthodoxy there was never that intellectualism, such as there was in the Catholic Scholasticism, and therefore there could not be such a motif of struggle against intellectualism, as there is with the modernists. For us there was no need to demolish the authority of Thomas Aquinas within religious thought. Closer to our blood is the mystical theology of Dionysios the Areopagite and Maximos the Confessor. Orthodox mysticism is pervaded by a spirit of supra-rationalism, to it is foreign both rationalism and irrationalism. The most remarkable Russian theologian-philosophers, Khomyakov, Vl. Solov'ev, V. Nesmelov, have brilliantly resolved problems, connected with disputes of faith and knowledge, they have bestown us a profound religious philosophy and they stand many heads higher than LeRoy and those like him. Khomyakov and

Solov'ev have organically adapted the idea of absolute reason, as developed by German idealism, and have transformed abstract idealism into a concrete idealism, and it was amidst the course of the greater reason that the matter of faith was played out for them. Only the lesser reason, prevalent in contemporary philosophy and modern culture, has subjected to doubt the rule of faith and the reality of dogmas. Khomyakov and Vl. Solov'ev are from the philosophic school of the greater reason and have continued with the great traditions, which stretch from Plato, through the neoPlatonists, to the teachers of the Church, to the philosophising mystics, through such medieval geniuses of thought, as John Scotus Erigena, down to the German idealists, Hegel and Schelling. LeRoy and the modernists tend to ignore this great tradition, they are from the school of the lesser reason, from philosophic modernism, which has given up on the great traditions of the past in the name of the spirit of positivism. And the modernists have been quite much tempted by this spirit of modern philosophy, the spirit of the lesser reason. The modernists could learn much from Vl. Solov'ev, but they are not even familiar with the French book of Solov'ev, entitled "La Russie et l'eglise universelle", which was devoted to the question about the reuniting of the churches and shows also the attraction of Solov'ev towards Catholicism. They are too much Catholics and too much the modernists, to understand the great Russian theosophy.

For the contemporary philosophic consciousness there exists only two points of departure -- intellectualism or voluntarism. Modern man is surrendered to either his own small human reason, or to his human will, in which he seeks salvation from rationality. The modern consciousness is fragmented apart, everything in it is dissociated, the organic centre is lost, and this centre can only be supra-human. Intellectualism and voluntarism, rationalism and irrationalism -- these are two sides of one and the same disintegration, of a sundering away from the supreme centre of being. The will affirms itself separately from the intellect, and the intellect likewise separately from the will, and both the intellect and the will affirm themselves fragmented off from the absolute reason, from the organic reason, in which the intellectual and the volitional are coalesced into an higher unity. The modernists are caught up entirely within the limitations of the antitheses of the contemporary consciousness, the will and reason for them are disunited, faith and knowledge are sundered apart, and the absolute reasonableness of the dogmas they do not see. They do not even suspect the possibility of that path, traversed by Russian philosophic and religious thought, the path of *supra-rationalism*. The dogmas are not theories, are not speculative teachings, -- in this LeRoy, certainly, is correct. He protests justly against the intellectualistic investigation of dogmas. The dogmas are facts first of all, facts not of the empirical, but of the mystical order. For LeRoy the dogmas have primarily a moral significance in life, they are necessary for actions, and appear as it were as practical norms. In the book of LeRoy there is a very interesting chapter concerning the Resurrection of Christ, in which he comes to a very characteristic conclusion. The dogma about the Resurrection means, that we ought to relate to Christ as to our contemporary. LeRoy many a time stresses, that in the capacity of a good Catholic he believes in the Resurrection as a fact, and he believes in all the dogmas. But the mystical sense of the Resurrection eludes him. Does he admit the cosmic salvific action of the Resurrection of Christ, as a victory over the primordial evil in the world, over death? With LeRoy the Resurrection is investigated in the sense of a subjective human relationship to Christ, and not in the sense of the relation of Christ to man and to the world. Moreover, in that the dogmatic-facts have an objective world significance, they disclose the relationship of the Divinity to the world, these dogma-facts lead thus to salvation.[14] The dogma-facts are reasonable in the utmost sense of this word. The contemporary consciousness, towards which the modernists are so inclined, ignores the tradition of a free

[14] Vide the interesting book of Brilliantov, "The Influence of Eastern theology upon the Western in the Works of John Scotus Erigena" -- in which is accurately noted the objectively Divine character of the Eastern evangelisation and the subjectively human character of the Western.

knowledge of God, the history of theosophy. The idea of reason, which can reconcile intellectualism and voluntarism, knowledge and faith, such as is connected with the teaching about the Logos, is quite foreign to the spirit of modernism and all the contemporary consciousness.

Amidst the discernment of the higher reason, miracle is -- reasonable, the order of nature -- is unreasonable, madness. The connection of cause with effect in the natural order -- is absurd, irrationalised, this order of nature itself has appeared as a result of the falling away from reason, the irrationalisation of being. The kingdom of necessity is not the kingdom of reason, for reasonable and meaningful only is the kingdom of freedom.[15] In this context it can be said, that in world life there was only one fact absolutely reasonable, absolutely meaningful -- the fact of the Resurrection of Christ. In this miraculous fact the world having fallen away from reason is returned to reason. The miracle of the Resurrection, having altered the order of nature subject to the law of corruption -- is meaningful, reasonable. When they speak about the incompatibility of miracle with reason, about the non-reasonableness and foolishness of giving credance to the miraculous, they are then judging with the lesser reason, with human judgement, which itself is non-reasonable, itself dissociated from the meaning of being. In the forefront of the contemporary consciousness of Europe there lives a legend about how there has been ultimately demonstrated and proven the incommensurability of the miraculous with reason, the impossibility and meaninglessness of the miracle. No one has ever proven anything like this and it cannot be proven.[16] Positive science simply does not concern itself with this, for this is outside its competency and for it not of interest. Science

[15] Kant understood this in the strongest part of his philosophy, in the "Critique of Practical Reason".

[16] N. Minsky in an article, "Absolute reaction" (in "Slovo") constructs his arguments against the possibility of miracle upon a naive confusion of reason with natural necessity. This is a typical point of confusion with the rationalists.

but speaks about what is from a scientific point of view, within the bounds of the order of the laws of nature, with which it deals, and in which the miraculous is impossible and wherein miracle never occurs. But religion itself likewise asserts, that as regards the laws of nature the miraculous is impossible, that it is possible only as an alteration within the order of nature, only but within the order of grace. Supernatural powers however lay outside the perspective of science, and about them science can affirm nothing either positive or negative. Philosophy however has an interest in the question about the possibility of the miraculous, and it explores this question. But that philosophy, such as has posited at its foundation the idea of reason, can particularly admit of the miraculous. A philosophy of reason, continuing with the tradition of reason, building upon the teaching concerning the Logos, the ontological teaching about the meaning of being, permits of the possibility of miracle; whereas an irrational philosophy does not permit of this possibility, denying as it does the very idea of reason. Certainly, either Schelling or Vl. Solov'ev have moreso acknowledged reason and have proceeded from reason, than Mills or Cohen. The modern scientific critical philosophy has cast aside the idea of reason as something outmoded and unnecessary. Reason however is an idea ontological, and not merely gnosseological, it is connected with an acknowledging of the positive meaning of being, its supreme centre and its supreme purpose. The positivist, critical, scientific philosophy does not have the right even to speak about reason, and for it there is no sort of meaning in a discussion about the non-reasonableness of the miraculous. The contemporary consciousness denies miracle both in its heart and in its will, it is frightened of the miraculous, as by a devil. The question about the relationship between knowledge and faith within the contemporary consciousness is not only not resolved, it is not even posited.

Science is a partial form of knowledge, not utmost and not ultimate, it is always directed to a delimited area, and in transgressing its bounds, it ceases to be science, and becomes a pseudo-philosophy and pseudo-theology. Thus, for example, with positivism, which expands its judgements beyond the bounds of scientific knowledge, and is hence a pseudo-philosophy, just as materialism can be termed a pseudo-theology. Faith includes within it a fullness of knowledge, it is not counter-scientific, but rather supra-scientific. The partial sphere of scientific knowledge does not negate religious faith, but the rather is made meaningful, and is led to a connection with the whole. The very object of scientific knowledge empirical nature, for religious faith is enlightened with the light of the supernatural. But faith cannot in any way stand dependent, nor can it in any sense be defined or delimited or negated by science. At the basis of knowledge likewise indeed resides faith. The world of knowledge and the world of faith obtain first of all for us as completely different orders, which can be and ought to be brought together on the same level, but upon the grounds of faith, and not knowledge. The question concerning the relationship of knowledge and faith stands very acute for the contemporary consciousness and for all forms of a modern religious movement. This is a matter for religious gnosseology, which has its foundations in the world of the developement of human self-consciousness. But religious faith can never be dependent upon scientific knowledge or to any degree be negated by it, and thereupon thus collapses the very possibility of the exegetical doubts of Christ. The exegetical doubts are based upon this presupposition, that the faith in Christ can be considered dependent upon the scientific investigations concerning Christ and Christianity. This is but a partial aspect of the general question about the primacy of science within human consciousness. If science should be the sole criterion of truth, if science be not only science, i.e. a partial and delimited sphere, but should likewise include philosophy, and religion, i.e. everything, then there is no other sort of relationship to Christ, besides the scientific-historical, and it cannot be such. The idolatry afront science, the transforming of it from a part into the whole, from a subordinate function into a supreme norm, would lead to idols of a "scientific" religion. But, it would seem, philosophy ought to be philosophic, religion ought to be religious, and science ought only to be scientific, if the scientific be not the sole and supreme criterion. But now it is in vogue to demand a scientific basis not only in philosophy, but also in religion. It is a demand, striking in its absurdity. Our philosophy and our religion deny the primacy of science, philosophy for us has its own independent source, and religion stands uppermost. How indeed can we "scientifically" ground the basis of our faith and our philosophy? The "scientific" is a pseudo-theological idol in our era, and it is impossible "scientifically" to shatter this idol. There is a vicious circle here. Philosophically and religiously we affirm only the scienceness of science, and science itself we regard as a sphere partial and delimited. The right of a free exegetical research, which is so dear to Loisy, is a sacred right, but the fate of faith cannot in any sense be dependent upon it. The faith of Loisy himself is however quite vulnerable to the pressure of his particular investigations. Catholicism renders man helpless against the threats of freedom of investigation, since actually it denies this freedom and fights against it.

Catholic modernism tends insufficiently to see, that in the world has coalesced a new consciousness, still quite newer than that, to which the modernists have gravitated and in which they see modernity, -- a religious consciousness. This consciousness is justified by an higher philosophy. But what however is it that transpires within contemporary philosophy? The voluntarism of contemporary philosophy (Bergson, James, and many a German reflects the crisis of positivism, it exposes the impossibility of positivist intellectualism to suffice, stretching as it does to infinity the whole of human striving. Bergson has exerted an influence even upon the French syndicalists, who are cut off from the Marxist intellectualism and who thirst for a philosophy of action. In the syndicalist "action directe" there occurs a mysteried action, there is as it were a revelation, acquired by an effort of the will and unintelligible to the sidelines. Bergson, LeRoy and those like them in essence assert, that *truth is born in action*, that there is also a truth which is created by the will and is necessary for the will.[17] This has analogy with the assertion of Marxism, in accord with which truth is but that which is necessary for the process of life, for action, within a given era for the proletariat -- the class mystique, which syndicalism developes further. Suchlike a philosophy is compelled to deny the reality and the presence of absolute norms in consciousness. If within consciousness the absolute be not really present nor appear as a source for truth, then there remains but to surrender oneself to the dark will, in the hope, that its efforts at action will lead to such results, which moreover might be termed truth. But this path leads from the false light of positivism to a total darkness, to a mystique of the blind. Action itself, the volitional effort itself can be accomplished only upon absolute grounds, in accord with a given revelation, a religious revelation within history and the natural revelation of reason and of conscience, then only is the action of the will purposive and leading towards light, to an absolute reality. The woeful aspect is in this, that the new voluntarism remains within the bounds of all that same rationalism, and the irrationalism is but an inverted inside-out rationalism. The sole light of reason, which permits of voluntarism and irrationalism, is all that selfsame old light of the lesser reason, all that selfsame rationalistic light. But this light cannot illumine other worlds, cannot extend into the religious sphere. The area of religion therefore remains unenlightened and is subject to danger on the part of the light of rational judgement, the light of science and philosophy. Faith is necessary for volitional life, for the practical, for action, but it is non-rational, it is shaken by the pressures of modernity, by the prevailing powers such as declared by an autonomous science and philosophy. That philosophy, which LeRoy and the modernists have seized upon, cannot justify faith, cannot open up into the possibility of religion and faith; this philosophy but lays bare the crisis of positivism and the crisis of Catholicism, nothing more.

---

[17] An analogous view can be found in Simmel [Georg, 1858-1918] and many other German thinkers.

Catholicism has long already been tempted by the secret of the "Grand Inquisitor" in its hierarchy. I speak, certainly, not about this or some other pope as a man, nor about this or some other hierarch of the Church, but about the spirit of the papacy, about a deviousness, employed by the Catholic hierarchy. Pope Leo XIII was a remarkable man and a genuine believer, and Pius X is certainly a believer, but they both shield themself with a secret of cunning deviousness. This weakening of truth by the Catholic Church has found expression in modernism. The modernists are incapable of a bold breaking with the pope, since they do not believe in absolute truth, nor do they believe in the ideal nature of man. They are relativists too much, opportunists too much. The Polish modernist Marian Zdzekhovskii [1861-1938] put in the *Moscow Weekly* an article entitled, "The Modernist Movement in the Roman Catholic Church", in which he makes a strange admission, but very characteristic of modernism. M. Zdzekhovskii -- is a fervent modernist, he delights in the modernist books, he extols Loisy, he is most doubtful on the mindset of Catholicism, but at the end he suddenly declares: "The intervention by the church authority lays in the interest of the common good, and a precautionary encyclical on the part of the pope was rendered necessary. And it became apparent: Pius X had fulfilled his duty". In these strange words is expressed all the dual mindset of modernism. The modernists are in a struggle against themself, they are not convinced, that freedom will lead them to something good, they suspect themself of a lack of religious insight. It is impossible to permit children to be too mischievous, it can be permitted somewhat, but then it is proper to put a stop to it and if necessary punish, else then the mischief lead to woe. One might permit oneself philosophic and exegetical investigations in the spirit of modernity, but upon this path there is no absolute criterion of truth, and one might readily plunge into the abyss. Pope Pius X is left as the absolute criterion and he can save one perishing from the excesses of freedom even in an instance, where one has lost the faith in Christ. Freedom, it would seem, leads to a loss of faith in Christ, but the faith in Pius X remains and saves from perdition. The whole horror of Catholicism, its whole pitfall -- is in this substitution for Christ by the pope. Christ -- is freedom, whereas the pope -- is authority. The Catholic Church -- is too legalistic, too completed an edifice, too materially rooted. Catholicism takes from man the burden of freedom, in this is its power and in this is its horror. In the Orthodox Church there is not this material tangibility, not the legalism, in it the weakness has been in historical dynamics. In Orthodoxy no one knows precisely, where the voice of the Church is, and where the borderlines of churchly teachings of faith reside. Herein is a weakness of Orthodoxy, but herein likewise resides possibly its strength. In the legend of the "Grand Inquisitor", Dostoevsky with an unprecedented and extraordinary power grasped the mystery of the substitution for Christ by the pope, of freedom -- by authority. The modernists desire as though to get free from the temptation of the "Grand Inquisitor", but they have not the wherewithal, since they have no hold on a faith in absolute truth, in the salvific aspect of freedom, in a religious realism. Catholicism has excluded the path of freedom, has surrounded man with impediments, and the spirit of modernity -- modernism -- has excluded absolute truth, it has deprived the religious life of reality. The Catholic modernists only then will have the ability to prevail over the reactionary authority of the pope and the false hierarchy and realise their revolutionary strivings, when they become less the Catholics and less the modernists, when they first of all freely will have affirmed Christ in themself and freely sense themself members of the Body of Christ -- the Church. I believe, that this religious process can readily start from Russia, from its Orthodoxy.[18] Within Orthodoxy has been preserved the sanctity of the Divine, though the human element has been weakly expressed. Within Orthodoxy there has not been the historical dynamics of the West, and this weakness can become a religious plus in that hour, when the exclusively human

[18] In the mystical, and not in the historical sense of the word.

dynamics become meaningless and there begins a Divine-human dynamic in history.

The religious tumult in Russia is quite more interesting, qualitatively higher, and more novel, than that in France and other lands. We have a greater boldness and sweep, a greater religious audacity. We have many an idea, we inspiredly demolish the old and prophesy about the new, but historical activity, the capacity for real action with us is so small, that it has become terrible. Our religious stirring is all still reminiscent of the conversation of Ivan Karamazov with Alyosha at the inn. And the impediments, which for us stand in the way for a rebirth of the Christian faith and the strengthening of a new religious consciousness, are altogether different from those in Western modernism. The chief hindrance -- is not in the consciousness, not in the intellectual spirit of modern science and philosophy, but in the will, the initiating element, in which has not yet occurred an ultimate choice of path. Our chief doubts are not exegetical and not philosophical, but moreso mystical. The Russian original philosophy does not posit any sort of impediments for faith. Almost all the Russian philosophers were believers, they conjoined knowledge with faith. The greatest Russian philosopher, Vl. Solov'ev, was a Christian philosopher and he provided a justification of faith better, than LeRoy gives now, or than the Scholastics gave formerly. Russian philosophy acknowledges the reasonableness of the Christian faith, it sees within Christianity the sole meaningful world-understanding, and alike foreign to it are an abstract intellectualism and an abstract voluntarism. The new religious consciousness ought to base itself upon the traditions of Russian philosophy, and not upon contemporary European philosophy. Bergson, James, Rickert and other modern philosophers -- are interesting and talented, yet they -- are symptomatic of the crisis of positivism, but they trouble not those who continue the deed of the worldwide revealing of the Logos and sense their bond with the great philosophers of the past.

In the Russian religious tumult lies concealed an immediate sensing of Christ, and equally also the spirit, opposed to Christ. This vital feeling of Christ for us has not been killed by the historical Church, as it has in Western Catholicism, and therefore it can become a basis of religious renewal. In our religious searchings there is a very strong social impetus, which is completely foreign to modernism, in it there is a vital expectation of the Kingdom of God upon earth, the onset of a true theocracy. All the Russian God-seekers, starting with Chaadaev, moved towards the universal Church, in which there would be the fullness of all and in which would be realised the Christian prophecies and promises. Chaadaev and Vl. Solov'ev -- our greatest religious thinkers -- had an inclination towards Catholicism. They believed, that within Orthodoxy obtains an absolute sanctity, the divine foundation of the Church, but within Catholicism they wanted to catch sight of that human constructive power, the historical power, which should realise the societal organisation of the Kingdom of God upon earth; within Catholicism they saw a means of transferring the Divine sanctity of Orthodoxy into world historical life. In an uniting of the churches, in the combining of the Eastern truth of Orthodoxy with the western truth of Catholicism, Vl. Solov'ev saw a way out into the Universal Church. The modernist Catholic movement has somewhat disenchanted us in this. In it is absent that social impetus, which attracted Chaadaev and Solov'ev. The official Catholicism however remains stagnant and reactionary, though all still quite mighty. Everything teaches us this, that the sanctity of the eternal, not the temporal, Orthodoxy, -- is the Divine basis of the Universal Church,[19] ought not to be united with the social organisation of Catholicism, but rather with European culture and with a liberative societal humanism, wherein already has occurred the affirmation of the human element, of volitional human activity, so unattained by the Christian East. The crisis of the contemporary consciousness points towards this conjunction.

---

[19] I believe, that this basis is common to both Orthodoxy and Catholicism, but the sacred within Catholicism mustneeds be sought not within the papacy as a social system.

ATTEMPT AT A PHILOSOPHICAL JUSTIFICATION OF CHRISTIANITY [1]

(Concerning the Book of V. Nesmelov "The Science of Man")

I.

The question about the possibility of faith, about its permissibility afront the judgement of reason, stands acutely again before human consciousness. The will and the heart of man draw him towards faith, but contemporary reason quite opposes itself to faith, as once formerly the pagan reason opposed itself, and for which the matter of Christ was folly. But is the matter of Christ genuinely, or is it facetiously in the court of reason, and is this reason indeed genuine, which would invest itself with the almightiness of the supreme court? People of a positivist mind consider it beyond doubt, that the matter of faith is facetious ultimately and that the religion of Christ ought to be repudiated even in the event, where the human heart might pine in longing for it and the human will strive fully towards it. And for the contemporary world, as once formerly for the pagan world, the matter of Christ continues to be a "temptation" and a "folly". The contemporary reason, having condemned the religion of Christ as irrational and folly, -- this is all but the old pagan reason, and essentially in its objections it makes use of all the themes of the old pagan arguments. But the traditional theology fights feebly against the temptations of pagan reason, and serves sooner as a support for the hostility to faith, than for faith itself. The spiritual baggage of contemporary "teachers" of the Church in a majority of cases is so

[1] A formal Paper, which was read at the Moscow, the Peterburg and the Kiev Religio-Philosophic Societies. Afterwards published in journal "Russkaya mysl'", September 1909.

wretched and deplorable, that with it there is no conquering the stormily blustering elements of this world. And it does not suffice to reminisce the old teachers of the Church, who converted the whole of pagan wisdom into a weapon in defense of the faith afront the court of reason, who with genius discerned that selfsame Logos in the philosophic presentiments of the pagan world, which in Christianity is manifest as the Logos in the flesh. Now ought anew ought to be continued the work of the great teachers of the Church, afresh there ought to begin a time for a philosophic justification of faith, and the very work of reason for the new history ought to be transformed into a weapon of defense of the Christian faith. The Logos in the history of the new thought is that selfsame eternal Logos, once but incarnated within world history. But philosophy cannot give faith or be a substitute for faith. Gnosticism is no less dangerous, than the hellishly dark denial of reason. For faith it is impossible to go the philosophic path, but after the experiential act of faith, a Christian gnosis is both possible and necessary. For a philosophic justification of faith there is needed quite a freedom of spirit and quite a breadth, such as is rather difficult to meet with among traditionalist apologetes of Christianity. Usually those apologists, long since bereft of the bond with the spirit of life, having lost the fire of soul, quite simplistically and with ease obliterate the recent history, they negate the work of reason and uproot it with an impassable chasm betwixt the religion of Christ and world culture and world reason. The official, the externalised Christians too often -- are pagan in their life and pagans in their consciousness, and for the sinful pagan world they provide not the opportunity to access the mysteries of the Christian religion. It is as though they intended, so that ultimately there should not be revealed to the world, that the mystery of the Christian religion is a mystery both of every human heart and the intellectual nature of man. The matter of the defense of the faith is posited in a position of being the opposite to the natural: the irrationality of history has set adrift this matter into poor hands. To justify the faith in Christ it cannot and ought not to be a matter in the everyday sense of this "spiritual-clergy" world, in which long since already has been quenched the Spirit of life, and that "secular" world, which is full of life, with the Spirit yet insufficiently comprehended. In Russia there have always been "secular" people with a deep religious thirst, with an authentic spiritual life, people inspired, and from them it is necessary to search out religious thought, the comprehension of faith.

I want to turn attention to a certain remarkable, "secular" in his make-up a religious thinker, but outwardly by virtue of his position belonging to the "spiritual-clergy" world, one who is mindful of the old teachers of the Church and who genuinely serves the revealing of this faith, in that the matter of Christ is a matter in the utmost sense rational, rather than folly. I speak about V. Nesmelov, author of the large work "The Science of Man", a modest and little known professor of the Kazan Spiritual Academy [trans. note, i.e. higher level seminary].[2] Nesmelov is very bold, very deep and original a thinker. He continues anew the matter of Eastern mystical theology, with which he unites a faith in the divineness of human nature, a faith foreign to Western theology.[3] In certain regards

---

[2] It is likewise impossible to deny the talent and originality of a professor of the Moscow Spiritual Academy, M. Tareev, who recently published a four-volume collection, "The Foundations of Christianity". But his interpretation of Christianity is but one of the forms of a *Protestant individualism.* The impotence of religious thought on the soil of Protestantism is clearly evident from a recently appeared booklet of R. Aiken, "The Fundamental Problems of the Contemporary Philosophy of Religion".

[3] Of the great teachers of the Church it was, evidently, St. Gregory of Nyssa who had the greatest influence on Nesmelov, and who allotted a large place to religious anthropology. Brilliantov as well has written an interesting book, "The Influence of Eastern Theology upon the Western in the Works of J. Scotus Erigena", and adeptly points out a distinction of Eastern theologising from that of the West: Eastern theologising is objective and it starts from the absolute givenness of the Divine, whereas the Western -- is subjective and starts from the human. Vide also the book of Nesmelov himself: "The Dogmatic System of St. Gregory of Nyssa".

he is more interesting than Vl. Solov'ev: he has not suchlike a scope nor brilliance, but there is a depth, an wholeness, an originalness of method and a vital sense of Christ. He is a singular thinker, standing afar off from life. His nobility of style and integrity are amazing for our tousled and fragmented era. In Nesmelov is the charm of his inner tranquility, an organic consciousness of what is right and the majesty of his work, the independence from whatever the petty powers of the times of his interests and breadth. In the restrained style of Nesmelov one senses the spirit of the extra-temporal, an orientation towards eternity. In him there is not that overwrought and fragmented feel, which one senses with people too caught up in our epoch, in its shifting moods, in its wickedness of the day. Nesmelov is totally absorbed by the wickedness of eternity, and therefore he did not squander his spiritual powers, he gathered them for a certain task. But these traits of Nesmelov make him foreign to the people of our generation. It is difficult to throw across a bridge from him to the contemporary restlessness in soul. He is altogether unknown of and unappreciated, and for the contemporary world he mustneeds be discovered and investigated.

Nesmelov called his two-volume work "The Science of Man". This -- is an unique in its kind attempt of a philosophic construct of religious anthropology. This work is broken down into a teaching about the essence of human nature, and derived from this teaching the necessity of redemption. Nesmelov gives to philosophy a redemption, strikingly profound and original, and he constructs it upon his teaching about man, which he regards as strictly scientific.

Nesmelov begins his work with an investigation of the question about the tasks of philosophy. Does philosophy have its own autonomous sphere, its own purpose, distinct from the purposes of all the other remaining sciences, or disciplines? If in philosophy there be viewed the teaching about the universal, then the boundaries, separating philosophy from the other sciences, become obscured, and it is deprived of its own specific object. But, according to Nesmelov, there is one object in the world, which in genuine manner cannot be investigated by any particular science and it presents an impenetrable mystery for the scientific manner of looking at the world. This object -- is man, and the mysteries are those lodged within his nature. This view has little in common with that which sees the task of philosophy in the gnosseological investigation of the subject and of the nature of cognition. The mystery of human nature is an ontological mystery, and not gnosseological, and the object, which philosophy proposes to investigate, is a fact of being, and not of intellect, a living mystery of the human being, and not a mystery of the knowing subject. The method of Nesmelov can be called ontologic-psychological, for he all the time starts out from lived facts, and not from cognition and ideas.[4] The abstract dialectic of concept is totally foreign to Nesmelov and it seemed to him scholastic. In this he quite differed from Vl. Solov'ev -- a dialectician foremost. This may seem strange, but as a thinker, as an apologete, Nesmelov has much in common with L. Feuerbach and he says straightoff, that the point of departure of Feuerbach is correct, and that he goes the same path that Feuerbach does, but arrives elsewhere. With Feuerbach, Nesmelov conceives of an identical understanding of the essence of all religion, and the Christian religion foremost. Just like Feuerbach, Nesmelov sees this essence *in the enigma concerning man.* Religion is the expression of the mystery of human nature, the reflection of the enigmatic-ness of human nature. "For man there does not exist in the world any sort of enigmas, besides man himself, and man himself is manifest for himself an enigma only in this sole regard, *that the nature of his person in regard to the given conditions of his existence be rendered ideal.* If it were possible to reject this sole regard, then together with it quite reasonably it would be possible to reject in the

---

[4] In the first volume of his work, Nesmelov gives a gnosseological basis to his religious philosophy, but gnosseology does not appear to be his very strong or original side. With an accurate instinct Nesmelov binds together gnosseology with ontology, but in this he is inferiour to Solov'ev, whom unjustly he ignores. With Nesmelov there is a stronger psychological side.

world both every wonder, and all mystery".[5] *"To realise oneself however in one's own natural makeup of one's unique person, not one man is in a condition to, in actual fact".*[6] And further on: "*The image of unconditional being is not created by man in any sort of abstractive thoughts, but in reality is given to man by the nature of his person*".[7] "Through the very nature of his person, man necessarily images his own unconditional essence and at that selfsame time he actually exists, as a simple being of the physical world".[8] This twofold aspect of human nature is also a great mystery, which ought to be investigated by philosophy and it ought to lead to religious anthropology, since positivist anthropology is not concerned *with the fact* of man's belonging to another world. Out of the things of the world man is unique, and man -- is the image and likeness of unconditional Being, of the Absolute Person-ness. This is the undoubtable initial truth, upon which all religion rests, and Nesmelov grounds it upon a scientific objectivism without anything of the fantastic.

It is from the *fact* of human nature, and not from the *concept* of God that Nesmelov comes to the awareness of God. He *anthropologically* posits the being of God and by this positing he philosophically affirms the objective verity of Christianity. God-awareness is a given by the ideal nature of the person as the image and likeness of God. The idea of God "is actually a given for man, but not only is it *not a given to him from somewhere outside, in the capacity of a thought about God, but factual-subjectively it is realised in him by the nature of his person, as a living image of God.* If the human person *were not* ideal in regard to the real conditions of

---

[5] Vide: "The Science of Man" ("Nauka o cheloveke"), Tom I, p. 241.

[6] Ibid., p. 242.

[7] Ibid., p. 246.

[8] Ibid., p. 246.

its own particular existence, man would be incapable of possessing the idea of God, and no sort of revelation would ever be able to impart to him this idea, since he would be in no condition to comprehend it. And if man *had not consciousness* by virtue of the ideal nature of his person, he would then be incapable of possessing any sort of consciousness about the real being of the Divine, and this consciousness would be unable to lodge within him any sort ever of a supernatural actuality, since by his human consciousness he would be susceptive only to the reality of the sense world and the reality of himself as a physical part of the world. But the human person is real in its being and ideal in its nature, and by the very fact of its ideal reality it without mediation directly affirms the objective existence of God as true Person-ness.[9] "The possibility of the consciousness of God is determined by the fact of the inner contradiction between the conditional being of man and the unconditional character of his person".[10] In such manner, Nesmelov decisively and victoriously refutes the mechanistic understanding of revelation, as something foreign and external to the inner nature of the human person itself. His method of discerning the being of God is more powerful and persuasive than all the discernments from intellect, and his proof -- is factual. But the fact of *an higher* nature of man is unprovable and positively inexplicable. Man as a person is conscious of himself as of an higher order, and not a thing of the natural order, and this consciousness cannot originate from a world of things, from the order of a lower nature. The consciousness of one's God-likeness is a consciousness not from this world, it is a consciousness, begotten from another world.

Within man, alongside his animate life, with his life as a thing of this world, there is alive a consciousness of life *true,* perfect, and God-like. *"The moral consciousness springs forth for man from the*

---

[9] Ibid., p. 256-257.

[10] Ibid., p. 261.

ideal nature of his person, and therefore it leads man not to the concept about the good of life, but exclusively only to the concept about the truth of life".[11] The consciousness of his belonging to another, to a Divine world, the consciousness of his vocation-call to a *true* and *perfect* life is the source of a tormenting dissatisfaction with this imperfect and false life. Man realises, that his unworthiness -- of God-like existence -- makes for the life of a simple thing of the natural world. Out of this is begotten the consciousness of guilt, the impossibility to be reconciled with this false and imperfect life, the thirst for the redemptive atonement of guilt and the attainment of the utmost perfection. For man is necessary not a pardoning of guilt, not an armistice with God, which would grant the hope for a semblance of a forgiveness, but rather the redemptive atonement of the guilt, the transfiguration of his nature in accord with the image of God, the attainment of perfection. Man himself cannot pardon himself his sin, his life in accord with the law of the animal world, he cannot reconcile with this his own God-like nature, his own consciousness of true life. And Nesmelov subjects to a deep analysis the idea of salvation, which is rooted in the depths of human nature.

The idea of salvation was not foreign to the pagan world, it was promulgated by the nature religions, but therein it was altogether different than in the Christian consciousness. The natural pagan religions were unable to arrive at the consciousness of true life. They looked upon God and the gods as means for the attaining of earthly happiness, as an help for their own purposes. True religion however requires the free assimilation of likeness to God. "The striving of man towards the justification of his existence upon the earth, amidst that hostile to the God-like life, gives rise to a juridical relationship to God and by this it directly and decisively negates the truth of religion, and the possibility of morality, since that in the grip of this relationship *religion is transformed for man into a simple deal with God, and like an ordinary worldly deal, it necessarily becomes*

[11] Ibid., p. 286.

subordinated to the principle of the happiness of life".[12] Such is the idea of salvation in natural religion. And this juridical theory was carried over also into the Christian world. In Catholicism and indeed in Protestantism also the juridical understanding predominates. The radical surmounting of it comprises the chief service of Nesmelov.

The pagan salvation is a seeking of help and the fulfilling of wishes, and the pagan relationship to the Divinity is a juridical contract with Him, a deal. Christian salvation is a transforming of man, the attaining of perfection, the realisation of God-likeness. The pagan idea of salvation Nesmelov sees not only in the pagan world, but also in the Christian world. Far too many a "Christian" understands the idea of salvation in the crudely pagan manner, they see in it only an heavenly projection of earthly greed, of earthly egoism. Man finds himself serving heaven, and imploring God, in atonements for his lower nature, and the attainment of blissful well-being. But the higher, the God-like nature of man calls him not to well-being, but to perfection, not to a life of making reparations, but to true life. The relationship of man to God ought to be defined by his thirst of perfective, of true life, by his ineradicable need to realise his eternal image, and not by his thirst for well-being and satisfaction. Therefore the relationship of man to God cannot be a juridical contract, it is impossible to cajole out of God forgiveness and well-being, God cannot be given hurt feelings by man, wherein either to pardon or to punish him. Christ revealed the truth about God-manhood, about sonship to God, about the God-likeness of man and He called people to this, -- that they should become perfect, as their Heavenly Father is perfect And God is not moreover Power, to be terrified of, which can either punish or befriend, and which it is necessary by bloody sacrificial offering to win well-being in life. God wants but the perfection of His children, and they themselves desire this perfection, this likeness to their Father. Herein there is no place for superstitious fears and terrors, for a contract, for pardons or punishments, of the crude transference of the humanly-relative to the

[12] Ibid., p. 296.

Divinely-absolute. This great truth which is Christ's, Nesmelov investigates and establishes, and he does a great service for the liberation of Christianity from pagan superstition.

Nesmelov recognises the possibility of an intellectual basis of the ontological significance of salvation, of a philosophic construct of an ontology of salvation. But his religious ontology is wholly based on religious anthropology, and religious anthropology is based on a scientific analysis of human nature, "on the psychologic history and critique of the fundamental questions of life". In such manner, Nesmelov attempts to provide a scientific-philosophic justification of the truth of Christ. Nesmelov -- is a remarkable psychologist, and he provides to psychology transcendent depths and extremes of the soul life. His psychology of the fall into sin is striking. The higher human nature is positively inexplicable, it remains an enigma for positive science, which acknowledges only the manifestation of the nature, only as a thing. Within human nature there is hid an enigmatic twofoldness, in man -- one of the things of the world, one of its phenomena, there is the image of absolute person-ness, there is the striving towards true and God-like life.

But there is a certain vagueness in the profoundly thought out teaching of Nesmelov. The dualism of human nature, the dualism of an higher nature in man, of a nature not of this world, and of a lower nature which is of this world, the dualism of God-likeness and beast-likeness is not a dualism of soul and body, or of the spiritual and the material. It is indeed incorrect to say, that man in soul belongs to the Divine world, but in body to the animal world, and that everything in him spiritual is of another world, whereas everything material is of this world. The soul and body, the spiritual and the material duality in man belongs simultaneously to two worlds. In his God-likeness man is transformed not only in his body, but also no less in his soul; the lower, the evil principle lies not only in the material sphere, but also in the spiritual sphere. The source of evil -- is in spiritual pride, and of hence is begotten the evil of the material fetters. But Nesmelov tends to express it, as though in the spirit he sees the sign of man's God-likeness, but in the body man's belonging to the animal world.

Nesmelov in the results of his analysis correctly arrives at this conclusion, that only a spiritualistic teaching about man withstands the test of philosophic and scientific demands. Spiritualism is the sole true philosophy, and this is so. But spiritualism can be varied, and least of all satisfactory for us is the dualistic medieval form of spiritualism. A spiritualistic monism is far and above more satisfactory a form of metaphysics. Together with this, a spiritualistic monism transfers the centre of gravity of the dualism of human nature from the area of philosophic ontology to the area of the religio-mystical. Philosophy can comprehend human nature only spiritually or vitalistically, but lodged within it is not so much the ontological dualism of soul and body, as rather the dualism of another order, the dualism of man's singular and complex spirit-(soul-bodily nature belonging to two worlds -- to a world Divine and free, and to a world bestial and of necessity. *This is a dualism foremost of freedom and necessity, the dualism of one's consciousness of belonging to a necessitated world of things, and one's consciousness no less of belonging to a free world of God-like existences.* Man -- is a thing in the world and both in his soul and his body he is subject to the necessity of the natural order, and man also -- is a free being, and he belongs both in his soul and in his body to the Divine world.[13]

[13] The principal dualism of spirit and flesh, as of the good and the evil respectively, is a teaching not so much Christian, as rather Manichaean and Gnostic. Manichaeanism was ultimately a product of Persian dualism, of two opposed gods, and Gnosticism taught, that matter is created by another, by an evil god, and that matter cannot become deified. Christianity however teaches about deification, transfiguration, the resurrection of the worldly flesh. For Christianity the consciousness of the materiality chaining us down is the result of the sinful corruption of the world, but there is no especial material principle that is of itself evil. This likewise distinguishes Christianity from Platonism. Vide: "The Collected Works of St. Ireneius of Lyons", 1900 [Russian edition]. [*Translator note*: for St. Ireneius in English, vide Vol. I of "The Ante-Nicene Fathers" Series, which is also now Online on the Internet.] St. Ireneius of Lyons with great

With Nesmelov there is not fully shown the character of the dualism of human nature. But here arises the possibility of yet other vagueness, connected with the ideas of D. S. Merezhkovsky. Merezhkovsky repudiates the metaphysical truth of spiritualism, on the basis that he wants to surmount the dualism of spirit and flesh, with which Christian history and Christian culture have been infused. This mistake is rather greater, than is the vagueness of Nesmelov, but it has the same root. Spiritualism is not a denial of flesh and the earth, and it does not have any sort of relation to the religio-moral or religio-cultural problem of "flesh", to the problem of an ascetic or non-ascetic relationship to the world. Spiritualism, or panpsychism, is but an understanding of the nature of man and the nature of the world as being spiritual, as comprised of living monads, from spiritised substances. The question about the religio-cultural dualism of spirit and flesh has therefore nothing in common with spiritualist metaphysics, because the principle of "flesh" in the moral, the cultural-historical and religious sense has nothing in common with matter, with the empirical, etc. The spiritual exists not only in Heaven, in an other world, but also upon the earth, in this world. It ought decisively to be stated, that the vulgar distinction between soul and body, the spiritual and the material, is neither possible to be identified with, nor to be brought into harmony with, a dualism between an other world and this world, a dualism of an higher and a lower, etc. Nesmelov is unable to detect the mistake of Merezhkovsky, since he himself but vaguely posits and resolves this question. "Spirit" thus indeed belongs to "this world", as also does "flesh", and in "spirit" there can however be a "lower", -- just as also in "flesh". The ontological dualism of spirit and matter does not at all

---

strength reveals, that it is Christianity namely that saves worldly matter and leads to the resurrection of the flesh, which all the while the Gnostic heresies with their pseudo spiritualism would but suffer and consign to perdition -- all the fleshly world, all the earth. From the *Incarnation of God,* i.e. *the Enfleshment of God,* St. Ireneius deduces the inevitability of the salvation of the *flesh.* St. Ireneius was an ardent defender of Chiliasm. Vide Bk. 5 of his "Against Heresies" ("Adversus Haeresis"), p. 445-548.

exist, but the moral and cultural dualism of "spirit" and "flesh" finds resolution in the religion of God-manhood; in the deification of mankind and the world in Christ.[14] Therefore the hostility of Merezhkovsky towards spiritualism is a simple misunderstanding, a vagueness of philosophic consciousness, and the association by Nesmelov of the twofoldness of human nature of soul and body -- this likewise is a misunderstanding.

With the question about human nature is closely connected the question about immortality and the resurrection. Nesmelov sees in this question a tremendous difference between the naturalistic, pagan mindset and the Christian mindset. For the pagan mindset there sufficed but the idea of a natural immortality, of a naturalistic passing-over from this world to another world. Death also appears as such a naturalistic passing-over. But the naturalistic teaching about immortality says nothing about the salvation of man nor does it point out a path of salvation. Upon the basis of such an idea of immortality there cannot be affirmed the meaning of life, nor can there be posited the purpose of life. Only the Christian teaching about resurrection provides this meaning and leads to salvation. The teaching of the natural religions about immortality only shows the impotence of man to save himself. Nesmelov very keenly discloses the impotence of natural religion and its fatal subordination to the principle of happiness, rather than truth and perfection.

II.

"Christianity appeared in the world, as an incredible teaching and an incomprehensible deed".[15] The human mind -- is pagan, and

---

[14] Already in Justin the Philosopher it is possible to find an excellent explanation of the Christian teaching about resurrection and the repudiation of a fleshless spiritualism. Vide: "Works of St. Justin", 1902, p. 479-484 [in English: Vol. I of Ante-Nicene Fathers].

[15] Ibid., Tom II, p. 7.

the naturalist temptations of the mind -- are pagan temptations. The naturalist human mind, left to its own devices, in natural religion readily reduces itself to this, that "the religion necessarily transforms itself into a simple implement for the attainment of its wishes, and the *natural transference* of the idea of a physical salvation onto the soil of religion necessarily is expressed for it only by *the invention of a supernatural method* towards the attainment of the purely physical interests and ends of life".[16] With a great depth of psychological analysis Nesmelov traced out, how in context of paganism people accepted the deed of Christ. Both Jews and pagans readily submitted to the preaching of Christ and the charm of His Person, but the mystery of this Person and the significance of His deed they were unable to grasp, misinterpreting it altogether. People awaited an earthly king, the establishing of an earthly kingdom, the saving of the physical life of people in accord with their interests, with their thirst for well-being. But Christ taught: "Be ye perfect, even as your Heavenly Father is perfect"; Christ said: "My kingdom is not of this world". The deed of Christ was salvation of another kind, a salvation incomprehensible for people, immersed in this world and having neither perfection nor happiness. Nesmelov says, that at the present time a tremendous multitude of the people, "Christians" namely, are situated in a stage of religious superstition, a pagan-Jewish superstition. The people have religion, since they think about their salvation, but not about their perfection, the fear of perdition disquiets them, but not the thirst to realise their God-likeness. People of a pre-Christian consciousness, "understanding their own salvation as a natural result of their own proper merits before God, would concern themselves and actually did concern themselves only about this, to discern for sure the will of God and for sure to define, what is particularly acceptable to God and what is unacceptable to Him, what

---

[16] Ibid., p. 25.

might please God and what might anger Him".[17] Upon this soil is begotten a juridical understanding of salvation, i.e. the interpretation of the Saviour's death on the Cross as a ransom payment for the sins of people, as the appeasing of an angry God.

Religious anthropology, having under it a purely scientific foundation, leads to a rational realisation of that great Christian truth, that man himself, by his own limited powers is unable to save himself. The world was created for the perfective God-likeness of the creation, for the free realisation of the Divine *perfection* of mankind, and not for the egoistic and greedy aims of people, and not for God to lord it up in dominion over us. Nesmelov penetrates to the intimate depths the psychology of sin and the psychology of salvation and redemption, and he has a grasp of transcendent psychological mysteries, as but few have had. People cannot themselves forgive sin, they cannot themselves make peace with their falling-away from God. "They thought not about that they had come to ruin, but only about this, that they -- were guilty before God, i.e. in other words, they thought not about themselves, but only about God; it came to be, they loved God more than themselves, and therefore they were not able to forgive themselves their transgression". And once there was such a psychology of sin, then also the psychology of redemption had to be included in the striving to merit the mercy of God, the forgiveness of sins, in the reconciliation with God from the fear of perdition. Nesmelov with indignation rejects the conceiving of God as an egoistical holder of power, and in such a view of God he sees the basis of the diabolical temptation. "God *did not threaten punishment* for the transgressing of His commandment, but beforetime forewarned man about what *would necessarily follow*, if His given commandment be transgressed by them. Consequently, the fulfilling of the commandment was necessary not for God, but only for people in the interests of their moral perfecting, and consequently, by the transgressing of the commandment, man could bring to ruin

[17] Ibid., p. 248.

only himself, since by this transgression he was however altogether unable to convey an infinite affront to God".[18] God cannot be indignantly insulted by man and therein either punish man, nor pardon him.[19] The will of God is in this, that man become perfect, like his Heavenly Father, to become likened unto Him, and it is altogether not in this, that man be made obedient to His formal will. Wherein therefore sin ought to be annihilated, and not merely pardoned, annihilated in the name of perfection. Man himself, conscious of the God-like nature within himself, recognises himself unworthy of forgiveness and thirsts to become perfect. The meaning of Christ's sacrifice -- is not in the ransom for sin, not in the appeasing of God the Father, but in a miraculous transformation of human nature towards perfection. The juridical teaching about redemption is an affront both to man, and to God. For Nesmelov, in what is the essence of the sin, and why have people, in gnawing the apple from the forbidden tree, committed transgression? Nesmelov provides a profound psychology of the primordial transgression. He always makes use of the psychological method, rather than one of abstraction. A "psychology of living facts", and not a "logic of concepts" -- in this is the originality of the method of Nesmelov in his religious anthropology.

People "desired, that their exalted position in the world should not be dependent on the free developement by them of their spiritual powers, but rather by their physical eating of certain fruits, it means that they essentially wanted this, that their life and fate should be defined not by them themselves, but by external material principle. And this desire of theirs they realised in actual fact. They actually turned for help to the forbidden tree in that particularly full confidence, that the somehow magical power of its fruits, without

---

[18] Ibid., p. 249.

[19] It would however be improper to misunderstand Nesmelov in suchlike a sense, as would negate the great significance of prayer, of this basis of religious life. Prayer is a non-avaricious devoting of oneself to the will of God, prayer mystically alters the nature of man.

any effort on their part, mechanically would render them all the more perfect. In these calculations of theirs they were of course crudely mistaken, but the fact of fulfilling their intention they nonetheless accomplished; and therefore the undoubtable mistakenness of their calculations does not itself in the least degree alter the actual significance and meaning of their fatal course of action: by their superstitious course of action people voluntarily subordinated themselves to external nature and themselves voluntarily destroyed that world significance, which they could and should have had in accord with the spiritual nature of their person".[20] People went their own particular godless way, reckoning to attain by this path a Divine condition, but they fell into a bestial condition, subjecting themselves to a restrictive material nature. Therefore the Biblical account about the fruits of the forbidden tree has deep metaphysical significance. Nesmelov emphasises especially, that the essence of the fall into sin -- is in a superstitious attitude towards *material things* as a source for power and knowledge. The deep truthfulness of this psychology of the fall into sin finds itself experientially confirmed in the consciousness of modern man, in the personal fall into sin of each of us. People "subordinated their soul life to the physical law of mechanistic causality, and it means, they put their spirit into common bondage with the world of things. In consequence of this, they can now essentially live only that life, which exists and is proper to the particular nature of the physical world, and under these conditions death appears inevitable. It means, that death is not something from somewhere from the outside that has come upon people, *in punishment, for example, God's punishment for sin*; it has come upon them from them themselves, *as a natural and necessary consequence* of that transgression, which people committed. In actual fact, this world, in which people wanted to live and in which they actually entered by fact of their transgression, God did not create and did not want to create, and all the appearances which exist in this

---

[20] Ibid., p. 251-252. And in the source-springs of history evil is all rooted in this superstitious attitude towards material objects.

world, as *in a world of transgression*, exist not in accord with the creative will of God, but rather in accord with the mechanistic forces of physical nature. That world, which actually was created by God, man spoiled by his transgression".[21] Why did God permit the mutilation of His creation? "By virtue of His almightiness, God undoubtedly was able to not permit the fall of the first people, but He did not want to stifle their freedom, since He would not distort His own image in mankind".[22]

"The holy human life of Jesus Christ speaks but to this, that *despite the existence of evil in the world*, the world nonetheless comes to realise the Divine idea of being. It means, by fact of His immaculate life, Christ manifested only *the justification of God* in His creative activity, and not a *justification of people before God* in their deviation away from God's law of life". [23] "Sin never and in no case can be excused man, since every pardoning of sin can only be a becoming reconciled with it, and not at all a liberation from it. For this, that man actually should be delivered from sin, he ought invariably annihilate it within himself".[24] But the salvation of man is bound up with the salvation of the world, and man himself even with a martyr's death cannot deliver the world from sin. Nesmelov understands Christianity as an universal deed, and not an individual one, and he affirms the religious meaning of history. The righteousness of Christ is also for him the righteousness of human nature in common. *The appearance of Christ was a continuation of the creation.* "Recognising Christ's resurrection as the efficacious basis and first expression of a general law of the resurrection of the

---

[21] Ibid., p. 257.

[22] Ibid., p. 268.

[23] Ibid., p. 305.

[24] Ibid., p. 306-307.

dead, we ought obviously to recognise in Christ suchlike a Man, Who being a true possessor of human nature, did not bear only an individual human person-ness, since that His righteousness was the righteousness not of a separate man, but the righteousness of human nature, completely independent of those who in particular partially possess this nature".[25]

Christ is also the appearance in the world of the God-like Man, a revealing of the religious mystery of the human being. The redeeming of the world by Christ is as it were a new creation: man comes to be in that position, in which he was situated before the fall, but enlightened and deified with experience. The Person of Christ is also a God-revelatory answer to the enigma of man: Christ is absolute and the Divine Man, the praeternally existing image and likeness of the Father. But the appearance of Christ in the world and His death on the Cross do not of themselves save, but rather only create the conditions for the possibility of salvation. Salvation is a deed of the will, and not of coercion by God.[26] Christ cleanses from sin those, who freely desire to be cleansed by Him, those who love in Him the image of the existent Divine perfection, to which man was fore-ordained.

"The death of Jesus Christ in actuality is not a ransom-payment to God for people's sins, but rather the sole means towards the *possibility* of the cleansing of people's sins, and furthermore not only of people's sins, but of the sins also of all the transgressive world in general. It actually and unconditionally cleanses all and every sin, yet still the sins of only those sinners, which Christ the Saviour seeks out, and He seeks out only those sinners, which acknowledge the need in the redemption of their sins and who believe in the actuality of the redemptive sacrifice of Christ. Whoever

---

[25] Ibid., p. 350.

[26] To Nesmelov was foreign the teaching of Bl(essed) Augustine about grace, which denigrated human freedom. But it would be unjust to accuse Nesmelov of this, that he belittles the significance of grace and falls into Pelagianism.

does not acknowledge the need in redemption, that one also cannot ultimately desire, that his sins be taken from him by Christ, and therefore he likewise remains in his sins. At the opposite, whoso desires the redemption of his sins and believes in the actuality of Christ's sacrifice for sin, and turns himself towards the saving help of Christ, that one, even though he should emerge from amidst the hosts of fallen angels, and even though he be Satan himself, it is all the same -- he can be cleansed and saved by the holy blood of Christ; since that even the devil likewise -- is a creation of God, since that he likewise was created by God not for perdition, but for life eternal in the radiant world of God's saints".[27] According to the noble teaching of Nesmelov, there can be cleansed and saved both pagans, and the dead, and even the fallen spirits. With a pervasive power of psychological intuition, Nesmelov repudiates the fear of hell's torments and the terror of perdition as un-Christian feelings, although eternal perdition he does not deny, and he defends the Christian character of fear of its own non-perfection and terror of its own beast-likeness. He saves the thirst for perfection, for God-likeness, he saves the love for Christ, the love for the Divine in life, but not the thought about punishment, chastisement, hell's torments, etc. "Whoso actually believes in Christ, and for whom the living source of moral energy in every instance is lodged not within thought about *the Dread Last Judgement of Christ,* but in the thought about *the love of Christ beyond intellection,* such that he would *fear* Christ's Judgement over himself only in this one regard, that with his own sinful impurity he might be manifest unworthy of Christ, and Christ might separate him off from living communion with Himself. This separation off for him is more terrible than any punishment, since the life with Christ is higher than any reward, and since he can conceive of his own life in Christ, evidently, not as a desire for heavenly rewards and not in terror of hell's torments, but exclusively and only through the moral imperative of his own pure and reverent love for

---

[27] Ibid., p. 337.

Christ. Such a man, reasonably, never would permit the immoral thought to this effect, that people might sin *in hope on God's mercy,* since that in *this hope* he could affirm only the undoubtable truth of his faith, that through the great mercy of Christ the Saviour that people *should be saved from sin.* Consequently, whoso recourses to God's mercy on the path towards licentiousness, such an one knows Christ not at all and thinks about the mercy of God not at all, -- he simply commits sacrilege *through the ignorance of foolish people,* and already it is reasonably apparent, that to put oneself upon the path of truth and render oneself virtuous is not a matter set upon the future threat of universal judgement, but only one's spiritual enlightenment by the ethical light of Christ's truth".[28]

Nesmelov raises Christian consciousness to an high degree, he cleanses the Christian consciousness from admixtures of crude paganism, from dark superstitions, from degrading fears, for those seeking the truth of Christ. Nesmelov teaches, that *the eternal truth of Christianity is identical with the eternal truth of the ideal and God-like human nature.*

III.

From the time of the infancy of mankind to our own time pagan idolatry and pagan superstition have been part of religious life. Paganism, ultimately, is not identical with idolatry and superstition, in paganism there was also a positive truth, a genuine sense of God, but the residue of paganism in the Christian world customarily bears an idolatrous and superstitious character. The strangest thing of all is this, that the most external aspect of Christianity, the most official ecclesiality not only does not heal this ulcer of religious life, but rather irritates it the moreso and intensifies it. The consciousness of the extra-temporal and ideal values is frequently strengthened in the mystic, in art, in creativity, outside the circle charted out by the official ecclesiality, and the organ of its conscious expression is

[28] Ibid., p. 420.

found in the heights of philosophy, which by this serves no little in the matter of the cleansing of the religious consciousness of mankind. The theoretical God-knowledge and the practical God-communion have taught about the higher, the God-like nature of man, while at the same time the representatives of the official ecclesiality and the official religiosity have fallen too often into an heavenly utilitarianism -- this as a projection of earthly utilitarianism. The pagan experiences within Christianity teach man to be guided by his own interests, they sustain within him the sense of fear and terror and by this they corrupt man, they evoke within him an indifference to the truth and the right. The rightful truth however of the eternal Gospel within the human heart and consciousness, the reflection of light from Christ teaches man to be guided by the thirst for perfection, by the striving towards God-communion and towards God-likeness, and it liberates from superstitious fears and terrors. The pagan superstition within Christianity is recognised wherein God is worshipped as an idol, rather than as the source of perfection, of truth, of true life, of value. And towards the Living God there can be an idolatrous and superstitious attitude, and it always is so, when the superstitious fear of perdition or the superstitious hope, that the interests of man be satisfied, takes precedence over the reverent love towards God and the striving towards that absolute perfection, which is reflected in the nature of man himself. *The will towards the realisation of perfective value,* towards the God-like manner of being is also the source of an authentic, a free, a non-superstitious and non-idolatrous religious life. The will towards value, towards the extra-temporal in regards to its own significance, the will towards the Divine, towards the true and the free is at the basis of life of all the great people as regards religion, of all the saints, the apostles and the prophets. Within their soul love hath conquered fear, the striving for perfection hath conquered private interests. The consciousness of extra-temporal values, the consciousness of their own higher nature provides deliverance from the pagan superstitions and fears, which abase and pervert the Christian faith. We cannot yet believe, that a man, deprived of consciousness of values, a man, never sensing in the depths of his nature the reflection of God, of filial sonship to God, -- that such a man by a superstitious and idolatrous falling to the levels of the external ecclesiality by this itself yet frees himself from guilt and sin and is rendered a member of the Divine world-order, of the Kingdom of God. Nor can we likewise believe, that a man with a rare escaping out of the ranks here by a consciousness of values, and having discovered within himself the Divine nature, is excluded from the Divine world-order, if he transgresses some aspect of the official ecclesiality. Nesmelov deeply understands this problem, and he says straight out, that everything of value, and true, and good in life is saved for eternity.[29] Nesmelov with a noble indignation repudiates the superstitious-magical attitude towards the sacramental-mysteries of the Church. The sacramental-mystery is not a conjuring, a magic spell, it is not a relict of the pagan darkness, and towards it there cannot be a mechanical attitude. A man, the whole life of whom is beast-like, does not become God-like through a mechanical communing of the mysteries. The partaking of the sacramental-mysteries is connected with an inner rebirth into new life, though the sacrament itself is independent of anything human. Evil-doers, who hope to receive pardon and absolution through a mechanical touching-upon by the Church, and who go to the sacramental-mysteries as a means to continue with their beast-like life and therein be freed of the fear of perdition and punishment, suchlike a malefactor does not participate truly in the sacramental-mysteries nor get truly into the Church. The Church is the world soul, conjoined with Christ the Logos, it is the congregate Divine consciousness of mankind, as a centre of the world, and it comprises all the positive fullness of being. The mystical essence of the Church cannot be confused with the historical sins of the empirical Church. The

---

[29] Catholics make a distinction between *the soul* of the Church (anima Ecclesiae), in which belongs everything that is of a will towards the good and towards Divine life, and *the body* of the Church, to which belongs all the faithful, subject to the hierarchy of the Church and in communion with its sacraments. (Vide the fine book of Abbot Peré, “Entretiens sur l’Eglise Catholique”, Tom II, p. 504-509).

abomination of desolation can also be in the place of the holy. About this one ought to bear in mind both the "right" and the "left" in the church question. The Church has preserved the image of the Crucified Christ and for the sacramental-mystery of communion to it -- only in this also mustneeds be sought the mystical sanctity of the true Church. Nesmelov -- is a pious member of the Orthodox Church, and yet is a merciless critic of the official religiosity, the exposer of the lie of the state church. The book of this faithful son of the Orthodox Church helps to surmount the crude paganism within "Orthodoxy".

"Be ye perfect, even as your Heavenly Father is perfect", i.e. realise within yourself the image of God. Herein is the eternal essence of Christianity, a setting in opposition to every pagan superstition and idolatry the thirst for a perfect, true, eternal and full life. But this essential core of Christianity cannot be transformed into moralism. Only through Christ, manifest as Person in the Divine truth of human nature, is to be attained God-likeness. By a path exclusively human man cannot attain to a condition of the Divine. Without the concrete truth about man, the abstract truth of idealism -- is dead and is not realism. The pretensions of a philosophic knowing to substitute for religious faith ought to be, not only religiously, but also philosophically repudiated. And the book of Nesmelov brilliantly lays bare the pagan limitedness of contemporary philosophy and of the whole contemporary mindset, for which the faith in Christ is folly and seduction. Nesmelov succeeded in philosophically showing, that faith in Christ is reasonable, and that only this faith is reasonable. Nesmelov speaks all the time about the "scientific" basis of faith, and his work he calls the "science" about man. This is not altogether precise. It would be more correct to speak about the philosophic justification of faith and about the philosophy of human nature. Nesmelov is very contentious against any scholasticism, he strives for a living knowledge and is proud of that his science of man is based on *facts,* and not on *concepts.* The tremendous merit of Nesmelov might in brief be expressed thus: *the fundamental thought of Feuerbach about the anthropologic mystery of religion is transformed by him into a weapon of defense of Christianity.* People come to religion through the twofoldness of their nature, through a lodged within them God-likeness alongside with a beast-likeness or nature-likeness. Man cannot be reconciled with this, not on the strength of his *subjective desires,* but only on the strength of his *objective nature.* Positivism, in the broad sense of the word, makes this point as regards another, a perfect world, this thirst of a Divine and absolute life, and for the subjective desires it is something which ought with caution to be explained positively. Positivism is correct, when it says, that the subjective desires never get accomplished fully, that essentially the world is not bound to be, such as we would wish to see it. But actually this manner of speaking addresses not the subjective desires of man, but it is rather about objective nature, and this objective nature proves itself much objectified, this nature is positively inexplicable, a mystery. Man -- is the member of another, a Divine world-order, he is not only of the natural world, and this -- is a fact, a mysterious fact, demanding another explanation. God, as Person, is perceived only anthropologically, within man; but in nature, cosmologically -- He is perceived as an impersonal creative force. A synthesis though of the cosmologic revelation of paganism and the anthropologic revelation of Christianity has religiously yet neither been investigated nor found. In this religious synthesis, which lies beyond the horizon of Nesmelov,[30] and there ought to be revealed the not yet revealed Christian mystery of God's creation.

Nesmelov reveals a new method of detection[31] of the being of God -- psychologically, or (more accurately anthropologically. This

---

[30] Just like Orthodoxy in general, Nesmelov -- is an opponent of Chiliasm. His exceptionally pessimistic view on the end of world history stands in contradiction with his avowal of the meaning of history and the necessity of history for redemption.

[31] I say *detection ("obnaruzhenie"),* since this word is a *demonstrative proof,* strictly speaking, and is not applicable to the being of

detection is distinct from the old ontological proof, which was based upon *an intellectual concept* and beyond the limits of intellectual concept it does not go, and it is distinct also from the rather newer moral demonstrative proof of Kant, which is grounded in *subjective duty*. Nesmelov's detection is grounded upon *the objective fact* of human nature. This, certainly, is not a new discovery of Nesmelov, for the whole religious and philosophic developement of mankind prepared this religious anthropology, it opened up the way to God. Furthermore, the teaching of Kant about *the moral-rational nature* of man and about its intelligible character has hidden within it the possibility not only of "religion within the bounds of reason", but also an authentic Christian religious anthropology. But Nesmelov gave clear and deep expression to the truth of religious anthropology.[32] The consciousness of *person*, as the image and likeness of God, the consciousness of his belonging to a true, perfect and free world *objectively* demonstrates also the being of God, and the necessity of the redemption of the world by the Son of God. The pathway to a Christian consciousness lies through a mysterious self-awareness of being a person. And there cannot be an understanding of Christianity for one in whom the person, -- the image of the Divine being, is still asleep, is still dissolved within fated being. But when man has become aware of his own person, he becomes conscious within himself of an higher being and a vocation to an higher life, and then there stands forth the image of Christ and nowise more can it be obscured.

For modern man at the vanguard of awareness, and especially for Russian man among the Intelligentsia, it is very difficult to accept

---

God. In acknowledging the being of God there is nothing logically compelling.

[32] I am myself given to think, that the "Critique of Practical Reason" is of Kant's greater merit, than is his "Critique of Pure Reason". But the religious rationalism of Kant weakened his profound teaching about the twofoldness of human nature and about man's belonging to the realm of freedom.

Christianity, there are obstacles waiting at every step, obstacles both of mind and of heart. This man has consented at times to accept each religion that pleases him, whatever a form of paganism, the religion of Babylon or Dionysianism, Brahmanism or Buddhism, even Mahometanism, but only not Christianity. In this turning away from Christianity is something strange and mysterious. And the man of our era is quite willing to become a pantheist, if the religious need has not ultimately gone numb within him. Pantheism and pantheistic mysticism is esteemed whether by the positivist, the atheist, the Marxist, or whatever the teaching of the contemporary time. Only Christian theism is esteemed by no one, and modernity does not accept it. Modern man thinks, that under pantheism he preserves his person, and that for mankind it betokens a tremendous significance, and freedom, and also other fine things, would result under it, but that here under Christianity the person is enslaved, and freedom vanishes, and mankind comes to naught. What s strange aberration! In actuality it is all just turned around backwards. Only the Christian consciousness is grounded in the sense of person, only it acknowledges the divineness of human nature and gives a central place in the world-order to mankind, only this consciousness affirms the freedom of man, his worth and his higher nature. Pantheism ultimately abolishes person, and freedom, and mankind, dissolving everything ultimately into the world's life, and imperceptibly passes over into naturalism and materialism. Pantheism cannot comprehend of our thirst for perfect and true life nor has it the ability to explain our higher nature and the twofoldness connected with it. Only Christianity acknowledges an absolute significance for man and his eternal destiny and no wise is he dissolved away, to nothing is he enslaved. And the profound self-consciousness of man is a Christian self-consciousness: in the depths of his self-consciousness man finds Christ -- the resolution of the enigma of his nature. But the Christian self-consciousness ought to be cleansed from paganism, the consciousness of person ought to be set off from the consciousness of the impersonal genus. And a sublime philosophy, like Nesmelov's, serves towards this important task. The renewed and eternal

Christianity transcends the relationship to God as idol, and man recognises within Him the absolute source of his thirst for *Divine perfection*, and within Christ the praeternally realised, Divinised humanity.

AN OPEN LETTER TO ARCHBISHOP ANTHONY [KHRAPOVITSKY] [1]

Your Eminence!

Your open Letter to the authors of the anthology "Vekhi" I have read through with the deepest trepidation, and an irresistible urge impels me, Vladyka, to express that which I thought and felt, in reading Your greetings. And like my "Vekhi" colleague, P. B. Struve, I sensed, that Your dealings towards us has opened up the possibility of a common ground, and has removed the former insurmountable obstacles between us.

By complicated and tortuous paths I have come to the faith of Christ and to the Church of Christ, which now I esteem as my spiritual mother. But I have not forgotten those obstacles, which stood in my way, and this does not permit me to forget the lot of those, who are unable to overcome the obstacles. The churchly actuality, the abomination of desolation in place of the holy, indicates how grievous is the nightmare for those seeking God and the truths of God. Many have come to doubt the sanctity of the place itself out of a love for truth and severe an accounting of the servitors of God, pronouncing the name of Christ but doing deeds, contrary to Christ. Everyone indeed knows and everyone is in agreement on this, that the deed of Christ -- is a deed of love. Is it not corruptive, that the officially Christian camp, confessing the right faith and therefore possessing before others so immeasurable a superiority, should in place of deeds of love commit deeds of malice and hate? People are weak, their religious will is overwhelmed by seductions and temptations, and it is difficult for them to hold out against a most terrible temptation, issuing forth from the faith, -- the spiritual decay

[1] Published in "Moskovskii Ezhenedel'nik", 15 August 1909.

and moral disintegration of the Church in its human, historical, empirical side (on its Divine and mystical side the Church is unshakable and preserves eternal truth). But woe to those, through whom such scandals enter into the world! The deeds of malice and hate are not being imputed to people that are non-believers in Christ and who spurn the legacy of love, but rather people that are believers in Christ who have accepted the legacy of love. The confession of the right faith would seem to obligate and impose an exceptional responsibility, unknown to naive pagans. I have deeply and with torment experienced the guilt of our atheistic society, have inquired into the consequences of this guilt, and have come to know the secret temptations. I have received the right and have become conscious of the obligation to expose the falsehood, by which our intelligentsia lives. The authors of "Vekhi", all of us, have done our duty as we have understood it to be, having turned towards that intelligentsia, with which we were intellectually connected in our past, and for which we desire a better future. But there is scarcely any one of us who has ceased to feel, that there is likewise guilt and sin also on the other side, in that camp, which is endowed with a superiority of outward power and can be a persecutor, and in its words it has the advantage of confession of right faith. The Church of Christ was strong with its Christian martyrs and saints, it showed the world the possibility of a victory over the world, the power of God's truth in a godless world. At present the Church has become enfeebled by christians inflicting the martyring, by the malice of servitors of the Church, having surrendered themself to the powers of this world and having lost faith in the power of God's truth. And how much the spiritual powers have fled in terror from the Church.[2] Everyone ought to repent, all the sides and all the camps, all have given themself over to malice and hatred, all have betrayed the legacy of love. Only then

---

[2] This decline cannot be justified, in it is a treason and betrayal of the Mother. But the guilt has to be shared.

will there ensue for Russian society a spiritual spring-time, a spring-time of love in place of the mutual hatred and malice.

The Russian revolution, nihilistic and atheistic at the core of its ideas, has intoxicated Russia with malice, has poisoned the blood of the Russia people with social and class hatred and spiritual hostility. But does the reaction not breathe with still greater a malice? Has it not with great force spilled blood and done violence? The "Union of the Russian People" -- is all malice, is all hatred, its deeds are terrible and scandalous, it promotes fratricidal discord in the Russian people and society, and most of all it is an obstacle to the religious rebirth of our native land. And how can the hierarchs of the Church possibly support a scandalous justification of this malicious, fratricidal, anti-Christian "politics"? Why do the deeds of love and the spirit of love not remain the rule of faith? Why do they not believe in the power of the truths of God, but rather believe in the power of the state, the material power? Why do they appeal to the powers of this world for a defending of that which is not of this world? All these questions torment the Christian conscience. Horrified we see, that the state coercive power of the Church is bound up with its religious and spiritual enfeeblement. Can the quenching of spirit be halted by coercive measures? We see, that the prevailing soul-intrusive and soul-coercive position of the Orthodox Church in the Russian state has led to a decline of faith, to the growth of sectarianism among the people and to unbelief within society, and to widespread hypocrisy and falsehood. Spiritual fruits, regretably, we however do not see. Our churchly hierarchy has become accustomed in everything to rely upon outward and coercive power, while the inner power of spiritual gifts has become almost dessicated within it.

Against the faith in Christ has begun everywhere in the world a spiritual persecution, everywhere the prince of this world, apparently, celebrates victory. But according to the Christian prophecies the Church has not been promised a governing and ruling position over the world. The persecution against Christ and His work can only be opposed by the power of faith in the truth of God, though the world be outraged. It is the martyrs, and not those doing the martyring, that witness to Christ. Those doing the martyring witness but to the prince of this world. I recognise, Vladyka, how easy it is to lose faith in man and in human society. But is not such a thing a degree of unbelief in man and in mankind, which already is incompatible with faith in the God-Man, in God conjoined with mankind, in the Saviour of the world. "For God so loved the world, that He sent His Only-Begotten Son". I tend to discern quite extreme unbelief in mankind with K. Leont'ev, a genius of a Russian thinker, whom I esteem deeply. But this unbelief of his in mankind, this godless attitude towards the world has taken on an anti-Christian and demonic character, spurning love. For Leont'ev, as for all that have lost faith in the image of God in man, Christianity then is not a religion of love, and for them Christ was God but was not man, -- which is contrary to the Orthodox confession of faith.[3] An absolute non-belief in man leads to this, that they want to guard the truth of God by force, by coercion, i.e. by non-truth, as condemned by Christ. Is a forced salvation possible and is it necessary, is it something pleasing to the Lord? Is force possible in matters of Christian faith, in matters of conscience, which ought to bear the burden of freedom? Do You remember, Vladyka, how with genius Your esteemed Dostoevsky spoke about the burden of Christian freedom in his "Legend of the Grand Inquisitor". Is not Christian freedom of conscience a duty, an obligation, a burden imposed by the Lord, and not a right, as is usually asserted? The New Testament of God with man is a testament, a covenant of love and freedom, and thus a forced salvation, in accord with the New Testament faith, is both impossible and not necessary.

Those, who do not believe in mankind and its earthly fate, are compelled to view Christianity as a religion of a few chosen ones, "which are inscribed by the Lamb into the book of life". But then it is a mere qualitative and not quantitative matter. The Church however,

---

[3] In this, it is impossible not to see an inclination towards the Monophysite heresy.

in wanting to hold dominion upon earth with the assist of the state, is concerned with the quantitative, with the masses. According to our faith, the gates of hell will not prevail against the Church of Christ, and therefore a fearing for the Church, the guarding of the Church by coercive measures is religiously unacceptable and scandalous. Neither a pessimistic nor an optimistic attitude towards the earthly fate of mankind can justify a violation of conscience, a coercion in faith. The Orthodox Church is sustained and given glory by a St. Seraphim of Sarov and those like him, but was there necessary for the appearance of St. Seraphim, for his dazzling white love and grace, was there necessary all the coercive churchly politics, the help by the sword of the state, with its pursuits and persecutions? In the oppressed and persecuted Church there appeared not some few Seraphims and by the power of God's truth they were victorious over the human non-truth. We have grown tired of hearing from the materialists, that only by a material power can anything in the world be created and initiated.

Let the state in worldly matters recourse to necessary measures of force. The sinful world, fallen away from God, cannot exist without the force of the state, always relative, and subject to historical developement. The Christian ought to be aware, that "the authorities do not bear the sword in vain" within the world, immersed still as it is in paganism. *But the Church of Christ is sustained upon faith in the Crucified One, and not by the power of the crucifier.* Why then in Christian history and churchly activity has the power of the crucifier won out over the truth of the Crucified One? Why has execution ceased to be a symbol of Christian martyrdom and become instead a symbol of Christian tormenting? The inauspicious shadows of the official churchliness torment us and many of us hesitate to enter into the Church. We thirst to hear the voice of the Church, an answer not human but the rather Divine, to all these questions. Where is the voice of the Church, Vladyka, the voice of the *Universal* Church of Christ, which also in everything I have become subject to and in the name of which I have disclaimed everything. What has become of the tradition of sobornost'-communality, as preserved within our Church? The voice of the Church has been drowned out by the human voices, has become distorted by human love for power and greed. We are returning to the native-land of our spirit, into the bosom of the Church of Christ, and there we are greeted by the felicitous greeting of Your Eminence, the most visible bishop of the Russian Church. This greeting is dear for those of us, who by faith belong to the Church. But our Christian conscience does not permit us to become reconciled with that abomination of desolation, which we have met with in our native land, in which we also are to blame and for which we are responsible. Our Christian conscience not only is not at peace, but compels us religiously to struggle against the transformation of the Christian faith into a tool of worldly politics, against capital punishment in a "Christian" state, against the justifications of these death sentences by the servitors of a religion of truth crucified and suffering, against violations of conscience, against the justification of the spirit of malice and of deeds of malice, where instead according to the Saviour ought to be love and freedom.

If we, as individual persons, have managed not to be devastated by the scandals of churchly authority, then still we are nowise proud of this and we remember always, that for many of our brethren this occurs likewise only with great difficulty, and that for many a little one these scandals are terrible. Religiously it is important to facilitate for the wide circles of the Russian intelligentsia their return into the bosom of the Church, but for this it suffices not to denounce and harangue the intelligentsia, for it is not alone blameworthy in everything. Even according to Your own words, Vladyka, many a soul of the Russian intelligentsia has fallen into the diabolical snares as it were gratis, and not out of any sort of greed. It would be proper to deal more severely with the greedy and the mercenary, but those dwelling officially within the Church are in communion with the earth, but not communing with God (words of St. Seraphim). Most Eminent Vladyka! I would be delighted, and indeed not I alone, if our meagre literary words might lead to a change of attitude among the Church hierarchy towards the Russian intelligentsia community. In Your openness towards us there is already heard sounds of love, and not hostility. It is indeed commanded us to love also the enemies. May this new common bond between us serve the work of Christ upon earth, to the regeneration of the Church of Christ, not "politics", not "The Union of the Russian People", not deeds of evil and violence.

I believe, that the victory of the Church of Christ in the world is a victory of truth crucified and suffering, over the power of those that crucify and torment. The power to crucify and to torture within the actions of church and state is a temptation of the Jewish kingdom of old, a temptation, wanting to see Christ not in the form of a lowly servant, crucified upon the cross, but rather in the form of a king powerful and outwardly mighty.[4] This is that selfsame temptation, which also is within socialism, in Marxism. We however have not our own earthly city. The truth of Christ, the "crucified truth" is external to any sort of "politics", it is neither reactionary nor revolutionary, neither of the "right" nor of the "left" camps, it is not of this world, and its power over this world is a power of love and freedom. Where Christ is, therein the deeds of love are victorious, and Christ is not in deeds of malice and violence.

Please pardon, Vladyka, that I have expressed to You my perplexity so openly and resolutely. And for the sake of Christ believe me, that in my words there is not a drop of "politics". In my words has been expressed a thirst for a freeing faith from "politics".
I entrust myself to Your prayers and I implore Your blessing, Vladyka!

---

[4] This is a false chiliasm, mixing up grace with law, the order of freedom with the order of nature. True chiliasm within the Church has however still not been revealed.

www.ingramcontent.com/pod-product-compliance
Lightning Source LLC
Chambersburg PA
CBHW031936090426
42811CB00002B/199

* 9 7 8 0 9 9 6 3 9 9 2 1 0 *